Crime, Disorder and Community Safety

Major changes are taking place in the crime control industry and by association in the discipline of criminology itself. These changes, which involve the adoption of local partnership approaches, new forms of managerialism as well as the blurring of distinctions between crime, disorder and community safety, have been described as constituting a watershed for criminology. Bringing together nine original articles from leading national and international authorities on these issues, this book is both a product of and a reflection on the changing state of play. The articles address, from a range of different perspectives, the changing nature of regulation in contemporary society and the simultaneous reconstruction of the communities which are being regulated. *Crime, Disorder and Community Safety* also offers a timely commentary on government attempts to address questions of inequality and social exclusion as well as issues relating to ethnic minorities and young people.

Roger Matthews is Professor of Sociology at Middlesex University. **John Pitts** is Vauxhall Professor of Socio-Legal Studies at the University of Luton.

Crime, Disorder and Community Safety

A new agenda?

**Edited by Roger Matthews
and John Pitts**

London and New York

First published 2001
by Routledge
11 New Fetter Lane, London EC4P 4EE

Simultaneously published in the USA and Canada
by Routledge
29 West 35th Street, New York, NY 10001

Routledge is an imprint of the Taylor & Francis Group

Typeset in Goudy by Taylor & Francis Books Ltd
Printed and bound in Great Britain by MPG Books Ltd, Bodmin

British Library Cataloguing in Publication Data
A catalogue record for this book is available from the British Library

Library of Congress Cataloging in Publication Data
Crime, disorder, and community safety: a new agenda?/edited by Roger
Matthews and John Pitts.
Includes bibliographical references and index.
1. Crime prevention. 2. Crime. I. Matthews, Roger. II. Pitts, John.

HV7431 .C7 2001
364–dc21   00-065337

ISBN 0–415–24230–4 (hbk)
ISBN 0–415–24231–2 (pbk)

Contents

Illustrations

Tables

Figures

Contributors

Adam Crawford is Professor of Criminology and Criminal Justice and the Deputy Director of the Centre for Criminal Justice Studies, University of Leeds. He is the author of *Local Governance of Crime* (1997), *Crime Prevention and Community Safety* (1998) and co-editor of *Integrating a Victim Perspective within Criminal Justice* (with J. Goodey, 2000). He has worked for both the New Zealand Ministry of Justice and the Northern Ireland Office in relation to crime prevention policy. He is part of a Home Office-funded team which evaluates youth justice reforms, introduced by the Youth Justice and Criminal Evidence Act (1999).

Marian FitzGerald is currently a Visiting Research Fellow at the London School of Economics and has researched many aspects of British race relations policies. Her earliest work was on relations between the main political parties and ethnic minorities, and she is the author of a report, entitled *Ethnic Minorities and the Criminal Justice System*, for the Royal Commission on Criminal Justice. Her recent publications include a major study of police searches in London and she is presently co-directing new research into police community relations in the capital.

Lynn Hancock is Senior Lecturer in Criminology at Middlesex University. Before moving to Middlesex in 1997, she was a Lecturer in Criminology at Keele University (1993–1996). She held a Leverhume Special Research Fellowship between 1996 and 1998. Her research 'Neighbourhood Change, Crime and Urban Policy' will be published in her forthcoming book *Crime, Community and Disorder*.

Tim Hope is Professor and Head of the Department of Criminology at Keele University, England. He has held positions at the Universities of Manchester and Missouri-St. Louis, CACI Ltd., and the Home Office, where he was Principal Research Officer. His research interests and publications lie in the fields of crime prevention, community safety, victimology and the evaluation of crime prevention programmes, where he is currently leading a consortium to evaluate the Home Office Reducing Burglary Initiative. He recently edited *Perspectives on Crime Reduction* (2000) and co-edited *Crime, Risk and Insecurity: Law and Order in Everyday Life and Political Discourse* (with Richard Sparks, 2000).

George L. Kelling is a Professor in the School of Criminal Justice at Rutgers University, a Research Fellow in the Kennedy School of Government at Harvard University, and a Senior Fellow at the Manhattan Institute. He is the co-author (with James Q. Wilson) of 'Broken Windows', published in *Atlantic Monthly* in 1982, and *Fixing Broken Windows: Restoring Order and Reducing Crime in our Communities* (with Catherine M. Coles, 1996).

Roger Matthews is Professor of Sociology at Middlesex University. His current research interests are centred around issues relating to toleration and public attitudes towards crime and justice. He has published a number of books including *Informal Justice* (1988), *Privatizing Criminal Justice* (1999) and *Rethinking Criminology: The Realist Debate* (with J. Young, 1992). His most recent book is *Doing Time: An Introduction to the Sociology of Imprisonment* (1999).

Ken Pease is Professor of Criminology at Huddersfield University. He has previously held Chairs at the Universities of Manchester and Saskatchewan. He is currently on secondment to the Home Office Crime Reduction Programme and sits on the Crime Panel of the DTI Foresight Programme.

John Pitts is Vauxhall Professor of Socio-Legal Studies at the University of Luton. He has worked as a 'special needs' teacher, a street and club-based youth worker, a youth justice development worker and a group worker in a Young Offender Institution. His recent publications include *Planning Safer Communities* (1998), *Working with Young Offenders* (1999) and *Positive Residential Practice: Learning the Lessons of the 1990s* (2000).

Nick Tilley is Professor of Sociology at the Nottingham Trent University and a consultant to the Home Office Policing and Reducing Crime Unit. He is the co-author of *Realist Evaluation* (with Ray Pawson, 1997) and co-editor of *Surveillance of Public Space: CCTV, Street Lighting and Crime Prevention* (with Kate Painter, 1999).

Paul Wiles is currently Director of Research, Development and Statistics at the Home Office. Previously, he was Professor of Criminology at the University of Sheffield. His recent research interests have been in the analysis of geographical crime patterns and more broadly in the ecology of crime. In the past he has worked in various areas of research on crime and socio-legal studies.

Jock Young is Professor of Sociology and Head of the Centre for Criminology at Middlesex University. His first book was *The Drugtakers* (1971) and his most recent book is *The Exclusive Society* (1999). He is the co-author of *The New Criminology* (with Ian Taylor and Paul Walton, 1973). His current research interests are in urban and cultural studies, and he is working on a book to be entitled *Strange Days: The Transition to Late Modernity*.

Acknowledgements

This book developed out of a series of seminars and workshops which took place in London and Luton in 1998. The seminar series was funded by the ESRC through their Research Seminar Series. We would therefore like to thank the ESRC for their support. We would also like to thank all those who took part in the seminar programme. The participants included Afshan Ahmet, Rob Allen, David Barrett, Jon Bright, Charlie Burr, Adam Crawford, Helen Edwards, Robin Fletcher, Roger Grimshaw, Lynn Hancock, Simon Harding, Tim Hope, Mike Hough, Michael Hutchinson-Rees, George Kelling, Alan Marlow, Kate Painter, Ken Pease, David Porteous, Nick Tilley, Norman Warner and Paul Wiles. We would also like to thank Julie Grogan for her assistance in organising the various meetings and the staff of Middlesex University who provided the necessary administrative support.

Roger Matthews and John Pitts
October 2000

Introduction

Beyond criminology?

Roger Matthews and John Pitts

Introduction

It used to be fashionable to claim that criminology was in crisis (Bottoms and Preston 1980; Young 1986). This diagnosis reflected a general mood of uncertainty and called for a reconsideration of the appropriate focus of criminological investigation. The mood, however, has changed over the past few years and a growing number of books and articles have appeared which suggest that criminology is currently in the process of fragmentation and dissolution (Ericson and Carriere 1994). These recent developments have been attributed to changes in the nature of social relations and to associated changes in the organisation of social control (Garland 1996; Lea 1998). No longer, it is argued, is the state purely concerned with individual acts of deviance. Increasingly, the focus is on security and the control of aggregate populations differentiated according to assessments of risk and dangerousness. The emergence of the so-called 'risk society' has brought in its wake new modes of inclusion and exclusion (Sibley 1995; Young 1999). Some critics propose that these changes have in turn eroded the conventional boundaries between social science disciplines as the objects of investigation begin to overlap and as narrow and parochial interests become less relevant.

Paradoxically, while some academics are beginning to mourn the demise of criminology as a discipline, the size of the crime control industry and the number of students studying criminology in many countries around the world is rapidly growing (Braithwaite 2000). In England and Wales the official annual cost of crime control currently stands at £8.2 billion, and this is projected to increase to £10.6 billion by 2003–4. These costs do not, of course, include the millions of pounds spent every year by private individuals and commercial organisations. Recent reports from the US indicate that in some states expenditure on crime control has exceeded that on education, while the amount spent by federal, state and local governments in 1996 was a staggering $120 billion for civil and criminal justice. This represented a 70 per cent increase over the previous year (Currie 1998; Bureau of Justice 2000).

The growing number of people studying criminology is on the one hand a function of the massive increase in media time dedicated to crime and punishment and, on the other hand, a result of the increased likelihood of employment within the burgeoning criminal justice industry. Thus, it would seem that while the debates in criminology are expressing a sense of exhaustion in relation to the subject area, the number of students studying criminology is increasing steadily, as is the annual expenditure on 'law and order'.

It must be said that there has for some time been growing doubts about the coherence of criminology as a discipline. Many writers have commented upon the elusive and narrow conception of 'crime' which is used among academics (Matthews and Young 1992; Muncie 2000; Schwendinger and Schwendinger 1975; Shearing 1989). If it is the case that the concept of 'crime' does not provide a solid enough base for the construction of the discipline, it might be suggested that its coherence lies in an established set of theories, or in a concerted body of knowledge, or alternatively in a particular tradition or mode of enquiry (Garland and Sparks 2000; Sparks 1997). Some commentators have asked whether criminology is better seen as a subset of a grander and more robust discipline, such as sociology, politics or psychology, or whether it should be seen as little more than an amalgam of knowledges pieced together from a range of disciplines. The answer depends on the degree of coherence one affords to the body of knowledges which have become identified as 'criminology'. Clearly the suggestion that criminology is in the process of fragmentation assumes a prior state of unity, which may be more imagined than real.

The uncertainty over the status of criminology has intensified as a result of a series of debates which have taken place over the past two decades questioning the proper object of enquiry of criminology from advocates of victimology, radical and critical criminology and from feminist criminologists. The victimology movement changed the primary focus from the offender to the victim and in the process drew attention to the limitations of purely offender-based criminology (Maguire and Pointing 1988; Mawby and Walklate 1994). The second level of critique came from radical criminologists who took issue with what they saw as the unduly narrow focus of conventional criminology, which paid relatively little attention to white-collar crime, corporate crime and crimes of the state. Together, these new radical and anti-criminologies demanded a fundamental review of the established agenda of criminological investigation, particularly where it was seen to deny progressive and emancipatory interests. The third level of critique was mounted by feminists who claimed that the assumptions of gender neutrality implicit in major criminological theories were in fact misguided (Leonard 1982). Traditional criminology was found guilty of being androcentric and gender biased. Moreover, it was argued that many key issues in criminology had been neglected by male researchers or defined in masculinist terms and that these issues required investigation from a feminist standpoint (Cain 1990; Smart 1990).

Most of these critiques, however, did not involve the negation of criminology as such, but instead called for the revision and a reorientation of the subject. These so-called anti-criminologies at their most constructive introduced new concerns, a wider range of issues and perspectives and generally enriched the subject area. At their worst they were irrelevant and indulgent. Much of the debate centred around the 'real' meaning of crime and the construction of a 'proper' criminology. While these critical, radical, feminist and realist criminologies attempted to change the focus of criminology, they succeeded in reshaping and to some extent re-legitimating, the subject. More recent contributions, however, have been concerned less with the reorientation of the subject and more with its demise. This change of perspective has been stimulated by widespread socio-economic developments and changing forms of governance which have been associated with globalisation and the transition from modernity to late modernity – or as some would have it, postmodernity (Bauman 1995; Harvey 1989). These changes, in turn, involve a unique historical mutation in which the distinctions between crime and disorder are becoming increasingly blurred and both are becoming incorporated within the wider framework of community safety. In this process it is becoming increasingly difficult to treat crime as a discreet object of study and to sustain criminology as a distinct academic discipline.

From crime prevention to community safety

The period from the mid-1970s to the end of the 1990s witnessed a shift in focus from situational to social crime prevention, to disorder and eventually to community safety. This development can be regarded as one of a gradual widening out of the analytic focus and at the same time a blurring of the distinctions between these processes.

The interest in crime prevention was given a new lease of political and academic life by Ron Clarke in the late 1970s. Clarke, who was Director of the Home Office, played a key role in developing situational crime prevention policies by seeking to provide a response to crime which was both cost effective and politically and socially acceptable (Clarke 1992). The enormous impact of these situational measures is difficult to gauge retrospectively since many of them have subsequently become an integral part of our everyday lives. By the mid-1980s, however, problems of displacement and of 'designing out' a range of serious crimes, including rape, domestic violence and racist attacks, indicated the limits of the situational perspective and encouraged the promotion of social prevention measures in the form of strengthening neighbourhoods by encouraging citizen involvement and fostering informal controls (Currie 1988; Rosenbaum 1986).

However, by the mid-1990s the promise of developing more effective social crime prevention measures was called into question by the observation that crime control strategies were most difficult to mobilise in the neediest areas and that dealing with crime in high-risk areas required a different type of approach. It was increasingly felt within British policy circles that the problem of crime required a more comprehensive and better co-ordinated response while retaining a local focus. A series of inter-agency initiatives were established during the 1980s to address the issue of crime, and a number of agencies have become increasingly involved in the prevention and reduction of different forms of crime. The logic of these developments was endorsed and extended by the Morgan Report (1991), whose recommendation that the responsibility for crime prevention and community safety should be devolved to local authorities was implemented by an incoming Labour government. The subsequent passing of the Crime and Disorder Act (1998) consciously linked crime control with disorder and saw both as part of a more comprehensive community safety strategy (Hughes 1998).

The shift from crime prevention to community safety has extended the terms of reference and made everything from crime and incivilities to environmental issues part of a more comprehensive agenda (Muncie 2000). The fact that community safety is as elusive and loosely defined a term as crime only serves to extend the open-endedness of this new agenda. Crime has increasingly become fused with disorder and both have become enveloped within the more general notion of community safety, despite the fact that the focus of the three terms, the nature of the events involved, the established forms of intervention employed and the characteristics of the victims is remarkably different. It is not so much that crime has become normalised but rather it has become absorbed within a more complex set of overarching relations. This widening of the frame of reference has been reflected in the language and concepts which have been used by policy-makers to address these issues. Such terms as 'dangerousness', 'anti-social behaviour', 'security' and 'social exclusion' are necessarily ill-defined (Brown and Pratt 2000). The wide-ranging terminology represents a shift away from the style of language that has been used in relation to the 'war against crime', which talks of 'targets' and 'campaigns'. From this 'get tough' crime control perspective, the claim is that there are a relatively small number of offenders, victims, groups, neighbourhoods ('hot spots') who are 'responsible' for a disproportionate amount of crime and victimisation. However, as the issue of crime becomes further integrated into the wider matrix of community safety the focus necessarily shifts to aggregate problem populations – the underclass, the marginalised and the socially excluded. Consequently, a hybrid discourse is emerging which at one moment identifies the problem as a limited number of deviant individuals, while at another regards whole sections of the population as a problem. Whereas the war against crime is seen as something which can be 'won' and criminals reformed or deterred, the terms 'underclass' and the 'socially excluded' come close to suggesting a permanent condition which has to be managed rather than eliminated (Feeley and Simon 1994). Policy-makers and practitioners espouse military metaphors and then in the same breath refer to social support and individual needs. This new hybrid discourse is appearing in various local authority-generated policy documents and in the newly established sites such as local authority community safety forums. The multi-agency forums are well situated to cultivate this ambiguous discourse since they typically incorporate the coercive powers of the police alongside the more welfare-oriented approaches of social services and education departments. The formalisation of these multi-agency interventions has created new alliances and new lines of responsibility. Importantly, the role of the key regulatory agencies is changing significantly in this process. The police in particular have been 'let off the hook' and can now legitimately claim that neither crime control nor community safety is their sole responsibility (Kinsey *et al.* 1986). At the same time, they are required to participate in a wider range of interventions which shifts the balance of their work away from crime control and towards public order and social work functions.

It has in fact been evident for some time that crime is related to almost every other negative indicator in society – poor health, limited educational facilities, unreliable transport, bad housing and the more serious environmental problems. Indeed, these negative indicators predictably overlap to the extent that high crime areas also rank high on every other scale of social and economic misfortune. Thus, multiple victimisation (the tendency for the same individual or household to be a victim of a range of hazards) is becoming a more appropriate point of reference than the more linear concept of repeat victimisation, which has shown that individuals and victims are subject to serial forms of victimisation (Genn 1988; Farrell and Pease 1993; Sparks *et al.* 1977). Multiple victimisation is the logical counterpart of multi-agency intervention, since one of the original justifications for developing a multi-agency approach was the recognition that a range of different agencies often intervene independently in the lives of certain individuals in response to the various manifestations of the same underlying problem.

The implications of this broader focus on the inter-related and the socially and geographically concentrated nature of social problems is threefold. The first is that crime may begin to lose its privileged position among other social problems. It may be the main problem in certain areas and for certain individuals, but in the majority of places it will only constitute one component of an integrated matrix of hazards. Second, it calls for a more comprehensive mode of theorising and a consequent shift away from the preoccupation with piecemeal and situational measures to forms of explanation which are more comprehensive and can account for the concentration and compounding of different types of victimisation. Social support theory provides one way of addressing these issues. Its basic proposition is that the best predictor of the areas and households with high levels of multiple victimisation are not those with low levels of social control, as conservative criminologists have argued, but rather those with low levels of social support (Cullen 1994). The difficulty, however, in a post-welfare era is that the traditional networks of state and social support are themselves in the process of dissolution and transformation. Consequently, introducing appropriate systems of support requires the development of new, innovative, interventionist strategies. The third implication is that because multiple victimisation moves beyond a preoccupation with specific crimes, it then raises the wider issue of social justice. The culmination of these processes may possibly result in the radical reorientation of criminology, both as a framework of intervention and of investigation. It will, however, almost certainly foster forms of enquiry that transcend strict disciplinary boundaries and encourage researchers to explore the relation between crime and other problems.

The shifting focus from crime prevention to community safety also raises the question of what is meant by 'community'. The assumption which lies behind much of the community safety rhetoric is that society is comprised of a number of fairly homogeneous communities expressing a high degree of consensus. But as Jock Young argues in Chapter 1, the notion of 'community' itself is becoming increasingly problematic, and any realistic community safety strategy needs to come to terms with the changing nature of these communities and associated forms of identity if they wish to address the issues of crime and community safety.

The integration of crime control and community safety signals that everyone is vulnerable to some degree, not only to the widely acknowledged forms of crime and victimisation but also to a whole range of unforeseen hazards. From the vantage point of community safety it follows that all citizens are more or less directly concerned with the issue of security. The shift in responsibility to local authorities potentially opens the door to new and broader forms of accountability since there is a perceived need to consult with a wide body of local opinion in order to identify priorities, elicit co-operation and establish support. However, rather than create greater transparency, the move towards local authority-driven community safety programmes has instead created new forms of complexity and opacity. This has been achieved through a combination of the development of new forms of managerialism as well as through decentralisation and privatisation.

The New Managerialism

The New Managerialism plays two important roles in this changing situation. First, it provides an ostensibly neutral language in which policy formation and decision-making can be located which serves to mediate the tensions generated by the emerging hybrid discourses. The second major attribute of the New Managerialism is its capacity to turn political and moral decisions into administrative and technical ones. In the name of cost-effectiveness, policy options are counted and discounted. Within the performance indicator culture, which is actively fostered by the New Managerialism, only that which is quantifiable is relevant. The fact that many of these performance indicators are uncertain is generally overlooked in the rush to produce figures and meet targets. The reliance, for example, on official crime statistics as a measure of the effectiveness of specific interventions or the efficiency of the relevant agencies is extremely dubious. Although there has recently been some recognition in official circles of the limitations of using official crime figures in this way, the general unreliability of many performance indicators is not routinely addressed (Home Office 2000). The performance indicator culture has encouraged new forms of expertise in the manipulation of figures and in prioritising those activities which are more directly measurable, irrespective of their overall contribution to designated objectives, the interests of the 'clients' or the realisation of justice (Loveday 1999). The requirement of local authorities to produce regular crime audits has also provided an example of how a body of unrelated figures, drawn from disparate and unchecked sources, based in many cases on dubious methodologies, can be cobbled together and used to provide a benchmark from which 'progress' is measured.

New Labour was quick to appropriate both the language and the principles of the New Managerialism. Its emphasis on the rationality of 'what works', 'joined-up solutions' and 'empowerment' fitted well with New Labour's avowed commitment to rational public policy and the devolution of power to 'local people'. As Anthony Bottoms (1995) has argued, the adoption of managerialism within criminal justice incorporates a significant actuarial dimension that presents policy choices as a function of competing risks which can be assessed on an objective scale as well as on the basis of cost-effectiveness. Balancing off these two apparently neutral and 'scientific' sets of criteria, however, opens up considerable latitude for interpretation and discretion. But the central appeal of the New Managerialism is that it offers a template for the new, more restricted role of government – a 'Third Way', which New Labour believed was necessitated by the unmanageability of the global economy and the privatisation of personal life precipitated by the radical changes in the class structure of Britain over the preceding thirty years (Giddens 1998). As Cooper and Lousada note:

> The state of affairs described here arises largely where government has vacated territory which it once organised, resourced, nurtured and presided over with *political authority* – even if contested authority – but for which it nevertheless will not or cannot abandon all responsibility. Where once it willed the means, now it tends to prescribe the ends while others are left to supply the means; and as with all instrumentally-oriented practices, the logic governing the attainment of ends is the logic of rules. In short, where government was, now audit regulation and management is. And so, inevitably, this social ego is pervaded by obsessional anxieties and behaviours about the loss of control.
>
> (Cooper and Lousada 2000: xx)

Thus, the Crime and Disorder Act (1998), in handing new responsibilities over to local authorities and local multi-agency partnerships, prescribes the goals they should pursue, the targets they should achieve and the time scales in which they should operate, but not the means for their achievement. However, as Cooper and Lousada (2000) suggest, the anxieties about the political legitimacy and electoral credibility engendered by this new form of 'hands-off' governance leads to an unprecedented concern with the management of implementation, which is specified in such detail that what at first sight appears to be an exercise in devolution upon closer inspection looks to be a franchising operation. 'Product support' is provided via a steady flow of 'evidence-based' data about 'what works' and 'pilot studies' of new administrative arrangements and modes of intervention, while 'quality control' is vouchsafed by statutory audits. Meanwhile, 'action teams', comprising senior officials from the relevant ministries, work on inter-ministerial synchronisation and the articulation of central government activity with that of the local authorities and multi-agency partnerships.

New Labour's community safety strategy similarly devotes an inordinate amount of time and energy to the detail of its day-to-day management and implementation – the development of partnerships, monitoring systems and the like – but little to any analysis of the origins and nature of the problems to which these elaborate, joined-up solutions are to be applied. In the 115-page Audit Commission report, *Safety in Numbers* (1999), for example, while only half a page is devoted to the origins of crime, David Farrington and David West's (1993) by now familiar 'risk factors' are presented as the appropriate mode of explanation, although it is noted in the report that: 'Risk factors are not causes of crime as such, but the likelihood of criminality increases as their intensity or clustering increases'. The origins of these phenomena, or why they are 'clustered' in the ways that they are, is apparently of little interest.

In the view of the government, the 'joined-upness' of solutions to youth crime and community safety consists in the simultaneous management of those 'risk factors' associated with the onset of crime and delinquency, and the application of 'evidence-based' technologies for the correction of familial, cognitive or behavioural deficiencies which lead to persistence. Alongside this, systemic anomalies are eradicated by rigorous audits and the imposition, by central government, of financial penalties upon local government, the police and the Crown Prosecution Service.

There is, however, an ongoing tension between the New Managerialism and multi-agency partnerships since interventions are not so much mobilised by the seriousness or urgency of the particular issue, but rather, in many cases, they are motivated by the availability of funding the interests of specific agencies. The actual decisions about priorities are often dependent upon personalised preferences or political priorities rather than a rigorous assessment of risk. Moreover, lines of responsibility in multi-agency networks are frequently blurred with the consequence that roles are unspecified and interventions may lack clear lines of command and decision-making. Consequently, interventions tend to be uncertain and poorly conceived, while active involvement may be short-lived, particularly where agency and individual interests compete (Crawford 1998). In many cases differences of objectives, styles of operation, and interests are played down in order to sustain a loosely constructed and fragile consensus. The increasingly diverse and amorphous nature of the object – community safety – is reflected in the equivocal nature of the mechanisms which are responsible for achieving it – multi-agency partnerships. As Adam Crawford argues in Chapter 2, the partnership approach, the New Managerialism and communitarianism form the three central strands of New Labour's 'Third Way' strategy, which aims to move beyond old-style statism, on the one hand, and a reliance on the operation of a free market economy on the other. Each of these separate strands has a certain logic and coherence on its own, but when 'joined-up' they produce unanticipated tensions.

Decentralisation and privatisation

A consequence of the political and academic onslaught which sought to limit the powers of the sovereign state in the 1960s and 1970s was the development of a decentralisation strategy through which state power would be dispersed and in which a series of more approachable, accountable and more efficient agencies would come to provide essential services. In the field of 'law and order' this decentralising impulse took the form of delegalisation, decarceration and deprofessionalisation. This resulted in the proliferation of different forms of privatisation, the expansion of the voluntary sector, the creation of greater autonomy among regulatory agencies and the devolving of responsibility for crime control to community organisations. In this process the aim was seen to be to gradually shed state power from a central axis to a wide range of regulatory bodies and for the state to become involved in 'steering' rather than 'rowing' (Cohen 1987).

This destructuring impulse provided the impetus for the development of new forms of decentralised community control which was seen to promote forms of inclusion by dealing with deviancy in more immediate and informal ways within the community (Cohen 1985).The optimism which had been associated in the early period with these destructuring tendencies, however, gradually turned into pessimism. Critics argued that what drove these more informal community-based interventions was not their greater effectiveness or benevolence. Rather, they were adopted because they were cheaper and provided a way of reducing state obligation to provide decent and consistent services, while serving to depoliticise the process of crime control by turning public issues into personal problems. At the same time, the proliferation of these apparently benign agencies meant that the depth and intensity of intervention in many cases was increased. As a result of 'net widening', it was argued, these interventions were seen as being largely counterproductive since a growing number of minor offenders were drawn ineluctably into the mainstream criminal justice process with a predictable proportion ending up in prison at a later date (McMahon 1990).Thus, rather than producing new forms of inclusion, the decentralising strategy resulted in promoting new forms of social exclusion and marginalisation. For some critics a disturbing consequence of the decentralising impulse was that existing forms of state control remained in place, and rather than curtail state power, this strategy produced an unwieldy complex of agencies and organisations which traversed the conventional distinctions between the public and the private realms and between state and civil society. Instead of a straightforward process of decentralisation, what seemed to take place was a complex blend of decentring and recentring processes, resulting in the proliferation of different sites of decision-making, increased bureaucratisation and a more diffuse set of interventions arising from a growing array of increasingly unaccountable agencies.

In retrospect, the model of the state power which the majority of criminologists held at this time was extremely limited. Consequently, most of the key concepts which were used to explain these developments remained underdeveloped:

> Take the very notion of decentralisation itself. This derives from a master metaphor which sees political power in terms of centre and periphery. We are asked to imagine such things as deviants being drawn away from the centre, or the periphery being awarded the power that belonged to the centre. But this metaphor rests on a largely unexamined view of state power, which at times leans towards the most extreme forms of elitist centralism, at other times towards the most amorphous forms of pluralism.
>
> (Cohen 1987: 377)

In relation to implementation there was also a *naïveté* about the role and interests of these newly formed or reconstructed agencies. It became apparent that the agencies had their own specific interests, not least of which was their own preservation and expansion. Less clear was the increasingly intricate network of policy formation and implementation, the financial links and pecuniary constraints which were imposed, the hierarchical relations which developed, and the growing pressure for these apparently autonomous and independent bodies to pursue the same goals and adopt the same management practices which had been previously developed in the existing state agencies. Alongside such uncertainties was a lack of clarity about the ways in which newly state-sponsored agencies were being established to monitor, assess, guide and regulate the 'independent' agencies, such that the apparent cost savings which were claimed were in some cases more than swallowed up by the costs of monitoring and supervision.

The criticisms of the decentralisation strategy which surfaced in the mid-1980s, however, did little to slow down this process, although they may have influenced its direction. Privatisation in its various forms continued to be promoted, particularly in relation to policing, crime prevention, the use of security equipment and the contracting out of prison management (Johnston 2000; Matthews 1989). The rapid development of multi-agency partnerships encouraged the involvement of the private sector alongside voluntary and statutory agencies.

In the UK in the 1990s the decentralising impulse took a slightly different turn following the implementation of the recommendation of the Morgan Report (1991) to devolve responsibility for crime control and community safety to local authorities. Emphasis was placed upon multi-agency partnerships and the establishment of community safety strategy groups which were to be responsible for assessing the nature of crime in each locality, developing a community safety strategy and monitoring interventions. During the 1980s, the

Thatcher-led Conservative government had tried to limit the powers of local authorities, which were seen as unreliable, but a decade later this policy was reversed by an incoming Labour government and local authorities in conjunction with the local police were given statutory responsibility for crime prevention and community safety. Local authorities were seen as uniquely placed to connect with the local population and thereby able to increase citizen involvement in crime control while mobilising the wide range of agencies which were deemed necessary to develop a comprehensive community safety strategy – housing, planning, social services, education, leisure services, youth services and others.

The potential problems associated with devolving responsibilities for crime control and community safety in this way received limited attention. The urge to shift responsibility to local authorities played down the existing unequal distribution of needy people in different areas, as well as the geographical concentration of victimisation. The placing of greater responsibility on local authorities for this increased range of problems has further burdened certain municipalities. Thus this development may be seen as a recipe for the consolidation rather than the alleviation of injustice. At the same time it should be noted that creating greater autonomy in local decision-making does not necessarily involve greater empowerment or increased accountability. Nor does it provide an alternative to the growth of a crime control bureaucracy, but instead broadens its base. Although crime in itself may be locally extremely variable, the level of crime in any particular area will also be a product of a wider process of deflection and displacement as well as a function of social and economic movements which affect the make-up and distribution of local populations (Barr and Pease 1990). Similarly, community safety in the vast majority of localities will be affected by environmental, health and transport issues which reach far beyond the geographical boundaries of local boroughs and over which particular local authorities may have little or no control (Young 1990). Therefore, in relation to crime and community safety there are unresolved issues about whether the local authority is the appropriate regulatory site and whether it might be more appropriate to locate these responsibilities in regional authorities if the aim is to achieve greater levels of distributive and social justice.

This shift of responsibilities is likely, as has been suggested above, to have a profound impact on the way in which crime control is perceived and carried out. Although it is too early to properly assess the impact of this form of decentralisation, the devolvement of powers and responsibilities to local authorities could take one of two directions. The first, which has been the main development to date, is that it could stimulate styles of management in which crime control and community safety are tied to narrow and short-sighted administrative concerns with community safety forums becoming victims of the New Managerialism and of the associated performance indicator culture. This could lead to a proliferation of bureaucratic processes and the overall expansion of an ever more opaque and impenetrable criminal justice industry. It could continue to be preoccupied with vertical forms of accountability, producing endless documentation, glossy brochures and the construction of audits which are designed to provide the basis of what is euphemistically called 'evidence-led' policy. As Nick Tilley suggests in Chapter 3, there are serious problems with the contention that policy and practice can simply be 'led' by evidence. There is a danger that this approach could lead towards a 'virtual war' against crime in which the reality of crime is reduced to a process of 'representations' based on forms of creative accounting, the massaging and recycling of figures, and the creation of forums in which those responsible for crime control and community safety are increasingly distanced from the messy business of victimisation and suffering (Ignatieff 2000).

The alternative option is that this form of decentralisation could open the door to wider public participation in both the decision-making process and in the setting of the community safety agenda. That is, local authorities could become a conduit for the development of new styles of participation and develop a real autonomy and independence in decision-making which is open and responsive to public interests. The potential of a more localised response in creating greater accountability remains largely unrealised and although the more democratically-minded local authorities may have a genuine desire to be responsive to the needs and views of the local communities, the lines of accountability appear at present to be mainly horizontal with the main pressure coming from the government, the Home Office, the Audit Commission and the police inspectorate.

Disorder

Since the 1980s there has been a growing concern in official circles, as well as in local communities, with the issue of disorder. This concern, however, has not entirely been stimulated by an increase in disorder in all its forms on our city streets. Certainly there has been an increase in the visibility of certain types of disorder, such as graffiti, vagrants and homeless people on the streets, aggressive begging, and more recently 'squeegee merchants', while a number of urban centres in Britain have become sites of disorder at the weekends involving predominantly young people (while other centres, in contrast, have become desolate and neglected). In many urban centres, however, the number of public demonstrations and riots and the level of public drunkenness has remained fairly stable, and in comparison to twenty or thirty years ago is more contained. Thus in explaining the growing concern with disorder we cannot identify a simple causal sequence which sees these responses, both by the general public and by official bodies, as a direct result of a general increase in disorder itself. The explanation instead must lie in the ways in which these incidents are perceived and the changing levels of toleration which is expressed by different groups in different localities. As Lynn Hancock and Roger Matthews argue in Chapter 4, the term toleration is a critical but largely unexplored concept in understanding changing public attitudes towards crime, disorder and community safety, since the level and nature of public tolerance will condition which activities members of the community are willing to put up with and those which they are not.

The changing conceptions and responses to street prostitution in the UK since the 1950s provides an example of how public tolerance and social sensibilities have changed. Although the visibility of street prostitution decreased in most urban centres following the implementation of the recommendations of the Wolfenden Report (1957), a number of residents groups across the country campaigned vigorously for the removal of prostitution from their neighbourhoods. This resulted in street patrols by residents, and in some localities vigilante squads were established. The groups involved a diverse mix of local residents and included individuals drawn from different religious and ethnic backgrounds. Their justification for establishing citizen patrols was that the police and local authorities were not interested in dealing with the problem. This was predominantly a 'bottom-up' community-based movement involving a number of like-minded but independent groups in a number of different urban locations.

The sociological question which arises is why these groups of residents, often living in poor transient communities – which the literature suggests should have low levels of informal control – mobilised so effectively around this issue in an attempt, as they saw it, to win back 'their' streets and neighbourhoods (Matthews 1993). Previous generations had put up with the noise and disturbance associated with street prostitution for years, but clearly a shift occurred in terms of public tolerance and this appeared to be bound up with changing conceptions of defensible space and changing expectations about privacy, security and risk. No small factor in this equation was the role of women living in 'red light' districts who felt they were living under a curfew and that they and their children should have the right to walk freely in public spaces without fear of harassment or intimidation. The mobilisation of local residents around this issue served to increase confidence and was a source of empowerment for many local residents groups. Dealing with disorder, as Zygmunt Bauman (1995) has observed, can have a cleansing and cathartic effect: it represents a form of social purification.

Because of the continuous and quasi-legal nature of prostitution, the police were ill-equipped to deal with the issue, and although a series of 'vice squads' were established in the 1970s, their methods relied mainly on the mobilisation of the criminal law which appeared increasingly heavy-handed, inequitable and inappropriate, particularly since many of the residents came to regard female prostitutes as victims rather than offenders (Benson and Matthews 2000). In many instances, residents were opposed to prostitution not prostitutes. Therefore, they looked for different, non-legal and more appropriate ways of addressing the problem which involved a combination of social and situational measures. In some ways the growing concern with disorder reflected both the increasing aspirations of citizens and the mobilisation of social movements which were interested in defending, and where possible, improving urban life. Increasingly, disorder in its various forms provides a bridge between crime on the one hand, and community safety on the other. Just as it is the case that certain forms of disorder involve illegalities (such as 'soliciting for the purposes of prostitution'), they also involve 'quality of life' issues which readily fuse with growing concerns about environmentalism, health, transport and community safety in general.

As George Kelling (1987) has pointed out, whereas crimes are mainly *events* or *acts* which occur in a specific time and place, disorder constitutes a *condition*. It represents not so much a direct confrontation between an individual victim and offender, but an ongoing process which affects whole neighbourhoods. The articulation of these concerns was presented in George Kelling and James Q. Wilson's article, 'Broken Windows: The Police and Neighbourhood Safety', published in *Atlantic Monthly* in 1982. The article hit a nerve, or rather a series of nerves, and its extensive international influence and the debate which it generated is testimony to its significance both as an attempt to explain the link between crime disorder and community safety and to provide a practical guide for intervention. The immediate appeal of the article was that it offered a way out which was both plausible and potentially cost-effective. The authors claimed that there was a clear link between low level disorder, crime and neighbourhood decline. They argued that the visible evidence of graffiti and public drunkenness indicates that an area is a vulnerable target for criminal activities. This prompts more mobile and respectable families to move away, with the consequence that the existing system of informal controls breaks down, crime and incivilities proliferate and eventually the neighbourhood slips into decline. Thus Wilson and Kelling argue that:

> at the community level disorder and crime are usually inextricably linked in a kind of developmental sequence. Social psychologists and police officers tend to agree that if a window in a building is broken and if it is left unrepaired, all the rest of the windows will soon be broken. This is as true in nice neighbourhoods as in run-down ones.
>
> (Wilson and Kelling 1982: 78)

The novelty and the attractiveness of this thesis lies in its emphasis on the added value of intervening at the most immediate and accessible level. In opposition to those forms of crime control which concentrated on serious crime, Wilson and Kelling offered a strategy which promised significant benefits by dealing promptly with low level disorder, incivilities and minor offences. In this way they promised to turn declining neighbourhoods around and to salvage those who were in danger of 'tipping' into decline (Hope 1999).

The 'Broken Windows' thesis was for many years held up as the new wisdom of criminology. However, it also became the object of criticism from a number of directions. These critiques generally took one of three forms. Most commentators took issue with the claimed developmental sequence between disorder, crime and urban decline. In opposition, they argued that this account captured at best only one side of the dialectic and at worst distorted the real developmental sequence which was in fact the opposite of the one proposed by Wilson and Kelling. Critics argued that it was urban decline which was more likely to affect the housing market, family stability and the composition of neighbourhoods and that as these elements changed informal controls would tend to break down and the vulnerability of affected populations would increasingly make them more attractive targets for crime and disorder (Matthews 1992). Second, it was suggested that the thesis did not clearly differentiate the significance and the social meaning of different kinds of disorder. Although it was accepted that disorder was a loosely defined category, the important differences between say prostitution and graffiti, or between homeless people sleeping in doorways and rowdy youths became blurred (Sampson and Raudenbush 1999). This conceptual slippage led to a third problem, the critics claimed, which was that Wilson and Kelling failed to distinguish between policing problems and welfare problems. Moving the homeless on or arresting them for loitering was seen by many as inappropriate – the problems were merely put out of sight and it failed to address the real causes, such as the shortage of available work or affordable accommodation. In Chapter 5, George Kelling provides a response to these critiques and restates the need to take issues of disorder seriously while providing some suggestions of the ways in which the 'Broken Windows' thesis might be developed and implemented.

Other critics have argued that disorder can have its uses and have pointed to the dangers of attempting to suppress every form of disorder since this can result in sanitised cities in which street life, in its various forms, becomes conspicuously absent (Sennett 1970). Alternatively, the fight against disorder can produce 'fortress cities', in which the use of public space is curtailed and law enforcement is built into the very bricks and mortar of the urban landscape. In Los Angeles, heralded by many as the city of the future, the fight against crime and disorder has resulted in what Mike Davis (1998) has identified as the creation of a series of 'social control districts' which embody new forms of spatial discipline. These include: *abatement districts*, in which the traditional police powers over nuisance are extended to the removal of graffiti and prostitution; *enhancement districts*, in which those committing certain offences within a specified radius of designated public institutions can have their penalties increased; *containment districts* which are designed to quarantine potentially endemic social problems and, more usually, certain social types; and *exclusion districts*, in which designated pariah groups are excluded from public spaces or even city limits. Engaging in urban life in cities like Los Angeles becomes a matter of moving between a series of 'security bubbles', which may take the form of malls, offices or gated communities. It is a world in which order is organised in relation to strict spatial divisions producing new geographies of inclusion and exclusion.

The underclass and social exclusion

A corollary of the shift from crime control to community safety is a change in focus from individual offenders to aggregate populations and a consequent interest in the development of an 'underclass' and the socially excluded. These two terms are used in different ways to refer to populations who are depicted as being excluded from useful or meaningful participation in mainstream society.

The concept of the underclass was developed and widely publicised through the work of the conservative critic Charles Murray (1994). Murray attributes the emergence of an underclass to the failings of a welfare system which creates dependency and indolence. He argues that not only is the present welfare system a disincentive for people to work, but it helps to foster a sub-economy of crime and promotes illegitimacy. This in turn sustains a 'culture of poverty' and intensifies the divisions between the haves and the have-nots. Whereas Murray locates the development of the underclass in a counter-productive welfare system and in the consequent lack of motivation of certain types of people to seek gainful employment and support their families, Ralph Dahrendorf (1994) and William Julius Wilson (1987, 1994) offer an alternative, 'structuralist' account of the emergence of an underclass by focusing upon the processes leading to social and economic polarisation in late modern societies (Crowther 2000). Wilson identifies the underclass as comprising the long-term unemployed, the persistent poor and the denizens of the 'ghetto' who have lost regular and guaranteed access to markets, especially the labour market, and effective political representation. In his later work Wilson uses the phrase the 'ghetto poor' in order to distance his critique from that of Murray.

Although contemporary politics and policy in the UK has increasingly been influenced by the underclass thesis in general, and particularly in its more voluntaristic variant as presented by Murray, in mainland Europe the notion of 'social exclusion' has gained far greater currency. The idea of social exclusion has its origins in France in the early 1980s. Upon his election as President in 1981, François Mitterrand faced nation-wide riots in the multi-racial *banlieue*. The analysis of these events proffered by Mitterrand's advisers suggested that French society was experiencing *une grande mutation* characterised by the dissipation of industrial society and the working-class movement, the supplanting of collectivism by individualism and subjectivism, mass unemployment and racial conflict (Wieviorka 1994). It was evident that the multi-racial *banlieue*, the site of the 1981 riots, was the place, *par excellence*, where the sense of French citizenship was at its weakest because its denizens were wholly or partially 'excluded' from participation in the key social, educational, cultural and political institutions of French life. As a result, Mitterrand's subsequent 'social prevention initiative' attempted not only to reduce crime and ameliorate material poverty, but also to include *les exclus* in the key institutions of the state and civil society in order to strengthen social cohesion and social order and re-establish the political legitimacy of the Republic (Donzelot and Roman 1991). As Graham Room observes, whereas:

> The notion of poverty is primarily focused upon distributional issues: the
> lack of resources at the disposal of an individual or household ... social

exclusion focus(es) primarily on relational issues, in other words, inadequate social participation, lack of social integration and lack of power.

(Room 1995: 5)

Defined in this way, 'social exclusion' is inextricably bound up with the notion
of citizenship. Further, it was the related issues of citizenship and 'exclusion'
which Jacques Delors, who was a close political associate of Mitterrand, introduced into the vocabulary of the European Union, most notably in the Delors
Report, *Growth, Competitiveness and Employment* (1993). Social exclusion and
citizenship both have a central role in contemporary political discourse in the
UK, but because the voluntaristic variant of the underclass thesis has such a
firm purchase within that discourse, there is always the sense that social exclusion may be self-inflicted and that discussions of citizenship accentuate the
responsibilities of young people at the expense of their civil, political and
economic rights (Pitts 2001). However, the question of citizenship, and more
particularly whether a citizen's race or culture has a bearing upon the service
he or she might receive from the police, was forcefully posed by the
Macpherson Report (1999) on the murder of Stephen Lawrence. Marian
FitzGerald, in Chapter 6, assesses the impact of Macpherson on the policing of
black and Asian citizens and the extent to which the policies which emerged
following the publication of the Macpherson Report have contributed to their
safety.

In order to respond to what is seen as the development of a more divided
society in which the gap between the rich and poor appears to be ever
widening, the Labour government established the Social Exclusion Unit. In its
major strategy document, it states that:

> Over the last generation, this has become a more divided country. While
> most areas have benefited from rising living standards, the poorest neigh-
> bourhoods have tended to become rundown, more prone to crime, and
> more cut off from the labour market. The national picture conceals pockets
> of intense deprivation where the problems of unemployment and crime are
> acute and hopelessly tangled up with poor health, housing and education.
> They have become no go areas for some and no exit zones for others.

(Social Exclusion Unit 1998)

In a society in which the structural and social divisions are becoming
increasingly pronounced, the ability of the Social Exclusion Unit to do more
than identify and possibly ameliorate certain pockets of poverty and deprivation
appear to be limited. The proposed interventions such as job training, the
development of 'more flexible' benefits, improved housing management,
measures to 'tackle' anti-social neighbours, youth crime and drugs, youth work,
improved local services and initiatives to get central government departments
working more closely together appear to be both overly ambitious and at the
same time inadequate.

In Chapter 7, John Pitts provides an overview and assessment of the Labour government's strategy for dealing with problem and excluded youth and argues that although this strategy may strive to tackle 'alienation' amongst the young it is unable to refurbish the structural links between impoverished, destabilised, neighbourhoods and local and regional labour markets; nor will it offer the financial incentives and tax breaks to the businesses and industries which would 'kick-start' moribund local economies into life.

It has also been suggested that there are conceptual problems associated with the use of the terms 'underclass' and 'social exclusion' in that, as with the notion of decentralisation, they suggest a simple centre–periphery relation and play down or ignore divisions and diversity in society. The implicit suggestion in much of this literature is that if the marginalised could be properly incorporated into the mainstream of society the problem would be resolved. This overlooks the fact that the so-called 'mainstream' is itself hugely fragmented and divided along class, gender, age and ethnic lines (Levitas 1998; Morris 1996). Similarly, the notions of underclass and social exclusion suggest that deprivation and inequality are peripheral in society rather than endemic. By playing down the potentially positive aspects of difference and diversity it fosters a moral authoritarianism which urges conformity with the contrived consensus of the mainstream. In reality, the stark dichotomy of inclusion and exclusion does not stand up to empirical investigation. Even those who live in poverty or who experience long-term unemployment may, as William Julius Wilson points out, endorse mainstream social values:

> Our research reveals that the beliefs of inner-city residents bear little resemblance to the blanket media reports asserting that values have plummeted in impoverished inner-city neighbourhoods or that people in the inner-city have an entirely different value system. What is so striking is that despite the overwhelming joblessness and poverty, black residents in inner-city ghetto neighbourhoods actually verbally endorse, rather than undermine, the basic American values concerning individual initiative.
>
> (Wilson 1996: 179)

The term social exclusion, however, fits well with the view that social deprivation is multifaceted and with the suggestion that the issues are wider than poverty alone and involve moral considerations and notions of identity. It also fits well with the commitment to multi-agency interventions. The implicit suggestion, however, that the problem is overwhelmingly one of distribution, or redistribution, has been challenged by those who see the focus on the underclass and the socially excluded as a distraction from the development of a more diverse and tolerant society, on the one hand, and by those who argue for a more thoroughgoing economic and social reorganisation, on the other (Bowring 2000; Young 1990).

The risk society

The advent of 'late modernity', it has been argued, marks the abandonment of the modernist dream, that through judicious intervention in health, crime and the environment, the state will progressively rid the world of risk. Instead, we confront the reality that both the natural and the social worlds are far less amenable to control than we had once supposed, and we can predict neither outcomes nor consequences with any degree of certainty. As Anthony Giddens (1992) comments:

> To accept risk as risk ... is to acknowledge that no aspects of our activities follow a pre-destined course, and all are open to contingent happenings. In this sense it is quite accurate to characterise modernity, as Ulrich Beck does, as a 'risk society', a phrase which refers to more than just the fact that modern life introduces new forms of danger which humanity has to face. Living in the risk society means living with a calculate attitude to the open possibilities of action, positive and negative, with which as individuals, and globally, we are confronted in a continuous way in our contemporary social existence.
>
> (Giddens 1992: 28)

Paradoxically, as Tim Hope observes in Chapter 8, the modernist attempt to understand the origins and nature of crime in order to devise social policy and rehabilitative responses which address the supposed causes of crime, is giving way to actuarial calculation, leading to categorisations of neighbourhoods and populations of actual and potential victims and offenders. In this way risk assessment is increasingly seen to displace the use of personal and moral criteria as a basis of intervention (Feeley and Simon 1992). Tim Hope also raises the issue of distributive justice and the distribution of crime and victimisation. This theme is further developed by Paul Wiles and Ken Pease in the final chapter. They argue that the issue of distributive justice is a fundamental but largely unexplored concept within criminology, since it relates both to questions about the relation between inequalities and punishment as well as to the possibility and desirability of achieving a more equal distribution of crime and victimisation throughout society.

The actuarial language of risk gives the impression of being objective, calculable and scientific. The reality is that the modes of risk assessment which have been developed to date in relation to crime are not particularly precise and consequently their predictive capacity is uncertain. Thus as tool for management or a guide for intervention, risk classification schemes are of limited utility. The value choices which guide decisions can, however, be effectively concealed, while most calculations of risk conveniently allow considerable leeway in the interpretation of the findings and the possibility of overriding outcomes when required. Of particular significance is the way in which the New Managerialism combines with actuarialism to redefine the meaning of certain categories. The way, for example, in which the meaning of 'needs' has become redefined in this discourse, such that it becomes virtually synonymous with 'risk' is instructive. The 'new penology' redefines needs of prisoners as those factors or deficiencies which are thought to be linked to an individual's criminal career. As Kelly Hannah-Moffat has argued in relation to risk assessment procedures in women's prisons:

> [However], an unintentional byproduct emerging in the correctional logic of the new women's prisons is that the concept of 'need' shifts from a vindication of a claim for resources (the feminist view) to a calculation of criminal potential (the risk of recidivism). Thus, correctional strategies and programmes now 'govern at a distance' by regulating women through their needs. Unlike past feminist narratives on women's needs that stress women's entitlement, the Correctional Service uses the language of needs to facilitate responsibilization. The prisoner is expected to 'cure' herself and manage her own risk by satisfying her crimogenic needs.
>
> (Hannah-Moffat 1999: 84)

Needs assessment, therefore, becomes a variant of risk assessment and serves as regulatory mechanism rather than a basis for therapeutic or welfare intervention. The potential for extending the logic of this form of needs/risk analysis outside of the correctional setting into community safety programmes is, of course, considerable.

The growing preoccupation with actuarial policies has also been heightened by the discovery, and dramatisation, of new forms of risk of which we may previously have been only dimly aware. Changing public sensibilities and awareness, a steadily expanding and ever news-hungry media, proliferating pressure groups, and a growing body of social and criminological research have been instrumental in revealing a much wider range of potential hazards. Moreover, hazards which we might once have regarded as rare and isolated aberrations increasingly appear to be endemic. Environmental pollution, contaminated foodstuffs, growing health problems and disease, violence in its various forms, drug use combined with other forms of crime and disorder appear as a major threat to the realisation of 'the good life' (Crimmens and Pitts 1999).

Conclusion

The shifting emphasis from crime control to community safety which has been institutionalised in local authority-based partnerships in the UK has been described as a 'sea change' and a 'watershed' with some justification. The formal coupling of crime and disorder in the Crime and Disorder Act (1998) and the incorporation of both within the wider framework of community safety has had a number of significant consequences, for criminology and for how crime is seen in relation to other hazards. Although the crime control industry continues to grow, the privileged position which crime has been accorded in recent years is coming under question. New styles of governance are emerging and the discourses through which interventions are being formulated are changing significantly. At the same time, policing strategies for crime are gradually being transformed.

In the course of these developments it seems probable that we will see existing divisions between administrative and managerialist approaches on the one side, and the more critical and sociological perspectives on the other, becoming wider and deeper. For the growing number of students and practitioners in the field, the focus of criminology will become broader but less precise while choices of orientation will become more difficult as debates become increasingly polarised and distanced.

The situation in which those of us who have come to identify ourselves as criminologists find ourselves is both disturbing and exciting. It is disturbing inasmuch that a great deal of what we have taken for granted for many years in criminology appears unreliable and uncertain. It is exciting in that new possibilities and questions are opening up. We are beginning to re-evaluate some of the old issues. There is, however, a problem in making sense of the changes and responding appropriately, not just because of the scale and depth of changes taking place, but also because of the pace of change. It is increasingly difficult to keep up with developments. The certainties of the past have become today's problems, and they demand solutions which conventional approaches no longer seem able to adequately grasp.

This book is a response to these changes. It represents an attempt to come to terms with shifting practices and changing policies, and it reflects current uncertainties and future possibilities. It is self-consciously diverse and uneven. In many of the articles there is a sense of reflection and taking stock. At the same time, however, there is evidence of a struggle to move on and to explore new ground.

References

Abel-Smith, B. and Townsend, P. (1964) *The Poor and the Poorest*, London: G. Bell and Sons.

Audit Commission (1996) *Misspent Youth*, London: the Audit Commission.

—— (1999) *Safety in Numbers*, London: the Audit Commission.

Barr, R. and Pease, K. (1990) 'Crime Placement, Displacement and Deflection', in M. Tonry and N. Morris (eds) *Crime and Justice: An Annual Review of Research*, Chicago: University of Chicago Press.

Bauman, Z. (1995) *Life in Fragments: Essays in Postmodern Morality*, Oxford: Blackwell.

Benson, C. and Matthews, R. (2000) 'Police and Prostitution: Vice Squads in Britain', in R. Weitzer (ed.) *Sex for Sale*, New York: Routledge.

Blagg, H. and Smith, D. (1989) *Crime and Social Policy*, London: Longman.

Bottoms, A. (1995) 'The Philosophy and Politics of Punishment and Sentencing', in C. Clarkson and R. Morgan (eds) *The Politics of Sentencing Reform*, Oxford: Clarendon.

—— and McWilliams, W. (1979) 'A Non-treatment Paradigm for Probation Practice', *British Journal of Social Work*, 9: 159–202.

—— and Preston, R. (1980) *The Coming Penal Crisis*, Edinburgh: Scottish Academic Press.

Bowring, F. (2000) 'Social Exclusion: Limitations of the Debate', *Critical Social Policy*, 20(3): 307–30.

Braithwaite, J. (2000) 'The New Regulatory State and the Transformation of Criminology', *British Journal of Criminology*, 40: 223–38.

Brown, M. and Pratt, J. (2000) *Dangerous Offenders: Punishment and Social Order*, London: Routledge.

Bureau of Justice (2000) *Expenditure and Employment Statistics*, US Department of Justice. On-line. Available: www.ojp.usdoj.gov/bjs/eande.htm

Cain, M. (1990) 'Realist Philosophy and Standpoint Epistemologies or Feminist Criminology as a Successor Science', in L. Gelsthorpe and A. Morris (eds) *Feminist Perspectives in Criminology*, Milton Keynes: Open University Press.

Clarke, R. (1992) *Situational Crime Prevention: Successful Case Studies*, New York: Harrow and Heston.

Cloward, R. and Ohlin, L. (1960) *Delinquency and Opportunity*, London: Routledge and Kegan Paul.

—— and Fox-Piven, F. (1972) *Regulating the Poor: The Functions of Public Welfare*, London: Tavistock Publications.

Cohen, S. (1985) *Visions of Social Control*, Cambridge: Polity Press.

—— (1987) 'Taking Decentralisation Seriously', in J. Lowman, R. Menzies and T. Palys (eds) *Transcarceration: Essays in the Sociology of Social Control*, Aldershot: Gower.

Cooper, A. and Lousada, J. (2000) *The Meaning of Welfare*, London: Venture Press.

Crawford, A. (1998) *Crime Prevention and Community Safety: Politics, Policies and Practices*, London: Longman.

Crimmens, D. and Pitts, J. (1999) *Positive Residential Practice: The Lessons of the 1990s*, Lyme Regis: Russell House Publishing.

Crowther, C. (2000) 'Thinking About the "Underclass": Towards a Political Economy of Policing', *Theoretical Criminology*, 4(2): 149–67.

Cullen, F. (1994) 'Social Support as an Organising Concept for Criminology', *Justice Quarterly*, 11(4): 527–59.

Currie, E. (1986) *Confronting Crime: An American Challenge*, New York: Pantheon.

—— (1988) 'Two Visions of Community Crime Prevention', in T. Hope and M. Shaw (eds) *Communities and Crime Reduction*, London: HMSO.

—— (1998) *Crime and Punishment in America*, New York: Metropolitan Books/Henry Holt and Company.

Dahrendorf, R. (1994) 'The Changing Quality of Citizenship', in B. van Steenbergen *The Condition of Citizenship*, London: Sage Publications.

Davis, M. (1998) *Ecology of Fear: Los Angeles and the Imagination of Disaster*, New York: Henry Holt and Company.

Donzelot, J. and Roman, J. (1991) *Le déplacement de la question sociale*, in J. Donzelot (ed.) *Face à l'exclusion*, Paris: Editions Esprit.

Ericson, R. and Carriere, K. (1994) 'The Fragmentation of Criminology', in D. Nelken (ed.) *The Futures of Criminology*, London: Sage.

Farrell, G. and Pease, K. (1993) *Once Bitten, Twice Bitten: Repeat Victimisation and its Implications for Crime Prevention*, Crime Prevention Unit Paper, no. 46, London: HMSO.

Farrington, D. and West, D. (1993) 'Criminal, Penal and Life Histories of Chronic Offenders: Risk and Protective Factors and Early Identification', *Criminal Behaviour and Mental Health*, 3: 492–523.

Feeley, M. and Simon, J. (1992) 'The New Penology: Notes on the Emerging Strategy of Corrections and its Implementation', *Criminology*, 30(4): 452–74.

—— (1994) 'Actuarial Justice: The Emerging New Criminal Law', in D. Nelken (ed.) *The Futures of Criminology*, London: Sage.

Garland, D. (1996) 'The Limits of the Sovereign State', *British Journal of Criminology*, 36(4): 445–71.

—— and Sparks, R. (2000) 'Criminology, Social Theory and the Challenge of Our Times', *British Journal of Criminology*, 40: 189–204.

Genn, H. (1988) 'Multiple Victimisation', in M. Maguire and J. Pointing (eds) *Victims of Crime: A New Deal?*, Milton Keynes: Open University Press.

Giddens, A. (1992) *The Transformation of Intimacy*, Cambridge: Polity Press

—— (1998) *The Third Way: The Renewal of Social Democracy*, Cambridge: Polity Press.

Graham, J. and Bowling, B. (1995) *Young People and Crime*, London: Home Office.

Hannah-Moffat, K. (1999) 'Moral Agent or Actuarial Subject: Risk and Canadian Women's Imprisonment', *Theoretical Criminology*, 3(1): 71–94.

Harvey, D. (1989) *The Condition of Postmodernity*, Oxford: Blackwell.

Hirschi, T. (1969) *The Causes of Delinquency*, California: University of California Press.

Home Office (2000) *Review of Crime Statistics: A Discussion Document*, London: HMSO.

Hope, T. (1999) 'Crime, Community and Inequality: The Rise of Disorder in British Public Policy', inaugural professorial lecture, University of Keele, October.

Hughes, G. (1998) *Understanding Crime Prevention: Social Control, Risk and Late Modernity*, Buckingham: Open University Press.

Ignatieff, M. (2000) *Virtual War: Kosovo and Beyond*, London: Chatto and Windus.

Johnston, L. (2000) *Policing Britain: Risk, Security and Governance*, Harlow: Longman.

Kelling, G. (1987) 'Acquiring a Taste for Order: Community and Police', *Crime and Delinquency*, 33(1): 90–103.

Kinsey, R., Lea, J. and Young, J. (1986) *Losing the Fight Against Crime*, Oxford: Blackwell.

Krisberg, B. and Austin, J. F. (1993) *Reinventing Juvenile Justice*, London: Sage Publishing.

Lea, J. (1998) 'Criminology and Postmodernity', in P. Walton and J. Young (eds) *The New Criminology Revisited*, London: Macmillan.

Leonard, E. (1982) *Women, Crime and Society: A Critique of Criminological Theory*, London: Longman.

Levitas, R. (1998) *The Inclusive Society? Social Exclusion and New Labour*, London: Macmillan.

Lewis, O. (1966) *La Vida: A Puerto Rican Family in the Culture of Poverty: San Juan and New York*, New York: Random House.

Loveday, B. (1999) 'The Impact of Performance Culture on Criminal Justice Agencies in England and Wales', *International Journal of the Sociology of Law*, 27: 351–77.

McMahon, M. (1990) 'Net Widening: Vagaries in the Use of a Concept', *British Journal of Criminology*, 30(2): 121–50.

Maguire, M. and Pointing, J. (1988) (eds) *Victims of Crime: A New Deal?*, Milton Keynes: Open University Press.

Marris, P. and Rein, M. (1967) *Dilemmas of Social Reform: Poverty and Community Action in the United States*, New York: Atherton Press.

Martinson, R. (1974) 'What Works? Questions About Prison Reform', *The Public Interest*, Spring: 22–54.

Matthews, R. (1989) *Privatising Criminal Justice*, London: Sage.

—— (1992) 'Replacing Broken Windows', in R. Matthews and J. Young (eds) *Issues in Realist Criminology*, London: Sage.

—— (1993) *Kerb-crawling, Prostitution and Multi-agency Policing*, Crime Prevention Unit Paper, no. 43, London: HMSO.

—— and Young, J. (1992) 'Reflections on Realism', in J. Young and R. Matthews (eds) *Rethinking Criminology: The Realist Debate*, London: Sage.

Mawby, R. and Walklate, S. (1994) *Critical Victimology*, London: Sage.

Morris, A., Giller, H., Swzed, E. and Geach, H. (1980) *Justice for Children*, London: Macmillan.

Morris, L. (1996) 'Dangerous Classes: Neglected Aspects of the Underclass Debate', in E. Mingione *et al.* (eds) *Urban Poverty and the Underclass*, Oxford: Blackwell.

Moynihan, D. P. (1969) *Maximum Feasible Misunderstanding: Community Action in the War on Poverty*, New York: Free Press.

Muncie, J. (2000) 'Decriminalising Criminology', in G. Lewis, S. Gewitz and J. Clarke (eds) *Rethinking Social Policy*, London: Sage.

Murray, C. (1994) *Underclass: The Crisis Deepens*, London: Institute of Economic Affairs.

Pitts, J. (2001) *The New Politics of Juvenile Crime: Discipline or Solidarity*, Basingstoke: Macmillan.

Preston, R. H. (1980) 'Social Theology and Penal Theory and Practice: The Collapse of the Rehabilitative Ideal and the Search for an Alternative', in A. E. Bottoms and R. H. Preston (eds) *The Coming Penal Crisis*, Edinburgh: Scottish Academic Press.

Room, G. (1995) (ed.) *Beyond the Threshold: The Measurement and Analysis of Social Exclusion*, Bristol: Polity Press.

Rosenbaum, D. (1986) *Community Crime Prevention: Does it Work?*, Beverley Hills: Sage.

Sampson, R. and Raudenbush, S. (1999) 'Systematic Social Observation of Public Spaces: A New Look at Disorder in Urban Neighborhoods', *American Journal of Sociology*, 105(3): 603–51.

Schwendinger, H. and Schwendinger, J. (1975) 'Defenders of Order or Guardians of Human Rights', in I. Taylor, P. Walton and J. Young (eds) *Critical Criminology*, London: Routledge.

Sennett, R. (1970) *The Uses of Disorder: Personal Identity and City Life*, New York: Vintage.

Shearing, C. (1989) 'Decriminalising Criminology', *Canadian Journal of Criminology*, 31(2): 169–78.

Sibley, D. (1995) *Geographies of Exclusion*, London: Routledge.

Smart, C. (1990) 'Feminist Approaches to Criminology or Postmodern Woman Meets Atavistic Man', in L. Gelsthorpe and A. Morris (eds) *Feminist Perspectives in Criminology*, Milton Keynes: Open University Press.

Social Exclusion Unit (1998) *Bringing Britain Together: A National Strategy for Neighbourhood Renewal*, Cm. 4045, London: HMSO.

Sparks, R. (1997) 'Recent Social Theory and the Study of Crime and Punishment', in M. Maguire, R. Morgan and R. Reiner (eds) *The Oxford Handbook of Criminology*, Oxford: Oxford University Press.

Sparks, R. F., Genn, H. and Dodd, D. (1977) *Surveying Victims*, Chichester: John Wiley.

Thorpe, D., Smith, D., Green, C. and Paley, J. (1980) *Out of Care*, London: Allen and Unwin.

Utting, W., Bright, J. and Hendrickson, B. (1993) *Crime and the Family, Improving Child Rearing and Preventing Delinquency*, Family Policy Studies Centre, Paper no.16, London.

Wieviorka, M. (1994) 'Racism in Europe: Unity and Diversity', in A. Ratsani and S. Westwood (eds) *Racism, Modernity, Identity on the Western Front*, Cambridge: Polity Press.

Wilson, J. and Kelling, G. (1982) 'Broken Windows: The Police and Neighbourhood Safety', *Atlantic Monthly* (March): 29–38.

Wilson, J. Q. (1975) *Thinking About Crime*, New York: Basic Books.

—— and Herrnstein, R. (1985) *Crime and Human Nature*, New York: Simon and Schuster.

Wilson, W. J. (1987) *The Truly Disadvantaged: The Inner-city, the Underclass and Public Policy*, Chicago: University of Chicago Press.

—— (1994) *Citizenship and the Inner-city Ghetto Poor*, in B. van Steenbergen *The Condition of Citizenship*, London: Sage Publications.

—— (1996) *When Work Disappears*, New York: Knopf.

Young, I. (1990) *Justice and the Politics of Difference*, New Jersey: Princeton University Press.

Young, J. (1986) 'The Failure of Criminology: The Need for Radical Realism', in R. Matthews and J. Young (eds) *Confronting Crime*, London: Sage.

—— (1999) *The Exclusive Society*, London: Sage.

1 Identity, community and social exclusion

Jock Young

Introduction

For the majority of social commentators, community safety programmes to control crime and anti-social behaviour are an exercise in the obvious. 'Community' is a wholesome, homogeneous entity waiting to be mobilised, 'safety' is a risk free end state – the self-evident goal of public desire – whilst 'crime' and 'anti-social behaviour' are entities which are readily recognisable by any decent citizen. Indeed, the trio – community, safety and crime – become elided together, each term defining each other. Thus the intense, socially rich interacting community is seen to be the very antithesis of crime and is indeed the place and source of all safety.

Nowadays, as Adam Crawford puts it, 'the attraction of the notion of "community" unites and transcends the established ... political parties' (1997: 45). He goes on to write that 'community ... is cleansed of any negative or crim-inogenic connotations and endowed with a simplistic and naïve purity and virtue' (*ibid*.: 153). Thus problems of crime and disorder are ascribed to a malaise of community and their solution is seen as the regeneration of community. Such a perspective can readily be seen as an aspect of modernity, in particular the social engineering characteristic of the post-war period. This was a period wherein slums were cleared, towns were planned and 'rational' communities were constructed – the apotheosis being the 'new town' developments, the more mundane and commonplace being the modernist tower blocks interspersed with family maisonettes and bleak gardens characteristic of the post-war city.

It has been the role of critical criminology to stand outside such conventional wisdoms and to problematise each of these seeming certainties. Community becomes seen as a reality lacking coherence, a rhetoric invoked to ensure the domination of one group over another, a key instrument of social exclusion. Safety becomes a curtain for fear, the miscalculation of risks, the denial of excitement and the excuse for xenophobia towards outgroups. Finally, crime and anti-social behaviour are social constructs which are bestowed by the powerful on disapproved behaviour but with no essential reality or core. In fact, their definitions are frequently contested within localities and adherence to criminal values can even be a dominant aspect of community.[1]

My concern in this chapter is not to reiterate these doubts but rather to point to the fashion by which the massive changes which have occurred in the last third of the twentieth century, in the basic building blocks of society – employment, the family and community itself – have transformed and magnified such doubts. For the shift from the modernity of the post-war period with its high (male) employment, intense communities and stable families, to the conditions of late modernity has been associated with a remarkable problematisation of each area.

The coordinates of order: class and identity in the late twentieth century

First, before mapping the terrain of late modernity, I wish to briefly establish coordinates. Nancy Fraser, in her influential *Justice Interruptus: Critical Reflections on the Post-Socialist Condition* (1997), outlines two types of politics: those centring around distributive justice and those centring around the justice of recognition – that is class politics and identity politics.[2] She points to the rise in prominence of the latter – a phenomenon which I will attempt to explain later in this chapter. However, what concerns me here is to develop and explain this distinction as a basis for an analysis of social order and political legitimacy. In my book *The Exclusive Society* (1999), I point to the two fundamental problems in a liberal democracy. First is the need to distribute rewards fairly so as to encourage commitment to work within the division of labour. Second is the need to encourage respect between individuals and groups so that the self-seeking individualism characteristic of a competitive society does not lead to a situation of war of all against all. Individuals must experience their rewards as fair and just and they must feel valued and respected.

I now wish to develop this distinction between the sphere of distribution and that of recognition. Central to distributive justice is the notion of fairness of reward, and in modern capitalist societies this entails a meritocracy in which merit is matched to reward. Recognition involves the notion of respect and status allocated to all, but if we stretch the concept a little further, it also involves the notion of the level of esteem or social status being allocated justly. Indeed, both the discourses of distributive justice and recognition have the notion of a basic equality (all must receive a base level of reward as part of being citizens), but on top of this rather than a general equality of outcome: a hierarchy of reward and recognition dependent on the individual's achievements.[3]

What terms are we to use when distributive justice or recognition is wanting? When material reward is unjustly allocated we commonly use the term 'relative deprivation', when recognition is denied someone we call this 'ontological insecurity'. But let us explore these further. We can talk of two aspects of unfairness – deprivation and insecurity, and two dimensions – economic and ontological. This gives us four bases of disaffection (see Figure 1.1).

How does this help inform us as to the genesis of crime and punishment? First, a major cause of crime lies in deprivation. That is, very frequently, the combination

	Insecurity	*Deprivation*
Economic	economic insecurity	relative deprivation
Ontological	ontological insecurity	misrecognition

Figure 1.1   The dimensions of disaffection

of feeling relatively deprived economically (which causes discontent) and misrecognised socially and politically (which causes disaffection). The classic combination is to be marginalised economically and treated as a second-rate citizen on the street by the police. Second, a common argument is that widespread economic and ontological insecurity in the population engenders a punitive response to crime and deviancy (see for example Luttwak 1995; Young 2000).

As we shall see in the process of the transition from modernity to late modernity, powerful currents shake the social structure transforming the nature of relative deprivation, causing new modes of misrecognition and exclusion, whilst at the same time being accompanied by widespread economic and ontological insecurity. The purchase of each of these currents impacts differentially throughout the social structure by each of the prime social axes of class, age, ethnicity and gender.

The journey into late modernity and mapping the terrain

> How can long-term purposes be pursued in a short-term society? How can durable social relations be sustained? How can a human being develop a narrative of identity and life history in a society composed of episodes and fragments? The conditions of the new economy feed instead on experience which drifts in time, from place to place, from job to job.
>
> (Sennett 1998: 26–7)

If one wishes to travel anywhere one must know what terrain one has to travel over, what means of travel are available and last, and by no means least, where one wants to go. In reality over the last twenty years the terrain, the structure of society, has radically changed, effective means of intervening in the social world have profoundly altered and, most important, the metropolis of possibility and desire in which we find ourselves has altered beyond recognition.

The last third of the twentieth century witnessed a remarkable transformation in the lives of citizens living in advanced industrial societies. The Golden Age of the post-war settlement, with high employment, stable family structures and consensual values underpinned by the safety net of the welfare state, has been replaced by a world of structural unemployment, economic precariousness, a systematic cutting of welfare provisions and the growing instability of family life and interpersonal relations. And where there once was a consensus of value, there is now burgeoning pluralism and individualism (see Hobsbawm 1994). A world of material and ontological security from cradle to grave has been replaced by precariousness and uncertainty, and where social commentators of the 1950s and 1960s berated the complacency of a comfortable 'never had it so good' generation, today they talk of a 'risk society' where social change becomes the central dynamo of existence and where anything might happen. As Anthony Giddens puts it: 'to live in the world produced by high modernity has the feeling of riding a juggernaut' (1991: 28; see also Beck 1992; Berman 1983).

Such a change has been brought about by market forces which have systematically transformed both the sphere of production and consumption. This shift from Fordism to post-Fordism involves the unravelling of the world of work where the primary labour market of secure employment and 'safe' careers shrinks and the secondary labour market of short-term contracts, flexibility and insecurity increases, as does the growth of an underclass of the structurally unemployed. It results, in Will Hutton's catchphrase, in a '40:30:30 society' (1995) – 40 per cent of the population are in tenured secure employment, 30 per cent in insecure employment, and 30 per cent are marginalised, idle or working for poverty wages.

Second, the world of leisure is transformed from one of mass consumption to one where choice and preference is elevated to a major ideal, and where the constant stress on immediacy, hedonism and self-actualisation has had a profound effect on late modern sensibilities (see Campbell 1987; Featherstone 1985). These changes, both in work and in leisure, characteristic of the late modern period, generate a situation of widespread relative deprivation and heightened individualism. Market forces generate a more unequal and less meritocratic society and encourage an ethos of every person for him- or herself. Together, these create a combination which is severely criminogenic. Such a process is combined with a decline in the forces of informal social control, as communities are disintegrated by social mobility and left to decay as capital finds more profitable areas to invest and develop. At the same time, families are stressed and fragmented by the decline in community systems of support, the reduction of state support and the more intense pressures of work (see Currie 1997; Wilson 1996). Thus, as the pressures which lead to crime increase, the forces which attempt to control it decrease.

The journey into late modernity involves both a change in perceptions of the fairness of distributive justice and in the security of identity. There is a shift in relative deprivation from being a comparison between groups (what Runciman [1966] calls 'fraternal' relative deprivation) to that which is between individuals (what Runciman terms 'egoistic' relative deprivation). The likely effect on crime is, I would suggest, to move from a pattern of committing crimes *outside* of one's neighbourhood onto other richer people to committing crimes in an internecine way *within* one's neighbourhood. In other words, the frustrations generated by relative deprivation become focused inside the 'community' rather than, as formerly, projected out of it.

Thus Roger Hood (Hood and Jones 1999) and his associates, in their fascinating oral history of three generations in London's East End, find a sharp difference between the 1980s generation, who left school in the late 1970s and 1980s, and those of the 1930s and 1950s. Again and again, the older respondents talk of their lack of fear of crime in the earlier periods, and make the distinction between the tolerated crime committed against shops, warehouses, rich outsiders and the anathema of crime against one's family, friends or neighbours. For the 1980s generation, all of this had changed:

> crime had formerly been seen as an activity on the margins of everyday relationships, something that a few segregated members of the community did to outsiders: the bosses and impersonal companies. It was now perceived to be increasingly an internal threat. Indeed some young men, as well as women described it as pervasive within their neighbourhoods.
>
> (Hood and Jones 1999: 154–5)

But it is also in the realm of identity that relative deprivation is increased and transformed. For here, on one side, you have raised expectations: the spin-off of the consumer society is the market in *lifestyles*. On the other side, both in work and in leisure, there has been a disembeddedness. That is, identity is no longer secure; it is fragmentary and transitional – all of which is underscored by a culture of reflexivity which no longer takes the world for granted. The identity crisis permeates our society. As the security of the lifelong job and the comfort of stability in marriage and relationships fade, as movement makes community a phantasmagoria where each unit of the structure stays in place but each individual occupant regularly moves, where the structure itself expands and transforms and where the habit of reflexivity itself makes choice part of everyday life and problematises the taken for granted – all of these things call into question the notion of a fixed, solid sense of self. Essentialism offers a panacea for this sense of disembeddedness.

The identity crisis and the attractions of essentialism

In *The Exclusive Society* (1999) I discuss the attractions of essentialism to the ontologically insecure and denigrated. To believe that one's culture, 'race', gender or community has a fixed essence which is valorised and unchanging is, of course, by its very nature the answer to a feeling that the human condition is one of shifting sands, and that the social order is feckless and arbitrary. To successfully essentialise oneself it is of great purchase to negatively essentialise others. That is to ascribe to the *other* either features which *lack* one's own values (and solidity) or which are an *inversion* of one's own cherished beliefs about one's self. To seek identity for oneself, in an essentialist fashion, inevitably involves denying or denigrating the identity of others.

Crime and its control is a prime site for essentialisation. Who, by definition, could be a better candidate for such a negative 'othering' than the criminal and the culture that he or she is seen to live in? Thus the criminal underclass, replete with single mothers living in slum estates or ghettos, drug addicts committing crime to maintain their habit and illegal immigrants who commit crime to deceitfully enter the country (and continue their lives of crime in order to maintain themselves), have become the three major foci of emerging discourses around law and order of the last third of the twentieth century. These types can be summed up as the welfare 'scrounger', the 'junkie' and the 'illegal'.

This triptych of deviancy, each picture reflecting each other in a late modern portrait of degeneracy and despair, comes to dominate public discussion of social problems. As the discourse develops, their ontologies become distinct and different from 'normal' people, their social norms absent or aberrant, their natures frequently racialised and rendered inferior. Crime, a product of our society, becomes separated from the social structure: it is viewed as a result of distinct aetiologies, it embodies differing values, it emanates from distinct and feared areas of the city. It is these areas that are contrasted with the organic community where social trust and harmony are seen to reside.

The organic community

The community of the post-war period was characterised by a sense of permanence and solidity. Placed there by the needs of capital around large-scale manufacturing industry or labour fixed to land for centuries, it involved the following characteristics:

- intergenerationality;
- an embeddedness of the individual in locality;
- intense face-to-face interaction;
- much direct information with regard to each other;
- high level of informal social control;
- provision of a localised sense of identity.

The obverse of the organic community is the anomic community, the locality without norms and the inevitable consequence of this is seen to be the proliferation of crime and anti-social behaviour. This formulation is wrong on two scores. First, there is no direct one-to-one relationship between strong community and crime. Second, even slum estates have strong social networks. Thus the organic community could easily support criminal values. As Adam Crawford nicely puts it:

> The logic behind this association between the lack of 'organized' community and crime is that, conversely, more community equals less crime. ... This benevolent understanding of community is highly misleading. In some instances 'community', i.e. its communal normative values, itself may be

the source of criminogenic tendencies. Recent British research into criminal subcultures has reiterated the long established criminological truism
that the collective values of a community may serve to stimulate and
sustain criminality.

(Crawford 1997: 153)

The recent research of Sandra Walklate and Karen Evans (1999) in Salford
corroborates Crawford's comments.[4] But the important conclusion from this is
that although intense community does not necessarily inoculate against crime,
it does exert considerable levels of social control – which may influence law-
abiding *or* criminal behaviour.

Conversely, the image of the sink estate, the inner-city ghetto or the satel-
lite slum is often seen as in a state of anomie. The immune system of informal
control is down and gross social pathology abounds. But even a brief visit to
one of these estates quickly dissipates such a notion. Mothers congregate
around the local school at delivery and collecting times, they discuss the
teachers, their kids, and this and that. Older children hang out at the entrance
to the tower blocks, or along the road by the shops, men meet in the pubs and
betting shops. Networks can be seen everywhere; *divided*, of course, by all the
axes of age, gender, ethnicity and economic situation, but certainly no lack of
an informal system or anomie in a sense of normlessness, or 'Broken Windows'
because no one knows each other (Wilson and Kelling 1982). Ironically,
because of structural unemployment, poverty and both geographical and social
immobility, the stigmatised estates of the so-called underclass allow greater
social interaction than on middle-class dormitory estates on the edge of cities.
Here, there is usually a quick turnover of residents, dual time-consuming
careers of husband and wife, the bussing of children to relatively distant schools
and little time except at the weekend to interact with anyone – even with one's
own family.

The work of Janet Foster has helped to dispel such images of the normless
community. In her study of the London housing estate 'Riverside', she notes:

> The differing types and composition of networks on Riverside aptly demon-
> strate that different forms of neighbourliness can occur in the same setting
> simultaneously among different groups of people. These networks played an
> important role in an environment where Asian, white, black and
> Chinese/Vietnamese households alike lived with an underlying suspicion
> about their neighbours and expressed concerns about their safety.
>
> The very existence of these networks suggests that popular perceptions
> of council housing – and the very poorest and most difficult-to-let estates in
> particular – as alienating environments in which there is little tenant inter-
> action and support, are too simplistic. Instead of condemning such places as
> 'dreadful enclosures' (Damer 1974) we should look more closely at the
> patterns of interaction between tenants in these contexts. We need to
> understand more about how they are characterised, in what ways they influ-

ence tenants' perceptions of the estates on which they live, and how different individuals and groups, who have had little or no choice in their housing allocation, manage to co-exist.

(Foster 1997: 126)

Crime and community: the one-to-one fallacy

The argument that there is no one-to-one relationship between strong community and little crime often teeters on the edge of suggesting that there is no relationship. This crucially mistakes the situation and it is worth turning for a moment to fundamentals. Crime occurs when there is motivation to commit crime (because of structural reasons such as those which engender relative deprivation) and where there are insufficient countervailing norms (chiefly informal, although enforced, legal norms are a vital backup). The major site of such informal norms is the community. Yet, of course, there are communities that have norms which are supportive or at least tolerant of crime and thus do not act in such a controlling fashion. Thus crime will occur when you have motivation and no community or where you have motivation and some level of support for criminal activity. Crime will be much less prevalent where there is no motivation even though there might be a lack of community or where there is strongly enforced communal norms against crime. In the Barbican in London or in the tower blocks of the Upper West Side of Manhattan, there may be little concept of community, yet no conventional crime may occur. In contrast, in the past, many poor communities were carriers of strong norms which stressed honesty and respectability, and this was underscored by intensive day-to-day, face-to-face interaction and underwritten by the disciplines of locally-based work and the fear of losing one's job. Hence crime, despite severe deprivation, tended to be low in these communities.

If, then, we are to make anything of the finding that the organic community sometimes supported crime and that conversely areas without a hint of *Gemeinschaft*, often have low crime rates – it is merely to register that there is no logical necessity of countering crime in this time-honoured fashion. The communitarian notion that the most effective means of tackling crime is to reconstitute the community (see Etzioni 1997) is, therefore, not only nostalgic (in the sense of a politics which is backward looking and difficult to achieve) but unnecessary. We know that communities of lightly engaged strangers can have low crime rates and, as we shall see, we know also that the phrase 'lightly engaged strangers' does not imply an atomistic and anomic society. What demands our attention is how the territory of community has changed and how we can find new and appropriate ways of fostering civility.

In late modernity, we face severe problems: the organic community is in decline, whilst the rise in change in the nature of relative deprivation gives greater motive to commit crime of a more internecine nature. Thus both the rise in motivation and the decline in informal control give rise to higher crime rates of a type which further fragments the already weakened community. The desire to 'maintain order amongst lightly engaged strangers' has, therefore, an urgency and this is further extended by the progressive demands of the new social movements to improve upon levels of civility in the areas of gender and ethnic relations and between diverse sexual, religious, and other subcultures which have flourished in late modernity.

The search for community

> One of the unintended consequences of modern capitalism is that it has strengthened the value of place, aroused a longing for community. All the emotional conditions we have explored in the workplace animate that desire: the uncertainties of flexibility; the absence of deeply rooted trust and commitment; the superficiality of teamwork; most of all, the spectre of failing to make something of oneself in the world, to 'get a life' through one's work. All these conditions impel people to look for some other scene of attachment and depth.
>
> Today, in the new regime of time, that usage 'we' has become an act of self-protection. The desire for community is defensive, often expressed as a rejection of immigrants or other outsiders – the most important communal architecture being the walls against a hostile economic order. To be sure, it is almost a universal law that 'we' can be used as a defense against confusion and dislocation. Current politics based on this desire for refuge takes aim more at the weak, those who travel the circuits of the global labor market, rather than at the strong, those institutions which set poor workers in motion or make use of their relative deprivation.
>
> (Sennett 1998: 138)

Here, Sennett notes that modern capitalism drives people to seek identity in community. But Hobsbawm counters that it is precisely the self-same late modern capitalism which has destroyed community and rendered destitute the bank of social trust that underwrote it. The local community becomes increasingly more invoked as a place of identity and moves to become a major part of the rhetoric of political mobilisation just at the time that it is transforming. In a well-known passage, Hobsbawm writes:

> We have been living – we are living – through a gigantic 'cultural revolution' an extraordinary dissolution of traditional norms, textures and values, which left so many inhabitants of the developed world orphaned and bereft. ... Never was the word 'community' used more indiscriminately and emptily than in the decades when communities in the sociological sense become hard to find in real life. Men and women look for groups to which they can belong, certainly and forever, in a world in which all else is moving and shifting, in which nothing else is certain.
>
> (Hobsbawm 1996: 40)

The organic community is, however, in decline, affected by both the globalisation of the economy and of culture. Manufacturing industries shrink and in many instances disappear leaving areas bereft of work, service industries proliferate often with small sizes, commuting increases to and from work, local cultures become less self-contained and more penetrated by the global. They become, in Giddens' (1990) evocative term, 'phantasmagoric', constituted by the ghostly presence of distant influences.

I argue that this paradox of a search for identity in community when organic community is failing, and whose failure to provide tradition and embeddedness is a core reason for the search for identity, is not nearly as cataclysmic as either Sennett or Hobsbawm maintain. In part, this is because they cannot envisage the notions of association and trust outside of the image of the face-to-face, organic community.

The privileging of community

Iris Marian Young has been one of the most ardent advocates of urban life as an ideal and, at the same time, an effective critic of the privileging of the organic community:

> Theorists of community privilege face-to-face relations because they conceive them as *immediate*. Immediacy is better than mediation because immediate relations have the purity and security longed for in the Rousseauist dream: we are transparent to one another, purely copresent in the same time and space, close enough to touch, and nothing comes between us to obstruct our vision of one another.
>
> This ideal of the immediate copresence of subjects, however, is a metaphysical illusion. Even a face-to-face relation between two people is mediated by voice and gesture, spacing and temporality. As soon as a third person enters the interaction the possibility arises of the relation between the first two being mediated through the third, and so on. The mediation of relations among persons by the speech and actions of other persons is a fundamental condition of sociality. The richness, creativity, diversity, and potential of a society expand with growth in the scope and means of its media, linking persons across time and distance. The greater the time and distance, however, the greater the number of persons who stand between other persons.
>
> (Young 1990: 233)

Young has no doubt about the oppressive nature of many relationships in modern urban societies and the real dangers of the city nor that the closest relationships are those of immediate intimates. But in its anonymity, the city allows deviance, freedom to develop (which I discuss in more detail below), its difference offers a *frisson* of excitement and entertainment, its access to such a huge bulk of people via the mediation of telephone and mass transit allows for the creation of vibrant new communities of difference. Let us first of all examine what changes have occurred in the late modern community.

The deterritorialisation of community

> The use of the term 'community' in crime prevention discourse commonly evokes images of localism and 'neighbourhood'; of territorially bounded communities in which it is assumed members also share other dense cultural and social bonds. But in 'modern' Western societies, high and increasing residential and spatial mobility among large sections of the population; high levels of functional specialisation mirrored in the spatial differentiation of social life; and sophisticated mass communications and transport systems, mean that the centrality of geography and the embed-dedness of existing social relations give way to the importance of other, 'deterritorialised' communities in the lives of many citizens. These are communities of interest and function related to work, leisure, education, taste, and so on, which increasingly owe little to geographical locale or residence for most citizens. These provide individuals with plural communities and identities, in and through which they live their lives. Crime prevention needs to be considered in relation to these 'deterritorialised', as well as the more familiar residential, communities.
>
> (Hogg and Brown 1998: 6)

Writers in cultural studies note the fashion in which the late modern community has lost its mooring in the locale – in the coincidence of the social and the spatial. Thus Mike Tomlinson (1999) talks of its 'deterritorialisation', whilst John Thompson (1995) refers to the notion of 'despatialised commonality' and, perhaps a little more elegantly, Joshua Meyrowitz (1989) talks of 'the generalised elsewhere'. Important here is the way in which people through the various media can share experiences and identity despite the separation of physical distance. This is not to deny locality – people after all must live somewhere – but it is to point to the diminution and transformation of the local community and the rise of the virtual community.

John Thompson (1995: 85) usefully classifies social interaction into three groups:

- Face-to-face interaction: the dialogical basis of the traditional community.
- Mediated interaction: which is two-way and dialogical, like face-to-face interaction, but occurs over space and time by telephone and e-mail.
- Mediated quasi-interaction: the conventional mass media which is monological, yet where there is audience selection, interpretation and interaction.

What is new are the developments in the latter two groups. Portable telephone companies are presently the fastest growing firms and e-mail communication has become part of everyday life for many people. But even before this, the old-fashioned landline telephone has had a major impact on people's lives. Thus Barry Wellman and other social network analysts have long pointed to the way in which social technology has liberated people from dependence on spatial locality. He argues that it makes more sense to perceive of *personal* communities and networks rather than communities of neighbourhood (Wellman 1982). Indeed, as Meyrowitz (1989) wryly comments: 'access to nonlocal people is now, via the telephone, often faster and simpler than access to physical neighbors'. Furthermore, within mass media the rise of multi-media and the vast expansion of choice in radio and television allow the development of niche audiences and subcultures (see McRobbie and Thornton 1995). Indeed the mass media take up a surprisingly larger and larger proportion of people's lives. In England and Wales, for example, watching television and listening to the radio constitute 36 per cent of the waking life of the average citizen (figures from *Social Trends* 2000).

Thus on one hand the local is penetrated by the global in terms of distant events, consumer choices and values (such as those emphasising lifestyle choice, feminism, meritocracy, etc.), and on the other hand, virtual communities develop on the back of the local which incorporate images, reference groups, favoured characters and celebrities from a global repertoire and involve both mass media and mediated interaction.

The community in late modern times

Tim Hope's (1995) excellent classification of images of community and crime prevention practices from community as disorganised (in the 1930s), to community as disadvantaged (in the 1960s) to community as frightened (in the late 1970s and 1980s) requires further reappraisal by the end of the twentieth century and the beginning of the twenty-first century. For all of these previous conceptions perceived a fixed entity which is variously disorganised, disadvantaged or frightened and consequently a thing which can be regenerated, redistributed or mobilised as strategies to regenerate itself and tackle crime. And, even more recently, the Social Exclusion Unit (1999a) carries the further image of the excluded community which needs to be included into citizenship in order to tackle crime and disorders. All of these images encompass facets of the truth but need to be drastically reviewed in the light of the late modern community. For the single entity has long gone and any notion of fixity has disappeared – there is no reified community out there to mobilise or repair, no fixed thing in need of incorporation. Nor can this situation be solved by adopting the conventional language of multiculturalism and communitarianism. Namely, that there is now a series of communities to reinvigorate and galvanise. That is to replace the fallacy of a single fixed entity with the chimera of the multiple community. None of this fully captures the fluidity and plurality of late modernity.

Let us delineate the basic features of the late modern community:

1   *Difference*: it is pluralistic, not just in terms of ethnicity but in terms of age, gender and class.

2   *Fragmentation, cross-cutting and hybridisation*: such a pluralism by combination of ethnicity, age, gender and class offers to create on the one hand fragmentation, and on the other hand, other cross-cutting alliances, for example gender across ethnicity and class. Furthermore, such subcultures *bricolage* from one another, creating hybrids of cross-over and reinterpretation.

3   *Intensity*: it is pluralistic in terms of intensity. The same locale can contain high intensity, disorganised and atomised groups. For example, around the school environment, single mothers can create intense coherent subcultures, at the same time as unemployed men can be atomistic and withdrawn.

4   *Transience*: such subcultures change over time in composition, intensity and coherence. Individual biographies are experienced as shifts backwards and forwards, from a sense of embeddedness to disembeddedness.

5   *Mediated*: it is highly mediated, the global penetrates the local, creating a series of virtual communities some of which are territorialised and rooted in the locale, and others which are considerably deterritorialised.

6   *Actuarial*: relationships are wary and calculative because of low information about a large proportion of the 'community'.

7   *Internecine conflict*: wealth and status is perceived as distributed in a chaotic fashion with no clear rationale or fairness. Relative deprivation, both materially and in terms of status, is widespread.

8   *Reinvention*: the history of the 'community/communities' is constantly reinvented and the boundaries redrawn and redrafted.

This late modern mixture of local and virtual community can clearly enhance people's ability to realise identity, yet it is also a prime site of misrecognition, and a threat to one's status and identity.

Freedom in the city

We have emerged from a world of neighbours and entered what has increasingly become one of strangers. Here we have the old theme in social science of a shift from *community* (crudely, the familiar, interpersonal and village-centred life of pre-industrialism) to *associations* which involve the mixing of people unknown to one another save in specific ways such as bus conductor, shop assistant, and newsvendor (crudely, the urban-oriented way of life of the modern). Ever since at least Simmel we have appreciated how disorienting and also often liberating the transfer from closed community to a world of strangers can be. The city may fragment and depersonalise, but in doing so it can also release one from the strictures of village life. With the shift towards town life comes about a decline in personal observation by neighbours and, accompanying this, a weakening of the power of community controls that are exercised on an interpersonal basis. Entering urban-industrial life from a country existence one is freed from the intrusions of local gossip, of face-to-face interactions, from close scrutiny of one's everyday behaviour by neighbours. … By the same token, in the urban realm one can readily choose freedom, to be as private as one likes, to mix with others on one's own terms, to indulge in the exotic without fear of reprimand, to be anonymous.

(Webster 1995: 56–7)

The breakdown of the organic community, the deterritorialisation of the local, is, on the face of it, an immediate gain in terms of personal freedom. Freed from the constraints of control of the organic community people become more free to change. Narrow chauvinisms, conceptions of masculinity rooted in the industrial plant and the local pub, respectabilities which were once policed by gossip and sanctioning, all begin to crumble.

It is conventional, particularly in liberal political philosophy, to think of that which is public as being good and that which is private as being concealed and possibly reprehensible. But such liberalism which sees freedom as bringing private problems into the light of public debate, however commendable, forgets the sociology of resistance and subterfuge (see Fraser 1997). For the public world, whether it is the local community or the wider polity, consists for the powerless of distinctly unequal partners and fellow citizens who can be potentially both censorious and coercive. Youth culture, for example, would be moribund and conformist if it did not learn to manoeuvre the restrictions of family by the device of deviance and half-truth. Teenagers are, in Dick Hebdige's marvellous phrase, 'hiding in the light' (1988). Similarly, from the black diaspora (see Gilroy 1993) to the gay community (see Plummer 1995), subcultures develop in the freedom of the urban landscape and spread into a virtual community of mass media and cultural artefact. The privacy, therefore, provided by the late modern city permits the exercise of freedom. Is it not more possible in this environment, then, to develop genuine identity and a sense of self than in the stifling atmosphere of the organic community?

Richard Sennett, in *The Conscience of the Eye* (1991), remarks that 'deviance is the freedom made possible in a crowded city of lightly engaged people'. But he then adds a pessimistic caveat: that the tolerance of diversity is not so much because the city encourages diversity but rather it permits it because it is merely indifferent towards it – in other words, it could not care less. And, indeed, if our mapping of the terrain of late modernity is correct, we can go further. Because indifference can very easily disintegrate into predation and punitiveness from both sides of the spectrum of criminal justice. Tony Bottoms and Paul Wiles capture this well when they write:

Recent technology means that neither time nor space is the fixed framework of our routines. … The result can be globalised cultures, no longer fixed in time or space, from which we choose and indeed make a series of different choices. Television representations based on the culture of

Australia or west coast America have taken on an autonomous existence and may be as 'real' to some British youth as anything else. Yet geographically localised cultures, in the sense of 'community' and spatially fixed, institutions, such as churches and families, have been regarded by much criminological theory as the main defences against crime: hence the Chicagoans' concern with community 'disorganization' and crime.

(Bottoms and Wiles 1997: 351)

I have argued that there is no one-to-one relationship between the organic community and the crime-free society. Yet how can we ensure that crime is diminished rather than enhanced by the freedoms of the city?

Similarly the disembeddedness of the self, the collapse of fixed, pre-destined narratives of biography, poses both problems and possibilities of progress. The dangers of essentialism of creating a fixed identity for oneself and a demonisation of the other is the premise for a punitive and exclusionary response to diversity. Yet, as we have seen, the freeing up from these constraints also presents precisely the opposite path: changes which might deconstruct the fixed categories of gender, age and ethnicity, for example – those which open up rather than fore-close on freedom. The question, therefore, boils down to how can we achieve and maintain a civilised society which minimises oppressive and predatory behaviour towards each other, in a world where the power of the localised organic commu-nity is diminished and replaced by the new community of late modernity?

From generalised other to generalised elsewhere

Now, physically bounded spaces are less significant as information is able to flow through walls and rush across great distances. As a result, *where* one is has less and less to do with what one knows or experiences. Electronic media have altered the significance of time and space for social interaction.

(Meyrowitz 1985: viii)

The notion of who you are becomes constructed on a much wider stage in late modernity. To understand this one must look at the late modern self and its reference points. Joshua Meyrowitz (1989), in a seminal article, develops the work of Charles Cooley and George Herbert Mead on the generalised other. The self according to the symbolic interactionist tradition is given reality by its reflections in the significant others around us. Cooley calls this 'the looking glass self', and Mead terms it 'the generalized other' – we see ourselves through our perceptions of others' perceptions of us. According to Meyrowitz, the rela-tive decline in community and the rise in the media has:

Extended the generalized other so that those who we perceive as significant others are no longer only the people we experience in face-to-face interac-tion within the community. People from other communities and localities also serve as self-mirrors. The 'mediated generalized other' weakens (but surely does not eliminate) our dependence on locality and on people in it for a sense of self.

(Meyrowitz 1989: 327)

We can expand this idea a little further, since the series of other reference points against which we judge ourselves fairly or unfairly treated in comparison with others, widen out as does our knowledge of what is fairness and unfairness and its distribution. Reference groups are much less attached to locality in late modernity, for instance, as Bottoms and Wiles (1997) pointed out, the culture of Australia or the west coast of America can be as 'real' to British youth as anything else.

How does this relate to crime and its control? What has happened is that people's notion of their self (and hence their sense of shame, of losing self-respect when certain norms are transgressed), the actual norms themselves – the informal mores which structure behaviour, the feelings of discontent which provide the wellsprings of criminality and the vocabularies of motive and justifying circumstances of crime – to a greater extent than ever before are a product of discourses which are of a global rather than a local nature.

Relative deprivation, for example, is global in its comparison points: aspirations jump frontiers, discourses about crime (including notions of fear, risk and danger) are a free-floating commodity of a world media, the informal mores of everyday life (including the introduction of new and more or less stringent definitions of deviance) are constituted within public cultures which are global in their reach. Indeed, the twin impact of cultural and economic globalisation penetrates the local, moulding aspirations and changing opportunities, so that the causes of crime can invariably be tied to global processes. All that is consistently local about crime itself (and here only conventional crimes) is its actual impact – the burglary of the dwelling, the violence on the street, the brutality in the home.

But let us return to the pressing problem: the maintenance of order among lightly engaged strangers. In late modernity the generalised other immediately presented to the self in the organic community by the reactions of neighbour and local friend becomes potentially more remote. Deviance is less likely to be directly observed, there are more nooks and crannies in the contemporary world, but the weakening of the local is accompanied by the rise of the 'generalised elsewhere': our notions of respectable and proper behaviour are then a product of a wider interaction and a more public discourse. Thus our feelings of shame and guilt are no longer solely constituted by the face-to-face encounter, but shame and guilt scarcely vanishes. Indeed it might well be argued that in a society where identity is both precarious and sought after, the need for the recognition of social worth is all the more pressing.

On the edge: the test case of the Philadelphian underclass

In *The Exclusive Society*, I examine the notion that the outcasts of US society are a distinct and localised entity. In particular I looked at Carl Nightingale's brilliant ethnography of the ghetto of Philadelphia. The conservative image is a spatially segregated underclass, whose values are different from the wider society, who have evolved a highly differentiated and dysfunctional way of life. They are a caste apart, a disgrace to the American dream (see, for example, Murray 1984). A common liberal image is not dissimilar to the conservative one: the underclass are the excluded, the people whom the economy has left behind, whose social behaviour is dependent and aberrant. The problem, they believe, is to resocialise them, retrain them, get them to work and back into society (see for example Social Exclusion Unit 1999a and 1999b).

Nightingale's research confounded these images. For here in the ghetto, at the bottom of this most segregated society, instead of a separate culture, what he found was the apotheosis of America. He discovered a community fully immersed in the American dream, a culture hooked on Gucci, BMW, Nike. They watched television eleven hours a day, shared mainstream culture's obsession with violence, backed, at the time of the study, Bush's involvement in the Gulf War, lined up outside the cinemas, worshipped success, money and status, and, in a perverse way, even shared the racism of wider society. The problem of the ghetto was not so much the process of it being simply excluded but rather one which was all too strongly included in the culture but, then, systematically excluded from its realisation. All of this is reminiscent of Merton – but where, in a late modern context, the implosion of the wider culture on the local is dramatically increased. We have a process which I have likened to a bulimia of the social system: a society which choruses the liberal mantra of liberty, equality and fraternity, yet systematically in the job market, on the streets, in the day-to-day contacts with the outside world, practices exclusion. It brands as 'losers' those who had learnt to believe that the world consisted of 'winners' and 'losers'.

None of this is to suggest that there is not a subcultural diversity within late modern societies, but this is what it is – *sub*cultural. Cultures criss-cross with each other, hybridise, transform and constantly change. They are not separate in any essentialist fashion. Nor, for that matter, are they separate in such a strict spatial sense as is frequently suggested. Thus Zygmunt Bauman writes of Washington, DC:

> One difference between those 'high up' and those 'low down' is that the first may leave the second behind – but not vice versa. Contemporary cities are sites of an 'apartheid à rebours': those who can afford it, abandon the filth and squalor of the regions that those who cannot afford the move are stuck to. In Washington D.C. ... there is an invisible border stretching along 16th Street in the west and the Potomac river in the north-west, which those left behind are wise never to cross. Most of the adolescents left behind the invisible yet all-too-tangible border never saw downtown Washington with all its splendours, ostentatious elegance and refined pleasures. In their life, that downtown does not exist. There is no talking over the border. The life experiences are so sharply different that it is not clear what the residents of the two sides could talk to each other about were they

to meet and stop to converse. As Ludwig Wittgenstein remarked, 'If lions could talk, we would not understand them'.

(Bauman 1998: 86)

This eloquent expression of the dual city thesis is wrong, not in its sense of division, but in its sense of borders. For the borders are regularly crossed and the language spoken on each side is remarkably similar. The most obvious flaw in this argument is that of gender: maids, nurses, clerical staff move across borders into work everyday. Women, as William Julius Wilson argues in *When Work Disappears* (1996), are more acceptable to the world outside of the ghetto than their male counterparts. It is after all 'home boys' who stay at home. But bell-hops, taxi drivers, doormen, maintenance men regularly ply their way across the invisible borders of Washington, DC. It is not, therefore, just through television that the sense of relative deprivation of the poor is heightened; it is in the direct and often intimate knowledge of the lives of the affluent.

Including the excluded

The decline of old industries and the shift to an economy based on knowledge and skills has given rise to a new class: a workless class ... Today the greatest challenge for any democratic government is to refashion our institutions to bring this new workless class back into society and into useful work, and to bring back the will to win.

(Tony Blair, speech at the Aylesbury Estate, Southwark, 2 June 1997, cited in Peck 1999)

In Britain the work of the Social Exclusion Unit (1999a), set up under the New Labour administration, explicitly regards its task as the integration of what it sees as socially disorganised communities into the mainstream. This task is explicitly aimed at reducing the levels of crime and disorder within society as a whole. So, once again, we have a notion of the dual city. But the political aim here is overtly inclusionist and can fittingly be seen as a social democratic attempt to tackle the correlate of social problems occurring in the poorest part of society. Here a key concept is the notion of the welfare dependency of the poor and the emancipating effect of work in transforming their lives.

Table 1.1 The binaries of social exclusion

Society at large	The underclass
The unproblematic	The problem
Community	Disorganisation
Employment	The workless
Welfare dependency	Independence
Stable family	Single mothers
The natives	The immigrants
Drug free	Illicit drug use

The danger of the concept of social exclusion is that it carries with it a series of false binaries: it ignores the fact that problems occur on both sides of the line, however much one has clusters in one area rather than another and, more subtly, it conceals the fact that the 'normality' of the majority is itself deeply problematic.

Thus in the first respect, as we have seen, unemployment, poverty and economic insecurity is scarcely unknown outside the designated areas – indeed quantitatively they are overall more prevalent in the supposedly secure majoritarian heartlands of society than they are in the selected minority of 'excluded' areas. And the same, of course, is true of illicit drug use, community disorganisation, unstable family structures, etc. In the case of the notion of 'the normal majority' it assumes that, in this world, class differentials are somehow insignificant, that paid work is an unambiguous benefit, that 'stable' family life is unproblematic, licit psychoactive drug use is less a problem than illegal drug 'abuse', and so on. Furthermore, it assumes that the transition from the socially excluded to the socially included majority via the vehicle of work will miraculously solve all these problems.

The centrality of work to the process of inclusion cannot be overemphasised. Being a member of society, being *included*, means being in work and *useful* work means paid work, labour sold in the market place. As Ruth Levitas clearly puts it:

> Under cover of a concern with 'social exclusion', and a rhetoric of solidarity, society dissolves into market relations. The importance of unpaid work to the maintenance of social life and human relationships is ignored. The possibility of integration into society through any institution other than the labour market has disappeared. There is no such thing as society – only individual men and women and their jobs....
>
> The concept of social exclusion as it is currently deployed places people either inside or outside mainstream society, synonymous with outside the labour market. The concept works both to devalue unpaid work and to obscure the inequalities between paid workers – not to mention the inequalities between paid workers and a property-owning class who can afford not to work at all, but who are apparently not among the ranks of the socially excluded. But then they do have a relationship with the labour market: it just happens to be one of exploitation.
>
> (Levitas 1996: 12, 19)

From community to public sphere

Having discarded the notion of a series of organic communities either actually in existence or, as in the communitarian dream, to be greatly regenerated and refurbished, as nostalgic and impractical can we, therefore, substitute a series of virtual communities with some territorial basis – a multiculturalism of a late modern sort? Thus we have the gay community, the Sikh community, the Irish community, the black community, women, etc. Such a formulation is a currency of contemporary politics and the media: events are publicly examined and debated by turning to representatives of various 'communities'. There can be no doubt that such a formulation has some foundation. A whole series of what Nancy Fraser calls 'subaltern public spheres' occur where genuine debates occur and which can by careful argument and presentation influence the debate within the more general public sphere. A key example which Fraser gives, is that of second wave feminism which as a new social movement has elaborated extensive networks, journals, activist groups and discussion centres. Furthermore, such activism has produced broad debate in the wider public sphere over a whole series of issues concerned with crimes against women: sexual harassment, rape, domestic violence, etc., many of which has resulted in changes in public attitudes and a broad raft of legislation. But it would be wrong to see such sections of the population as late modern equivalents of the organic community.

Nancy Fraser, in her essay 'Sex, Lies and the Public Sphere' (1997), discusses the 1991 struggle over the confirmation of Clarence Thomas as an associate justice of the US Supreme Court who was nominated as only the second African American on the Court in US history. Thomas was accused of sexual harassment by Anita Hill, a black female law professor who had served as Thomas' assistant at the Equal Employment Commission in the 1980s. Fraser takes us through a fascinating account of the discourses surrounding this struggle: for discourses of gender, race and class each entered the public arena as the debate developed. What became clear was that there was no clear line from women, from blacks, from the middle- or working-class white males. It was not that self-conscious 'communities' of a sort existed, particularly in this context of American multiculturalism, but that each divided and crossed in their alliances. A result was what Fraser (1997) called 'the fracturing of the myth of homogeneous '"communities"'. As a result, she continues, it would be better to consider:

> Replacing the homogenizing ideological category of 'community' with the potentially more critical category of 'public' in the sense of a discursive arena for staging conflicts ... In these respects, the concept of a public differs from that of a community. 'Community' suggests a bounded and fairly homogeneous group, and it often connotes consensus. 'Public', in contrast, emphasizes discursive interaction that is in principle unbounded and open-ended, and this in turn implies a plurality of perspectives. Thus, the idea of a public, better than that of a community, can accommodate internal differences, antagonisms, and debates.
>
> (Fraser 1997: 118)

We start then from noting how the notion of 'community' has changed remarkably in late modernity but, further to this, that what takes its place is not simply a series of discrete multicultural communities with both local and virtual dimensions, which both criss-cross and are contested. The community loosens its mooring in the locality and the various public discourses no longer have any one-to-one relationship to a specific section of the population.

Conclusion

It is now time to bring the threads of this discussion together. The problem of crime is inevitably one of order, to tackle crime we must, therefore, involve the politics of distribution and the politics of recognition. We must, in short, intervene both on a material and a symbolic level. This chapter has been concerned largely with the latter although it has been argued that without some form of redistribution any considerable reduction in crime is unlikely. The significance of the symbolic level has changed remarkably with the transition to late modernity. First, a more individualistic society generates greater and greater demands for self-actualisation and recognition. Second, the increased sense of disembeddedness makes, at the same time, a sense of secure identity more and more precarious. Third, a potent solution to this ontological uncertainty is that of essentialism. Fourth, such a fake sense of solidity is more easily achieved by denigrating others. And finally, such a dehumanisation of others can be a potent facilitator both of crime (particularly violence) and a punitive attitude towards the criminal. It is therefore crucial that we attend to the problems of identity, arguing for policies which ensure a sense of self-worth and actualisation yet which do not rest upon the fake premises of essentialism where others are systematically denigrated and then abused. Not the least reason for this is that such a sense of identity brings with it the informal norms which apportion praise and shame and help control predatory crime towards others.

Nancy Fraser, in *Justice Interruptus* (1997), develops an extremely useful typology of the politics of reform based on the two dimensions of redistribution and recognition. Reform, she argues, must recognise the necessity of changes in both these areas, assuaging the failings of distributive justice *and* misrecognition and devaluation. But to this dichotomy she adds a further distinction: between the politics of affirmation and the politics of transformation. Affirmative politics merely involves the surface transfer of resources without changing the basic underlying divisions whereas transformative politics seek to eliminate the basic underlying structures of injustice (see Young 1999; Mooney 2000). Thus in the area of redistribution affirmative remedies involve, for example, coercing the underclass into the labour market at extremely low wages. Their underclass position is merely reproduced this time within the lower reaches of the market place (see Levitas 1996). This dragooning of people from one category of exclusion to another ('getting the people to work', as the Social Exclusion Unit [1999a] put it, with its cheerless *double entendre*) is experienced all too frequently, not as inclusion but as exclusion, not as the 'free' sale of labour but as straightforward coercion. Relative deprivation would, of course, not be solved by such 'inclusionary' politics and the sources of discontent which are liable to generate high crime rates would be unabated. Transformative redistribution, on the other hand, would involve such measures as retraining so that jobs could be gained and then rewarded on a meritocratic basis – thus putting a genuine element of equality into equal opportunity policies, the recognition of non-paid work (e.g., child rearing, caring for ageing parents) as of vital importance for social reproduction, the creation of viable childcare infrastructures for women with children, and the enforcement of a minimum wage on a level which allows the individual an existence which is neither demeaning nor severely straitening in circumstance. Above all, it would not fetishise paid work – it would not view such work as the vital prerequisite for full citizenship, for acceptance and inclusion in society.

An affirmative politics of recognition does not question the various essentialisms of difference. That is, in the case of conventional multiculturalism, what is stressed is the need for the positive recognition of various groups on equal terms, for example: Irish, African-Caribbean, gays, women, etc. In contrast, transformative politics seek to break down and destabilise the categories by questioning the very notion of fixed identity and essence. Thus the invented notion of tradition is challenged, the overlapping, interwoven nature of what are supposedly separate cultures stressed, and the ambiguity and blurred nature of boundaries emphasised. Diversity is encouraged and, where non-oppressive, celebrated, but difference is seen as a phenomenon of cultures in flux not essences which are fixed.

In the case of crime and punishment, the critique of essences both in criminal victimisation and in punishment is a high priority. The category of hate crimes must be widened out in the realisation that a considerable proportion of acts of violence involve vocabularies of motive which debase and dehumanise the victim (see Young 1990). Thus not only crimes against gays and blacks, but against women, the elderly, the poor, etc. In terms of our response to crime it is vital that the essentialism which runs through the discourses about crime and its causes is thoroughly debunked. Important, here, is to confront and shatter the triptych which locates crime spatially and socially in three loci – the underclass, the drug user and the immigrant. Such a combination, portrayed as interdependent and very frequently racialised, is presented as the major source of crime and disorder in our society.

Against this we must emphasise that crime occurs throughout the structure of society and that its origins lie not in a separate aetiology but in the structure of society and its core values. The identification of a distinct criminal class is an endeavour bound to failure. Politicians forget this at their peril. As I write, the British Prime Minister Tony Blair roundly castigates drunken hooligans one week and calls for robust legislation to bring them under control when in the next week his own 16-year-old son is arrested for drunkenness in London. A year previously, the Home Secretary, Jack Straw, famous for his tough on crime approach and the appointment of a drug Czar, is awakened from sleep by a telephone call from the police informing him that his son has been arrested for selling drugs. As the perceptive journalist Joan Smith (2000) put it:

> The Government's responses are off the cuff and authoritarian ... Again
> and again it reveals an us-and-them mentality as though there are only two
> Britons: decent God-fearing folk whose only transgression is the occasional
> parking ticket and a violent, anti-social sub-class whose members habitually
> exploit drugs and alcohol and deliberately go out deliberately looking for
> trouble.

(Smith 2000: 13)

At the start of this chapter I discussed the need to chart the journey into late
modernity. It was necessary to examine the terrain, chose our means of travel
and be clear as to our destination. We have seen how the terrain has changed
dramatically: employment, family, community – the structure of society, has
become less secure, boundaries blur, identities are less and less fixed, place and
social category become less determinate in prescribing behaviour, vocabularies
of motive lose their mooring in discrete parts of the structure – we have entered
the period of what Bauman (2000) graphically calls 'liquid modernity'. And this
terrain has become a more risky place both in terms of crime and disorder and
in terms of demonisation and scapegoating. On the one hand, the organic
community has diminished and fragmented becoming much less capable of
controlling the rising tide of crime and discontent, whilst on the other hand,
community itself becomes reinvented as a mythical *Gemeinschaft* which serves
to exclude and essentialise others.

Yet the organic community of the past is in terminal decline, although not
into a black hole of atomistic individuals devoid of trust as the more dystopian
of commentators would have it. For it has reformed into the late modern
community: virtual and mediated in part and global in its reach which touches
down at the local sometimes substantially but always intermittently in the biography of each individual. It is in this new community, the 'generalised
elsewhere', where old identities are discarded and new identities reconstructed.
It is here both in the more general public sphere and the host of subaltern
publics where concepts of appropriate and inappropriate behaviour, and the
criteria of social worth and opprobrium are regularly debated. Never have so
many people looked at so many people: never in human history has there been
such a degree of reflexivity about human behaviour. The paradox of identity, of
course, is that it is precisely at the point in history where it becomes most
apparent as a social construction that there is a widespread desire for essence
and fixity. The importance of the new social movements here is vital. For they
become the key axes of the debate about gender, ethnicity, or relations with
other species and the environment. The worry, of course, even here, is the
tendency to essentialise whether it is anti-racists who give credence to 'race',
radical feminists who essentialise masculinity and femininity or gay rights
activists who begin to believe in the biological basis of homosexuality.

Furthermore, as Fraser (2000) points out in a recent essay, it is necessary to
recognise the need to tackle the institutionalised patterns which maintain such
essences. For example, the institutionalised racism within police practice which

causes such disproportionate focusing on African-Caribbeans, the Irish, etc. (see also Mooney and Young 2000).

The terrain has changed and, of course, with it the available means of change. Thus as Hans Hofman (1996) pointed out, the worthy social demo-cratic critiques of society which link crime and punitiveness to lack of stabile employment, community and family life assume that we can nostalgically bring these entities of the 1960s back into existence by an act of political will. We have seen how, in the case of community, this is an implausible dream, possible only for a minority. Artificially created communities, such as Disney's new town Celebration in central Florida (Ross 1999), are the exceptions which prove this rule. But this is true of the other institutional areas. Take paid work as an example, an important site both of distributive justice and of identity. Herein, as Andre Gorz trenchantly puts it:

> Is an enormous fraud. There is not and never will be 'enough work' (enough paid, steady, full-time employment) for everyone any longer, but society (or, rather, capital), which no longer needs everyone's labour, and is coming to need it less and less, keeps on repeating that it is not society which needs work (far from it!), but you who need it, ... Never has the 'irreplaceable', 'indispensable' function of labour as the source of 'social ties', 'social cohesion', 'integration', 'socialization', 'personalization', 'personal identity' and meaning been invoked so obsessively as it has since the day it became unable any longer to fulfil *any* of these functions ... Having become insecure, flexible, intermittent, variable as regards hours and wages, employment no longer integrates one into a community, no longer structures the daily, weekly or annual round, or the stages of life, and is no longer the foundation on which everyone can base his/her life project.
>
> The society in which everyone could hope to have a place and a future marked out for him/her – the 'worked-based society', in which he/she could hope to have security and usefulness – is dead. Work now retains merely a phantom centrality: phantom in the sense of phantom limb from which an amputee might continue to feel pain.
>
> (Gorz 1999: 57–8)

Work in the sense of that which involves self-realisation and creativity, is not, of course, dead but secure, paid, full-time employment for life is considerably diminished and where it exists does not have this quality. Hence the title of Gorz's book 'Reclaiming Work'. Work, like the community, needs to be refor-mulated if we are to seek to provide the basis of identity and social worth.

Lastly, let us look at our final destination. The transition to late modernity is one which involves the most dramatic changes in the fabric of society. Anthony Giddens (1990) describes it like a juggernaut sweeping all solid institutions aside, Francis Wheen (1999), in his recent biography of Marx, wryly notes how the images of globalisation and the metaphor of the 'melting' of all that seemed solid in the Communist Manifesto is prescient more of the present time than in the nineteenth century. Indeed there is more than a slight resonance of today when we read of a world where there is 'uninterrupted disturbance of all social conditions, everlasting uncertainty and agitation ... fixed, fast-frozen relations, with their train of ancient and venerable prejudices and opinions are swept away'. Such changes with heavy irony swept away the fossilised state socialist regimes of Eastern Europe just as they transform our lives in the West. Community, work, the family – all the major institutions of social order, face a transformation. Whether this is in the direction of greater equality and a sense of self-worth or towards inequality and essentialism is the central hub of the politics of the future.

Notes

1   And, of course, such a process of deconstruction has been characteristic of critical analysis throughout the humanities and the social sciences. What is worth noting is that the period in which critical criminology emerged in the late 1960s and early 1970s was at the cusp of change within which dramatic transformations were occurring throughout the social fabric of advanced capitalist societies. The early critiques were, so to speak, a harbinger of what was to come and what, at that time was a relevant yet perhaps technically peripheral critique of modernity, has become a pressing and key concern of any social analysis of late modernity.

2   In fact she points to a shift from one to the other so that 'the struggle for recognition is fast becoming the paradigmatic form of political conflict in the late twentieth century' (Fraser 1997: 11). Her predictions as to the decline of the social democratic politics of class are undoubtedly incorrect: what her own work vividly shows is that the discourses of both class and identity politics co-exist even in the United States (see, for example, her remarkable essay on the Clarence Thomas case in her book *Justice Interruptus* [1997]), as also does her discussion of methods of social transformation lean heavily on the co-existence of both dimensions (of which more later). Indeed, her distinction between the politics of distribution and recognition and the strategies needed to overcome maldistribution and misrecognition are of great use and versatility.

3   I have paired the concepts of distributive justice and relative deprivation and misrecognition and ontological deprivation. Fraser's distinction echoes the traditional Weberian distinction between class and status and it is significant that Runciman (1966) in his original, although largely unexplored, discussion of deprivation utilised as I am doing here relative deprivation on both these dimensions. In a recent essay, Fraser (2000) acknowledges the Weberian influence on her work.

4   Of course, all of these authors rediscover that which was a mainstay of traditional subcultural theory. Such is the amnesia in criminology that the pivotal work of Cloward and Ohlin (1961), particularly in their discussion of the organised and disorganised slum, is not built upon.

References

Back, L. (1996) *New Ethnicities and Urban Culture*, London: UCL Press.

Bauman, Z. (1998) *Globalization*, Cambridge: Polity Press.

—— (2000) *Liquid Modernity*, Cambridge: Polity Press.

Beck, U. (1992) *Risk Society*, London: Sage.

Berman, M. (1983) *All That's Solid Melts Into Air*, London: Verso.

Bottoms, A. E. and Wiles, P. (1997) 'Environmental Criminology', in M. Maguire, R. Morgan and R. Reiner *The Oxford Handbook of Criminology*, 2nd edition, Oxford: Clarendon Press.

Campbell, C. (1987) *The Romantic Ethic and the Spirit of Modern Consumerism*, Oxford: Blackwell.

Castells, M. (1994) 'European Cities, the Informational Society, and the Global Economy', *New Left Review*, 204 (March–April): 19–35.

Cloward, R. and Ohlin, L. (1961) *Delinquency and Opportunity*, London: Routledge and Kegan Paul.

Crawford, A. (1997) *The Local Governance of Crime*, Oxford: Oxford University Press.

Currie, E. (1997) 'Market Society and Social Disorder', in B. MacLean and D. Milanovic (eds) *Thinking Critically About Crime*, Vancouver: Collective Press.

Damer, C. (1974) 'Wine Alley: The Sociology of a Dreadful Enclosure', *Sociological Review*, 22: 21–48.

Davis, M. (1990) *City of Quartz*, London: Vintage.

Elias, N. (1982) *State, Formation and Civilisation: The Civilising Process*, trans. E. Jephcott, Oxford: Blackwell.

Etzioni, A. (1997) *The New Golden Rule*, London: Profile Books.

Featherstone, M. (1985) 'Lifestyle and Consumer Culture', *Theory, Culture and Society*, 4: 57–70.

Foster, J. (1997) 'Challenging Perceptions of "Community" and Neighbourliness on a Difficult-to-Let Estate', in N. Jewson and S. MacGregor (eds) *Transforming Cities*, London: Routledge.

Fraser, N. (1997) *Justice Interruptus: Critical Reflections on the Post-Socialist Condition*, New York: Routledge.

—— (2000) 'Rethinking Recognition', *New Left Review*, 2/3: 107–20.

Giddens, A. (1990) *The Consequences of Modernity*, Cambridge: Polity Press.

—— (1991) *Modernity and Self-Identity*, Cambridge: Polity Press.

Gilroy, P. (1993) *The Black Atlantic*, London: Verso.

Gitlin, T. (1995) *The Twilight of Common Dreams*, New York: Henry Holt.

Gorz, A. (1999) *Reclaiming Work: Beyond the Wage-Based Society*, Cambridge: Polity Press.

Harvey, D. (1997) 'Contested Cities: Social Process and Spatial Form', in N. Jewson and S. MacGregor (eds) *Transforming Cities*, London: Routledge.

Hebdige, D. (1988) *Hiding in the Light*, London: Routledge/Comedia.

—— (1990) 'Fax to the Future', *Marxism Today* (January): 18–23.

Hobbs, D. (1988) *Doing the Business*, Oxford: Clarendon Press.

Hobsbawm, E. (1994) *The Age of Extremes*, London: Michael Joseph.

—— (1996) 'The Cult of Identity Politics', *New Left Review*, 217: 38–47.

Hofman, H. (1996) 'Kritische Criminologie en Preventie in het Licht van een Postmoderne Conditie', *Tijdschrift voor Sociale Wetenschappen*, 41(2): 109–205.

Hogg, R. and Brown, D. (1998) *Rethinking Law and Order*, Annandale, NSW: Pluto.

Hood, R. and Jones, K. (1999) 'Three Generations: Oral Testimonies on Crime and Social Change in London's East End', *British Journal of Criminology*, 31(1): 136–60.

Hope, T. (1995) 'Community Crime Prevention', in M. Tonry and D. Farringdon (eds) *Building a Safer Society: Strategic Approaches to Crime Prevention, Crime and Justice. Crime and Justice 19*, Chicago: University of Chicago Press.

Hughes, G. (1998) *Understanding Crime Prevention*, Buckingham: Open University Press.

Hutton, W. (1995) *The State We're In*, London: Cape.

Jacobs, J. (1961) *The Death and Life of Great American Cities*, New York: Random House.

Levitas, R. (1996) 'The Concept of Social Exclusion and the New Durkheimian Hegemony', *Critical Social Policy*, 16(46): 5–20.

Luttwak, E. (1995) 'Turbo-Charged Capitalism and its Consequences', *London Review of Books*, 17(21): 6–7.

McRobbie, A. and Thornton, S. (1995) 'Rethinking Moral Panic for Multimediated Social Worlds', *British Journal of Sociology*, 46(4): 559–74.

Matthews, R. (1988) 'Reassessing Informal Justice', in R Matthews (ed.) *Informal Justice?*, London: Sage.

Meyrowitz, J. (1985) *No Sense of Place: The Impact of Electronic Media on Social Behaviour*, New York: Oxford University Press.

—— (1989) 'The Generalized Elsewhere', *Critical Studies in Mass Communication*, 6(3): 326–34.

Mooney, G. and Danson, M. (1997) 'Beyond Culture City: Glasgow as a Dual City', in N. Jewson and S. MacGregor (eds) *Transforming Cities*, London: Routledge.

Mooney, J. (2000) *Gender, Violence and the Social Order*, London: Macmillan.

Mooney, J. and Young, J. (2000) 'Policing Ethnic Minorities', in B. Loveday and A. Marlow (eds) *Policing After the Stephen Lawrence Inquiry*, Lyme Regis: Russell House.

Morley, D. and Robins, K. (1995) *Spaces of Identity*, London: Routledge.

Murray, C. (1984) *Losing Ground*, New York: Basic Books.

Nightingale, C. (1993) *On the Edge*, New York: Basic Books.

Peck, J. (1999) 'New Labourers? Making a New Deal for the "Working Class"', *Environment and Planning Government and Policy*, 17: 345–72.

Plummer, K. (1995) *Telling Sexual Stories*, London: Routledge.

Robins, D. (1992) *Tarnished Vision*, Oxford: Oxford University Press.

Ross, A. (1999) *The Celebration Chronicles*, New York: Balantine.

Runciman, W. (1966) *Relative Deprivation and Social Justice*, London: Routledge and Kegan Paul.

Schelsky, H. (1957) 'Ist die Dauerreflektion institutionalisierbar?', *Zeitschrift für Evangelische Ethik*, 1: 153–74.

Sennett, R. (1991) *The Conscience of the Eye*, London: Faber.

—— (1998) *The Corrosion of Character*, New York: W. Norton and Co.

Smith, J. (2000) 'Mr Blair gets a wake-up call from the real world', *Evening Standard*, 6 July: 13.

Social Exclusion Unit (1999a) *Bringing Britain Together: A National Strategy for Neighbourhood Renewal*, London: The Stationery Office.

—— (1999b) *Teenage Pregnancy*, London: The Stationery Office.

Social Trends (2000) *2000 Edition*, London: The Stationery Office.

Thompson, J. (1995) *The Media and Modernity*, Cambridge: Polity Press.

Tomlinson, M. (1999) *Globalization and Culture*, Cambridge: Polity Press.

Walklate, S. and Evans, K. (1999) *Zero Tolerance or Community Tolerance*, Aldershot: Ashgate.

Webber, J. (1992) 'Individuality, Equality and Difference: Justification for a Parallel System of Aboriginal Justice', in R. Silverman and M. Nielsen (eds) *Aboriginal Peoples and Canadian Criminal Justice*, Toronto: Butterworths.

Webster, F. (1995) *Theories of the Information Society*, London: Routledge.

Wellman, B. (1982) *Studying Personal Communities in East York* (research paper no. 128), University of Toronto: Centre for Urban and Community Studies.

Wheen, F. (1999) *Karl Marx*, London: Fourth Estate.

Willis, P. (1990) *Common Culture*, Milton Keynes: Open University Press.

Wilson, J. Q. and Kelling, G. (1982) 'Broken Windows', *Atlantic Monthly* (March): 29–38.

Wilson, W. J. (1996) *When Work Disappears*, New York: Knopf.

Young, I. M. (1990) *Justice and the Politics of Difference*, Princeton, NJ: Princeton University Press.

Young, J. (1992) 'Ten Points of Realism', in J. Young and R. Matthews (eds) *Rethinking Criminology*, London: Sage.

—— (1999) *The Exclusive Society*, London: Sage.

—— (2000) *Globalization, Chaos and the Narcissism of Minor Differences*, Middlesex University: Centre for Criminology. Paper first given at The American Society of Criminology, Toronto, 1999.

2 Joined-up but fragmented

Contradiction, ambiguity and ambivalence at the heart of New Labour's 'Third Way'

Adam Crawford

New Labour's Third Way

The 'Third Way' has become a term which has both sociological (academic) currency as an analysis of the 'modern times' in which we live (Giddens 1998; 2000) and political currency (Blair 1998) as a banner under which an evolving set of 'new' political ideas – with associated programmes of action – coalesce. The Third Way refers to the construction of a political agenda in response to, what are perceived to be, profound changes unfolding across the world. Traditional politics, it is argued, are inadequate to respond to contemporary needs, including required responses to cultural diversity, scientific and technological change, globalisation and ecological concerns. Contemporary conditions, it is also argued, have caused a transformation in, and blurring of, traditional political boundaries, as many issues cut across the Left–Right divide. Hence, the Third Way seeks a social analysis and political response which goes 'beyond the Left and Right'.

Crudely put, the Third Way as identified by Anthony Giddens and Tony Blair represents a quest to transcend social democracy, on the one hand, which looks to the state for answers, and neo-liberalism, on the other hand, which looks to the market for solutions. It is argued that, whilst neo-liberals historically have wanted to shrink the state, social democrats have been keen to expand it. What is necessary, rather, is to reconstruct a 'new democratic state' (Giddens 1998: 70). The reformed state, it is argued, will establish a new relationship between risk and security, on the one hand, and individual and collective responsibility, on the other.

The Third Way accepts anxieties and worries about civil decline as both real and tangible within many sectors of contemporary societies, not just the inventions of conservative politicians or the media. Hence, the loss of a sense of community, weakening sociability, urban decline, fear of crime and the break-up of marriages and families are seen as real problems needing to be addressed by the Third Way. However, as Giddens suggests, 'it is just as wrong to reduce civic decline to economics, as the old left often did, as to deny the influence of poverty and underprivilege' (1998: 79).

Whilst the over-interventionist welfare state has removed individual responsibility by (inadvertently) producing a 'culture of dependency', it is argued, the neo-liberal marketisation of everyday life, in which the 'public good' has become defined as merely the outcome of individual market-driven decisions and choices, has left little sense of, or space for, public responsibility and civic duty.

> The life of any family and any community depends on accepting and discharging the formal and informal obligations we owe to each other. The politics of 'us' rather than 'me' demands an ethic of responsibility as well as rights.
>
> (Blair 1998: 14)

In sum, the Third Way is premised upon the short-comings of traditional social democratic ideals that the 'good life' can be delivered through the (Keynesian) welfare state, whilst seeking simultaneously to tame, ride and steer the apparently 'inevitable' juggernaut-like pressures of globalisation, including the free flow of capital, finance, trade, technology and information. Alongside these global pressures is a growing salience of 'place' and locality. Global pressures, it is argued, are refracted and interpreted through local meanings, identities and sensibilities (Giddens 1991). As a result, there appears to be an increasingly profound relationship between globalised conditions and local circumstances in which the nature of the nation-state's capacity to exercise political control is called into question. In this sense, community safety both reflects a field of policy that it is saturated with wider concerns about contemporary social change and is a referent for an unfolding form of governance.

The Third Way for crime control

In the field of crime control and criminal justice policy the Third Way has been captured by the infamous phrase, first used by Tony Blair in an interview for BBC Radio 4 in 1993, namely: 'Tough on crime; tough on the causes of crime'. This catchphrase evocatively suggested a break with a 'soft on crime' stance traditionally associated with Labour. Downes and Morgan (1997) note that, for a Party historically tainted with many 'hostages to fortune' with regard to law and order (albeit paradoxically with a record in government which was no worse than that of the Conservative Party), this shift constituted a potential political vote winner. Moreover, it marked a 'watershed' in so far as it broke with the discourses associated both with the traditional Left of societal responsibility for crime and with that of the Right which emphasised the purely individual responsibility for crime (Downes 1998: 192). In so doing, it borrowed selectively upon the pragmatism of Left Realist criminology in its proclamation to take crime and the victims of crime seriously, focusing upon the 'lived realities' of ordinary people within a framework of moral responsibility (Young 1992). In the politics of the Third Way, obligations are both social and individual. Giddens reduces this to a further catchphrase: 'One might suggest as a prime motto for the new politics, no rights without responsibilities' (Giddens 1998: 65).

The New Labour government, elected in May 1997, wasted little time in identifying and selecting crime control as a major plank of public policy upon which its fortunes in office would hinge and upon which it should be judged. It clearly sees 'flagship' pieces of legislation such as the Crime and Disorder Act (1998) and the Youth Justice and Criminal Evidence Act (1999) as key elements in the implementation of Third Way politics in the field of law and order. The Home Secretary, Jack Straw, has suggested that the statutory community safety partnerships established by the Crime and Disorder Act (1998) alongside measures such as the anti-social behaviour orders (ASBO) and child curfews will help bind together and empower communities to fight crime. Through these and associated measures he declared:

> We are trying to develop the concept of 'the Active Community' in which the commitment of the individual is backed by the duty of all organisations – in the public sector, the private sector and the voluntary sector – to work towards a community of mutual care and a balance of rights and responsibilities.
>
> (Straw 1998: 16–17)

The proactive prevention of crime is a central and recurring theme in New Labour's policies. The duty on local authorities and the police to establish and promote community safety partnerships and to put in place crime and disorder strategies, has been acknowledged by many commentators as possibly the most important elements of the recent legislation. It represents a fundamental acknowledgement that the causes of crime lie far from the traditional reach of the criminal justice system. This is a theme which also resonates with the transformations to the youth justice system introduced by the 1998 Act and extended by the 1999 Act. Youth justice now has the prevention of youth crime as its over-riding central aim (s. 37). Moreover, the new community safety partnerships and strategies recognise the need for social responses to crime which reflect the nature of the phenomenon itself and its multiple aetiology through a multi-agency perspective. This approach is reinforced through reforms to youth justice which have introduced youth offending teams and other proposals such as the joint local approaches to truancy (s. 16 of the 1998 Act). Moreover, the establishment of inter-departmental bodies at central government level constitutes an important new addition to the institutional landscape with which to advance 'joined-up government'. The Social Exclusion Unit (SEU), for example, has established 'action teams' to develop a national strategy to tackle social exclusion and launched the New Deal for Communities, which funds programmes of intensive regeneration of targeted small neighbourhoods (SEU 1998).

Importantly, section 17 of the Crime and Disorder Act (1998) imposes a duty on local authorities to consider the crime and disorder implications of their various functions and the need to do all that they reasonably can to prevent crime and disorder in their area, thus requiring local authorities to anticipate the potential crime consequences of their policies. As the Home Office Consultation Document noted, this will 'give the vital work of preventing crime a new focus across a very wide range of local services ... putting crime and disorder considerations at the very heart of decision making, where they have always belonged' (Home Office 1997: para. 33). Consequently, some commentators have gone so far as to suggest that like 'a wolf in sheep's clothing' this section could come to constitute one of the most important parts of that Act (Moss and Pease 1999).

Moreover, through the required community consultation processes in the implementation of community safety strategies and community representation in local partnerships there is the potential to encourage a stronger and more participatory civil society. This theme is continued through the restorative justice elements in the youth justice reforms and particularly the involvement of voluntary panel members on youth offending panels (under the 1999 Act, currently being piloted), which attempt to reproduce forms of 'community conferencing' at the heart of the youth justice system in England and Wales.

Together, many of the reforms inspired by Third Way politics potentially afford a more holistic and problem-oriented approach to crime prevention and community safety (Crawford 1998a). As such, they may allow a fundamental shift in the way we govern crime and its prevention. Moreover, they challenge, both implicitly and explicitly, many of the taken-for-granted modernist assumptions about professional expertise, hierarchical competence and specialisation, as well as state paternalism and monopoly. In their place, the new politics offers more plural understandings of and social responses to crime, drawing together a variety of organisations and stakeholders, in the public, voluntary and private sectors as well as from among relevant community groups in ways which are problem-focused rather than defined according to the means most readily available for their solution. As such, they may allow a systemisation and co-ordination of effort, expertise and information and a democratisation of control through greater community empowerment.

Nevertheless, in this chapter I want to focus upon a number of sites of tension, ambiguity and ambivalence in both Third Way politics and the manner in which they are being implemented. I do so because it is in these conflicts and tensions that we find some of the key determinants of contemporary law and order policy and practice, as well as central components guiding the future shape of crime control.

Central ideas at the heart of Third Way politics

Within Third Way politics, notably the crime and disorder elements, we can identify three broad dominant influences, namely: communitarianism; managerialism and a partnership approach. This is not to suggest that these are the only dynamics which infuse New Labour's crime control policies (see Downes 1998; Newburn 1998) nor do they exhaust the range of influences upon change, but it is my contention that they are key elements within these, both of specific import and worthy of particular attention. Moreover, they expose and reveal some of the central and broader tensions, ambiguities and ambivalences in Third Way thinking more generally.

Communitarianism

As the above quotes already suggest, Third Wayism draws upon a communitarian philosophy, notably that espoused by Amitai Etzioni (1993; 1997a), whose work has explicitly sought to influence (Etzioni 1997b), and has impressed, the Labour leadership (Blair 1995; 1996). Such ideas have been advanced in Britain by the Demos think-tank (see Leadbeater 1996) and such commentators as Henry Tam (1998). This influence expresses itself in the diverse appeals to 'community' as a focus of moral renewal. As Etzioni suggests:

> Communities often have strong moral voices and hence can help maintain a social order that draws significantly on value commitments ... communities also share sets of values and reaffirm them, encourage members to abide by these values, and censure the members when they do not.
> (Etzioni 1997a: 123)

This form of 'communitarian moralism' asserts the need to restore communities and their moral voices, requiring a greater emphasis upon individuals' responsibilities towards, rather than rights over, their communities. As such, it attempts to reactivate institutions of civil society – notably communities, schools and families – into forms of vibrant social control. It is concerned with a 'remoralisation of justice', through community as moral order (Etzioni 1997c). Communitarianism is premised upon the notion that individuals are members of one another, they are ontologically embedded in a social existence. Thus, we gain our initial moral commitments from the communities into which we are born, which over time are reinforced by other forms of community membership. For communitarians 'the social' and the 'community' are no longer necessarily complementary aspects of the same broad rationality of rule, but constitute different and potentially 'competing problematics of government' (O'Malley and Palmer 1996: 140). As Etzioni notes: 'Society, as a community of communities, should encourage the moral expectation that attending to welfare is the responsibility of the local community' (1993: 146). Such communitarian ideas infuse New Labour's thinking and policies, as Jack Straw notes: 'Concepts such as community and personal responsibility, which have so long been buried in the futile arguments between Left and Right, are at the centre of everything we do' (1998: 17).

Managerialism

Second, there is both an explicit and implicit managerialism at the heart of New Labour's reforms. In many ways, recent policy initiatives have intensified the New Public Management (NPM) reforms introduced under previous Conservative governments since the mid-1980s. These reforms have seen a significant restructuring of the public sector and the role of the state, as well as the introduction of a new regulatory style and managerial culture. NPM reforms represent a cluster of ideas and strategies which variously have sought: to hive off certain traditional aspects of public service delivery to the private sector; introduce private sector management methods to the public sector; flatten bureaucratic hierarchies; measure performance by results set against clear objectives; disaggregate separable functions into quasi-contractual or quasi-market forms; introduce purchaser/provider distinctions; open up provider roles to competition between agencies and private interests; and advocate a 'closeness to the customer' (see Hood 1991; 1995; Clarke and Newman 1997).

Under New Labour the managerialist urges to objective setting, performance measurement and output-fixation, notably through 'league table' comparison, has reached a new zenith. This is particularly apparent with regard to crime control in the Crime and Disorder Act (1998) and the managerial processes introduced to implement the local crime and disorder strategies. Lord Warner, a senior policy adviser to the Home Secretary during the conception and passage through Parliament of the Crime and Disorder Act (and now the Chair of the Youth Justice Board of England and Wales), described the Act as reflecting 'a much more managerial feel about how you implement election promises' (Warner 1998).

Partnerships, networks and joined-up government

A third influence, as already noted, is the appeal to 'joined-up' and 'holistic' government through partnerships with cross-cutting approaches to problem solving. This has implications both within the state (as a critique of 'departmentalism') and across the traditional state-civil society divide. With regard to the former concern, the government declared in a recent White Paper, entitled 'Modernising Government', that 'To improve the way we provide services, we need all parts of government to work together better. We need joined-up government. We need integrated government' (Cabinet Office 1999: 5). With regard to the latter concern, according to Giddens, 'state and civil society should act in partnership, each to facilitate, but also to act as a control upon, the other' (1998: 79). Hence, a partnership approach reverses the dominant assumption of a single agency (notably police) 'solution' to crime. The appeal to a partnership approach to community safety is premised upon the belief that crime prevention lies beyond the competency of any one single agency. Traditional segmented and compartmentalised social responses fail to provide coherence, co-ordination and synergy. Partnerships, by contrast, propose an holistic approach to crime and disorder which is problem-focused rather than bureaucracy-premised.

> The Third Way recognises the limits of government in the social sphere, but also the need for government, within those limits, to forge new partnerships with the voluntary sector. Whether in education, health, social work, crime prevention or the care of children, 'enabling' government strengthens civil society rather than weakening it, and helps families and communities improve their own performance ... New Labour's task is to strengthen the range and quality of such partnerships.
>
> (Blair 1998: 14)

Networks of interlaced agencies drawing from the public, private and voluntary sectors are heralded as alternatives to a primacy upon bureaucracies and markets as the bedrocks of the new governance.

Sites of contradiction, ambiguity and ambivalence

It is my contention that these three dynamics, as well as being important in their own right in understanding the direction of Third Way policies, constitute what I have elsewhere described as 'an unholy Trinity' (Crawford 1998b: 242). These visions are deeply embedded within the politics of the Third Way but clash in many important respects. In so doing, they yield and reflect a number of important sites of contradiction, ambiguity and ambivalence all of which have significant implications for the future. I will consider a number of these in turn under the following seven aphorisms:

- joined-up but fragmented
- arm's length but hands on
- wide-angled but tunnelled vision
- growing demands for trust and the institutionalisation of distrust
- co-operation and negotiation in a cold climate of competition
- nostalgia disguised as modernisation
- ambivalent political responses

Joined-up but fragmented

At the heart of appeals to partnerships and policy networks is an ambiguity as to what partnerships entail and their purpose, inclusiveness, responsibilities, working relations and lines of accountability. The discussion tends to treat partnerships as if the public sector, voluntary organisations, private businesses, communities and groups are undifferentiated clusters of organisations, as if they present the same issues and opportunities as well as difficulties. There is little sense of the diverse priorities and forces as well as the plural traditions, cultures and practices which differentiate such clusters of interests. Little concern is given to the problematic task of managing such networks, particularly in light of the reality that conflicts are overlain by very different power relations and access to resources (both human and material). It would appear that there is little consideration as to what partnerships, as a Third Way between the state and the market, actually entail. Giddens, for example, identifies but fails to resolve this problem. He suggests that:

> Reinventing government certainly sometimes means adopting market-solutions. But it also should mean reasserting the effectiveness of government in the face of markets.
>
> (Giddens 1998: 75)

Far from wrestling with this conundrum, Third Way proponents sidestep it, leaving a vacuum too easily filled with today's dominant managerialist dogma, which often resembles little more than the 'marketisation of the public sector', through the injection of private sector management ideas, such as those popularised by Osborne and Gaebler (1992).

More fundamentally, the 'unholy Trinity' has encouraged a pluralisation of services and service providers. Managerialist reforms and appeals to community involvement in policing and crime control have enticed new actors and active citizens into what was once perceived as the sole responsibility of the public police. As a consequence, we have witnessed the fragmentation and dispersal of policing and control. Fragmentation, itself, has been encouraged by the introduction of privatisation and quasi-markets through purchaser/provider splits where services could not easily be privatised. We can no longer speak (if we ever could) of a state monopoly in crime control and policing (Jones and Newburn 1998). They have become shared, as diverse agencies, organisations, groups and individuals are implicated in these tasks. This has produced a complex array of networks, partnerships, interlaced alliances of organisations and active citizenry that transcend the 'public' and 'private' spheres constituting hybrid mixes of plural agencies, places and functions.

In many senses, the establishment of the new community safety partnerships, by the Crime and Disorder Act (1998), will encourage and entrench this process of fragmentation of service delivery (and service providers) at a local level. The logic of the Act and the Guidance (Home Office 1998) which accompanies it is to encourage a pluralisation of local service providers and networks. It does so, not only by transcending the traditional workings of particular local agencies, but also by opening up new policy arenas, encouraging partnerships across and between the public, voluntary and private sectors. In addition, the emphasis upon a locally-grounded, problem-solving methodology encourages new local players to enter the field. However, the (unintended but logical) consequence of this is to exacerbate co-ordination and undermine the effectiveness of steering mechanisms.

This process of fragmentation itself has generated a demand for co-ordination and the conditions for the emergence of ever newer networks and partnerships which attempt to draw together the diverse services in new 'tangled webs' (Charlesworth *et al.* 1996). The task of co-ordination is itself undermined by the expanding complex of networks. As Rod Rhodes notes with irony: 'the competition-based fragmentation which undermined existing networks created pressures to form new networks which, in turn, undermined the competitive rationale of marketisation' (2000: 353). Perversely, government policy has encouraged fragmentation, not only by fostering the disaggregation of purchaser/provider roles, sub-contracting and the introduction of quasi-markets, but also through its response to earlier fragmentation in the form of new networks. This has produced what the Social Exclusion Unit, in its report into services for socially deprived neighbourhoods in Britain, referred to as 'initiative-itis' (SEU 1998: 38). As Rhodes also suggests: 'Such trends make steering [by central government] more difficult, so the mechanisms for integration multiply' (2000: 349).

In the community safety field the new partnerships in England and Wales must jostle for their own position on an already crowded terrain which includes Drug Action Teams (DATs), Drug Reference Groups, Youth Offending Teams (YOTs), Child Protection Committees, and Single Regeneration Budget (SRB) partnerships, as well as in some areas, New Deal for Communities pilots, Sure Start initiatives, Crime Reduction programme pilots and pathfinder projects and health, education and employment action zones. In addition, the community safety strategies are required to share a local arena with statutory demands for a plethora of other local management 'plans': for health, education, housing, policing and youth justice as well as police force objectives and probation strategies which are clearly related but often remain uncoordinated. Moreover, there is often no hierarchy of control or clear lines of accountability between the various services and networks: they lack overall coherence and correspondence. It is unsurprising, therefore, that according to Home Office research evaluating recent youth justice changes introduced by the Crime and Disorder Act 1998, 'the experience of YOT managers in the pilot areas who have responded to the range of requests for "joined up government" at the local level has highlighted an apparent lack of co-ordination at national government level' (Hines *et al.* 1999: 7).

The massive transformation of inter-organisational relations that a partnership approach and 'joined-up government' entail have in part been hindered, rather than advanced, by a managerialist culture. The baronial interests that historically have structured agencies and organisations within and around the criminal justice system have been disrupted only in part by managerialist reforms. In the late 1980s Joanna Shapland (1988) likened the integration of victims into criminal justice to a medieval baron system, whereby each baron or criminal justice fiefdom jealously guards its piece of criminal justice processing, only negotiating reluctantly with others. The particular difficulty for victims, she argued, is that their needs span several fiefdoms who rarely communicate with one another. As a consequence, trying to effect real change, even with regard to simple and uncontroversial needs of victims, becomes heavily problematic. The same analogy applies equally well to community safety – and other so-called 'wicked issues' – which, as the Morgan Report reminded us, 'is a peripheral concern for all the agencies, and a truly core activity for none of them, even those agencies which explicitly include crime prevention within their objectives such as the police and the probation service' (1991: 15, para. 3.15). However, the managerialist reforms which increasingly have pervaded criminal justice organisations with their emphasis upon performance measurement, financial control and responsiveness to 'customers' for whom services are delivered have not disrupted this image significantly and perversely may have strengthened it (Shapland 2000). They have strengthened intra-organisational control but often at the expense of concerns for inter-organisational relations (a point to which I return below), thus exacerbating fragmentation. The supreme paradox of managerialist reforms is that they are increasingly undermined by plural partnerships and networks while simultaneously weakening the effectiveness of the partnerships and networks that they spawned. They induce a landscape which is simultaneously joined-up but fragmented.

Arm's length but hands on[1]

As already noted, one of the primary managerialist techniques has been the separation of purchaser and provider functions with regard to public services. The rationale behind this has been to redraw the role of government to that of policy-making which should be disentangled from the administration and operational delivery of services. This is a relationship in which government 'steers' by leading and setting agendas, as well as catalysing and facilitating change. It leaves the task of 'rowing', on the other hand, the 'doing' of things, to others. It is a relationship of 'less government but more governance' (Osborne and Gaebler 1992). As the state attempts to 'steer' more and 'row' less it authorises, licenses, audits and inspects the doings of others. Hence, they necessitate processes of control and verification which allow those that 'steer' to monitor and correct the activities of those that 'row' (*ibid.*: 32). This shift in regulatory style demands new flows of information to fill the gulf created by the redrawing of state functions. Contracts, performance indicators, audits and inspections are some of the practical tools used to deliver this relationship of 'governing at a distance'. This 'revolution' in the relationship between state and civil society suggests a situation in which the former asserts a form of control through the setting of norms and the correction of deviations from them.

However, in practice there are difficulties implicit in observing effort and performance and in obtaining information. For example, the experience from the UK in health service reforms suggests that: 'The purchaser is often dependent on the provider for knowledge of what has been done, or even what should be done, so that information becomes a key battleground in service management' (Deakin and Walsh 1996: 37). The lesson is that delivery systems once set up may begin to exhibit a life of their own, which become increasingly difficult to rein back or control. This internal momentum can end up pulling contract-based systems in directions that were not always anticipated by those that set them up. Furthermore, partnerships once established tend to become increasingly autonomous and resist central guidance. Hence, in practice, it is often harder to distinguish those who are 'rowing' from those who are 'steering'. Inadvertently, government may be producing 'self-steering networks' (Rhodes 1997: 110).

Often the implication of these harsh realities for governments is that they tend to fall back upon interventionist strategies. Fuelled by the pluralisation and fragmentation, outlined above, a perception on the part of central government can develop for the need to maintain a 'hands on' approach to the networks and partnerships it has helped spawn. In this context, as Rhodes notes, for government ' "hands off" is the hardest lesson of all to learn' (2000: 361).

This ambiguity for central government is illustrated in the content of the Home Office (1998) *Guidance on Statutory Crime and Disorder Partnerships*. The government has preferred to leave local partnerships to decide the content of strategies. It 'deliberately avoids attempting to define the terms "crime" or "disorder" and goes on to declare that "within reason, nothing is ruled out and nothing is ruled in" ' (Home Office 1998: para. 1.43).[2] Nevertheless, the *Guidance* goes on to identify a variety of issues which local partnerships would do well to consider. More recently, however, the government has retreated from its abstentionist position and been highly critical of the new community safety partnerships for not sufficiently complying, in its view, with the guidance. Moreover, the Home Secretary has chastised local authorities and the police for under-utilising certain powers given to them by the CDA, such as the controversial anti-social behaviour orders (ASBOs) and youth curfews.[3] At the Local Government Association conference in Bournemouth in June 2000, Jack Straw criticised councils for not making greater use of ASBOs. He claimed ASBOs to constitute a 'powerful weapon' which 'should be used swiftly where circumstances demand it, not just against the very hard cases of unacceptable behaviour' (*Independent*, 29 June 2000). Moreover, he suggested that councils should ignore concerns over conflicts with the recent Human Rights Act (which incorporates the European Convention on Human Rights into UK law) commenting that 'no drunk on the street who has his can of Tenants lager taken off him is going to take us to the court in Strasbourg' (*The Times*, 29 June 2000). This 'hands on' central government interventionism runs counter to the spirit of locally sensitive and problem-oriented approaches adopted by community safety partnerships.

Networks and partnership arrangements require 'hands off' management and 'governance at a distance' which are often undermined by the practice of intervention on the part of government. This can produce significant conflicts and tensions between local initiatives and central steering. The reality of trying to separate purchaser/provider functions has been much more complex than managerialist gurus suggest, often fusing and blurring roles and responsibilities, and producing forms of government which are simultaneously 'at arm's length but hands on'.

Wide-angled but tunnelled vision

The innovation of managerial reforms in many ways runs counter to the elaboration of a partnership approach. As one political commentator notes, these reforms:

> had one overriding failure – they left government less, rather than more, able to solve the important, 'wicked' problems that most concern electors: how to cut crime. ... The vertical links between departments and agencies in any one field and professional groups such as the police, teachers, doctors and nurses are strong. The horizontal links are weak or non-existent.
>
> (Perri 6 1997: 9–10)

Managerialist reforms have served, perversely, to increase the isolation and introspection of many criminal justice agencies and other public sector organisations drawn into community safety partnerships. They have done so in four principal ways. First, managerialist reforms focus upon efficiency, economy and value for money, on hierarchical control and on the clear distribution of authority and responsibility (Rhodes 1997: 55). They are primarily concerned with internal re-organisation. Managerialist reforms encourage an intra-organisational focus that pays little attention to the task of managing inter-organisational relations. Scant regard is afforded to the more complex process of negotiating shared purposes, particularly where there is no hierarchy of control. Managerialism may suit hierarchical line management structures but is largely inappropriate for managing horizontal inter-organisational networks. There are fundamental tensions between a 'partnership' approach and aspects of the intra-organisational focus of managerialist reforms.

Second, the intra-organisational focus on 'outputs' and performance measurement can make agencies concentrate their energies upon their core tasks and activities at the expense of peripheral ones. Managerialist reforms focus attention upon narrowly construed service delivery to 'customers' of a particular segment of criminal justice at a given time and place within the process, rather than upon cross-cutting, horizontal accountabilities and responsibilities. Where a partnership approach envisages corporate decision-making on behalf of a number of actors, managerialism conceives of compartmentalised and independent responses coupled with an intra-organisational focus on objectives and results. The emphasis upon intra-organisational performance measurement fails to recognise that partnerships inherently blur the boundaries between, and the roles of, the incorporated organisations, such that individual contributions cannot easily be separated off and disentangled from each other without undermining the nature of that contribution.

The recent development of 'corporate' performance indicators has gone some way towards tying diverse agencies into the production of collective goods which transcend the competency or capacity of individual agencies – such as community safety. Yet, this does not resolve two dilemmas. First, there are problems that arise with regard to any conflicts between intra-organisational and inter-organisational performance indicators and where priorities should lie. Second, there are significant problems with regard to account-ability for corporate performance indicators, given the very nature of partnerships, their multiple layers of authority and complex interdependency. Joint and negotiated decisions tie the various parties into corporate policy and outcomes but often fail to identify lines of responsibility. Institutional complexity further obscures who is accountable to whom, and for what. This gives rise to what Rhodes has identified as 'the problem of many hands, where so many people contribute that no one contribution can be identified; and if no one person can be held accountable after the event, then no one needs to behave responsibly beforehand' (1996: 663). As authority is 'shared' it becomes difficult to disentangle and can become almost intangible. As Peters comments:

> Under the present conditions authority can hardly be located any more: it has become shared, parcelled, delegated, conditioned, subjected to approval and correction … In a word: authority has become elusive.
>
> (Peters 1986: 34)

Third, managerialist reforms place a growing emphasis upon organisationally defined outputs as distinct from outcomes. 'Outputs' are service activities whereas 'outcomes' are the impacts or consequences (intended or unintended) of these outputs on the wider environment. 'Outputs' frequently refer to inter-nally defined organisational goals over which organisations have considerable control. These may depart significantly from 'outcomes' – the effects of an output, or set of outputs, upon the community. Hence, output measurement and outcome evaluation are not the same thing. Given the control that organisa-tions can assert over defining their own outputs there are questions to be asked about the validity of output measurement as a central aspect in the monitoring of community safety. The concern is that the gulf between the two may grow larger under managerialist pressures. There is a danger that 'outputs' may take precedence over 'outcomes', so that social goals are eclipsed by organisational ones. This can express itself as 'measure fixation' whereby greater concentration is given to the measure, rather than the service which the measure is intended to signify.

Fourth, while it is clear that managerialist reforms have generated much more information about public organisations and services and the way in which they work, the quality, value and utility of the information produced remain uncertain. There is a danger that the application of performance cultures to public sector organisations drawn into community safety partner-ships focuses attention upon 'target management' rather than upon the quality of performance itself. This can produce the unwelcome dangers of 'gaming' through the strategic management of information as well as the manipulation and obfuscation of data, all of which can result in the demoralisation of staff and public cynicism (see Tilley 1995). More fundamentally, it can encourage a concentration upon 'easy' or 'soft' targets: those which are more likely to yield positive results, consequently diverting attention and resources away from (and possibly writing off all together) more problematic areas or intractable crime problems.

In sum, managerialist reforms are essentially hierarchical and as such antithetical to the management of complex networks: they emphasise inward-looking and myopic forms of performance measurement and output fixation which often work against holistic governance. As a consequence, they often fail to address 'wicked issues', focusing upon narrowly defined, measurable elements of a problem. They are simultaneously wide-angled but tunnelled vision.

Growing demands for trust and the institutionalisation of distrust

The construction and maintenance of trust, as I have argued elsewhere (Crawford 1997: 112–23; 1998a: 179–80), is a central dynamic in effective community safety partnerships. This is particularly evident where structural conflicts exist, where partners are steeped in divergent cultural ideologies and/or where there is a legacy of mistrust or misunderstanding. Fostering relations of trust between partner agencies, as well as among and between lay representatives, can take time and the investment of considerable effort. As such, partnerships have 'life-spans' during which they adapt and change. They need to develop and mature as circumstances alter. As trust develops and partnerships become more established different ways of managing conflict may become more appropriate. A crucial element in establishing trust relations is making people aware of the limitations of their own and other agencies' contribution, such that they neither try to 'do it all' nor do they have unrealistic expectations of what others can deliver. Consequently, there is a need for mutual respect for different types of contributions.

The crucial nature of inter-organisational trust is increasingly recognised within government guidance and by influential policy bodies such as the Audit Commission. In a management paper, the logics of which inform the *Safety in Numbers* Report, the Audit Commission declared: 'For most partnerships, building trust between partners is the most important ingredient in success' (1998: 26, para. 69). And yet, the wider context of managerialist reforms have tended to problematise trust, most notably trust in professional expertise. Managerialist reforms have introduced various 'rituals of verification': contracts, performance indicators, audits and inspections. Most notably, as Michael Power (1997) has shown, the audit has become a central instrument in the transformation of modes of governance and control. As the state has redrawn its functions and become increasingly committed to a supervisory role, audit and accounting practices have assumed a more prominent place. The 'hollowing out' of the state by NPM generates a demand for audit and other forms of inspection to fill the void. As Power notes:

Audit has become a benchmark for securing the legitimacy of organisational action in which auditable standards of performance have been created not merely to provide for substantive internal improvements to the quality of service but to make these improvements externally verifiable via acts of certification. As the state has become increasingly and explicitly committed to an indirect supervisory role, audit and accounting practices have assumed a decisive function. The state cannot play this indirect role without assuming the efficacy of these practices at the foot of a regulatory hierarchy.

(Power 1997: 10–11)

Despite its technical discourse, the audit is also a system of values and goals which are inscribed in the official programmes which both demand and encourage it. It helps shape public conceptions of the problems for which it is the perceived solution. As such, 'it is constitutive of a certain regulatory or control style which reflects deeply held commitments to checking and trust' (*ibid.*: 7). Audit is not merely a technical solution to a problem: 'it also makes possible ways of redesigning the practice of government' (*ibid.*: 11). Audits have as their primary object organisations and their sub-systems of control, as such audits are concerned with the control of control (*ibid.*: 128).

It is unsurprising, therefore, that the community safety partnerships have, at their very heart, a process of audit. In many senses, this process differs from traditional financial audits, but nevertheless the core idea of independent checking through informational evidence remains a key factor. Moreover, the audit process incorporates wholesale the language of managerialism, thus constructing afresh the nature of local crime problems: how they should be measured and managed. It seeks to shape public expectations, redefine success and failure and construct new forms of authority and legitimacy.

Appeals to 'community participation', 'active citizenry' and 'consumer sovereignty' also imply a scepticism of professional expertise. They feed off critiques of 'self-serving professional élites' and claim to represent a challenge to the 'cosy cultures of professional self-regulation' (Power 1997: 44). Here lies an appeal to open up a new circuit of power between the demands of communities and individuals as against those of criminal justice agencies. Where once we were told to 'leave it to the professionals' now we are enjoined to active participation in a 'self-policing society' (Leadbeater 1996). As concerns over 'vigilantism' have demonstrated, this circuit of power is a problematic and volatile one.

Paradoxically, technologies such as audits and inspections are contrived, in part, in the hope of restoring trust in organisational competence. Moreover, they presuppose and necessitate trust in themselves as instruments of verification and control. And yet, rather than resolving trust deficits they tend to multiply and disperse these into the fabric of the organisational environment. They disrupt trust relations by replacing traditional forms of trust in the professional use of discretion with forms of audit and inspection. Relations of trust in, and between, functionaries which have traditionally allowed large scope for policy discretion have been significantly curtailed in recent years by managerial reforms. They have encircled trust, by reducing the boundaries of discretion and rendering it subject to inspection and budgetary constraint.

As such, managerialist reforms institutionalise forms of distrust. However, recourse to audits, performance measurement, contracts and inspections does not necessarily destroy trust – as some have argued (Broadbent *et al.* 1996) – but rather reconfigures it. Trust and the contractualisation of relations are not mutually exclusive. In many senses, contracts presuppose a certain degree of trust. The new governance does not obliterate trust altogether, in fact it necessitates that trust is placed in new 'guardians of trust': auditors and inspectors. But this is a different form of trust, involving a 'second order' relationship. Ultimately, however, these systems of control are themselves the subject of questions as to their competence. The trust that new technologies demand must itself be the subject of 'verification' (Crawford 2000b).

Whilst it is the government's explicit intention that the audit process should be a developmental one, in that the Crime and Disorder Act (1998) establishes a strategy cycle in which the audit process is revisited every three years, there are legitimate concerns that in practice this may be undermined by competing pressures. These arise in large part because the veracity of the audit process becomes bound up with target setting and performance measurement. It would seem that the quality of the data which informed the first round of audits published in early 1999 was both limited and variable. Nevertheless, the very process of striving to meet the targets set on the basis of the audit baseline lends a legitimacy to the audit itself and shrouds it from critical gaze. For, to question the baseline is to question the process, and hence the very purpose of measurement. Rather than providing a foundation for informed dialogue and negotiation, the audit process demands that its efficacy is trusted. The concern is that in the 'audit society' the strategy cycles will become less a process of institutional learning and problem-identification or merely the basis for discussion but more, in Power's words, 'ritualised practices of verification whose technical efficacy is less significant than their role in the production of organisational legitimacy' (Power 1997: 14).

Moreover, the reality is that, once set up, baselines and audit processes exert a dynamic of their own. Continuity and comparability often rein back innovation and development. These problems are compounded by difficulties of measurement and the inadequacies of information available. Setting meaningful targets and determining performance indicators for dealing with 'disorder' or 'anti-social behaviour' are inherently problematic. Public definitions of disorder and community safety are inconsistent. Different audiences define the same behaviour differently. Furthermore, many of the neighbourhoods with high levels of crime and incivilities are inscribed by a general lack of consensus about such issues. In England and Wales, the Crime and Disorder Act (1998) provides no statutory definition of disorder nor is it defined in the accompanying *Guidance* (Home Office 1998). In practice, no standard systems for monitoring anti-social behaviour exist. In particular, there is no formal process for making decisions about what counts as an instance of anti-social behaviour. Consequently, the increased monitoring of non-criminal anti-social activity – through nuisance-related calls to the police and complaints to housing and environmental health departments and the development of more sophisticated methods of measurement – may actually result in an increase in recording. Expanding the focus of official regulation into non-criminal incidents, perversely, may produce an apparent increase in the phenomenon itself, at least in the short to medium term.

As Mollie Weatheritt noted some time ago with regard to performance measurement in policing, that it

> is primarily a way of formulating and asking further questions and promoting a dialogue with service providers about the prospects for service improvement. That dialogue may well turn out to be no more than a sterile tussle over disputed meanings.
>
> (Weatheritt 1993: 41)

In sum, managerial reforms exhibit factors which make trust more valuable and simultaneously render it more difficult to sustain. They corrode trust and encourage distrust at the moment in which trust is perceived to be a precious commodity – as the basis for communal self-regulation, managing networks and inter-organisational negotiation – such that the increasing demand for trust coexists alongside the institutionalisation of distrust. Moreover, the new technologies which seek to respond to trust deficits themselves demand that their efficacy is trusted, whilst generating information which is of limited use.

Co-operation and negotiation in a cold climate of competition

Since its inception in 1982, the Audit Commission has played a central role in the spread of managerialist ideas throughout public sector organisations, with a particularly significant impact on the field of crime control and policing. Along with the National Audit Office and Her Majesty's various Inspectorates, the Audit Commission has been crucial in encouraging the spread of objective-driven performance and generating a performance conscious culture, most notably within senior management, but ultimately throughout public sector organisations.[4] This 'value for money' approach has encouraged competition and comparison within and between public sector agencies.

In mid-1997, after the publication of the highly influential report into the youth justice system, *Misspent Youth* (Audit Commission 1996), the Audit Commission announced an eighteen-month national investigation and analysis of 'community safety'. The subsequent report *Safety in Numbers* (Audit Commission 1999) brings the Audit Commission's influential version of managerialism to the heart of community safety debates. In place of the rather crude totem of 'value for money' it advances the notion of 'best value' as a key element of managerial accountability. The logics of the report correspond with, and are inscribed into, government policy and guidance (see the Local Government Act 1999). The Audit Commission (1999: 23) defines 'best value' as requiring:

- *challenging* authorities to be clear and open on their service objectives,
- *consulting* local people on these objectives,
- *comparing* performance with other authorities,
- *competing* – demonstrating that services are competitive against alternative providers in the market place.

Hence, competition and comparison are seen as key criteria through which to require authorities to demonstrate improvements in services. And yet, unlike the first two criteria they appear particularly problematic with regard to community safety partnerships.

First, there is a contradiction between competition between service providers, on the one hand, and the process of managing networks of service providers – notably on the basis of negotiated equilibrium – on the other hand. Managerialist reforms by creating quasi-markets and injecting competition into community safety can serve to produce new sites of inter-agency conflict (Raine and Willson 1997: 88). They encourage low levels of interdependence, which may leave inter-organisational networks unstable. Moreover, competition can serve to undermine both reciprocity and trust. The cultures conducive to managing collaborative partnerships and constructive networks are rooted more in the identification of shared values, mutual trust and the respect of common principles and diverse contributions than in competitive market mentalities or managerial performance comparison. The skills necessary for co-ordinating and steering horizontal networks are more concerned with enhancing commitment through management by negotiation. Rhodes (2000: 355–6) likens such skills to those of 'diplomatic virtues' which are far removed from those of the 'head-kicker macho-manager', the 'individualist entrepreneur' or the 'bureaucrat'.

Second, comparison as an element of competition can introduce negative dynamics into community safety given the capacity of crime and disorder to divide populations and excite fears and anxieties. Moreover, there are significant difficulties in drawing meaningful comparisons given the very different nature of local crime and disorder problems in differing communities. Certain forms of crime and associated problems are heavily concentrated in specific geographic areas. Furthermore, there are dangers that community safety is not a rationalistic 'zero sum' endeavour. Safety is relative and relational: one area's sense of security and 'place' within the city, may be defined, in large part, in contradistinction to the perception of other areas' insecurity. In other words, to feel safe in your own area may necessitate the identification of other, less safe areas or urban 'badlands'. Hence, competition and comparison in community safety may serve to fuel dynamics of social exclusion and ghettoisation.

Comparison, in a context of appeals to community as a force for moral order and social control, can promote a disaggregating social force. An emphasis upon comparison can encourage boundary disputes and the formation of new communities around defensiveness and exclusivity, increasing social polarisation. There are dangers that contemporary quests for security will encourage the flight of people and capital out of certain localities as they become associated with, and stigmatised by, high levels of recorded crime and disorder. This can produce increasing social dislocation of a fundamentally spatial nature, in which disorder is a dynamic in a vicious spiral of decline and 'market residualisation'. The concern is that 'security differentials', fuelled by crude area-based comparisons, may become increasingly significant characteristics of wealth and status as communities solidify around defensive exclusivity (Crawford 1997).

This can be further exacerbated by the central paradox in crime prevention: the existence of an often inverse relationship between activity and need with regard to community crime prevention. Years of research have shown that community responses to crime are easiest to generate in exactly those areas where they are least needed and hardest to establish where the need is greatest. This paradox is compounded by problems of spatial displacement. As such, the role of community as a force for social cohesion can be undermined by the increasing extent of social and geographic dislocation, as a result of which the wealthy retreat into disaggregated, defended communities of affluence and withdraw from participation in, and contribution to, public services. In this context, the image of communities as exclusive islands of self-regulation raises concerns about the relationship between community and social justice. Partnerships, in this context need to address the vexed question: to what extent is local community safety a public good rather than a club good serving the interest of its members?

If community safety partnerships are to play a role in reconstructing the institutional bedrock of inner-city communities by assisting in building institutions of social solidarity, governments – both central and local – will need to provide the conditions under which genuine partnerships and networks can flourish. This requires policies and an infrastructure which foster reciprocity and interdependence between organisations and interests, not insularity and competition. The challenge for government is to cultivate such conditions and to nurture new forms of co-operation and shared values, rooted in mutual acceptance of difference and reciprocity on the basis of inter-organisational trust.

Hence, (quasi-)markets, competition and crude comparisons can inject pernicious dynamics into inter-community and inter-agency relations. They can encourage boundary disputes and the formation of new communities around defensiveness and exclusivity, increasing social dislocation and polarisation. As such, environments of co-operation and negotiation, so necessary for constructive partnership and inter-community relations, must exist in an unfavourable cold climate of competition.

Nostalgia disguised as modernisation

Inherent in much of the appeal to community in Third Way politics, under the communitarian influence, is a nostalgia which harks to a different age of tradition and authority. At a psychic level, it allows people to delve into the nostalgic 'imagined communities' of tradition. Underlying policy initiatives around community crime prevention is the prevailing idea that crime results from a failure or breakdown of community life. Appeals to community assume that there is a direct relationship between a lack of 'community' and the existence of high levels of crime. Disorganised communities – which lack a sense of mutuality and cohesiveness, where people are unwilling to intervene in support of communal order as 'no one cares' – are associated with high levels of crime and, inversely, low crime areas are associated with well-organised and cohesive communities. Yet, contemporary communities are not synonymous with social order. 'Organised' communities can produce both disorder and foster high levels of crime. Collective values of a community may serve to stimulate and sustain criminality. Communal values themselves can be crimogenic. Moreover, strong communities can be pockets of intolerance and prejudice. Nevertheless, appeals to community retain a profound emotional legitimacy in that they hold out the fantasy of genuine human identity, connectedness and reciprocity precisely at a moment in time at which they appear most absent.

This 'wilful nostalgia' (Simon 1995) has been particularly notable in the debate about 'zero tolerance' policing. The idea of 'zero tolerance' – warmly embraced by the New Labour government – offers a strategy through which to re-assert sovereignty, impose discipline and order and reclaim the streets from the deviant (Dennis 1997). 'Zero tolerance' policing evokes a nostalgic reassertion of moral authority through more aggressive and assertive strategies (see Bratton 1997). Wilson and Kelling's (1982) 'Broken Windows' thesis, from which zero tolerance draws its intellectual legitimacy, implicitly evokes a nostalgia for a secure and consensual world of the past. Signs of disorder are the enemy of community. Disorder, it is argued, violates a community's expectations of what constitutes appropriate civil behaviour (see Kelling in this volume). What is deemed necessary, therefore, is for the community to reassert its 'natural forces' of authority and control. The role of the police and other formal agencies is to support a community's political and moral authority. To do so, the police must accommodate those 'natural forces'.

This nostalgic re-imagining of community appears to run in stark contrast to the 'modernisation offensives' of New Labour and Third Way politics, for whom 'modernisation' stands as a short-hand for the need to embrace the 'inevitable' consequences of contemporary (global) conditions. Furthermore, the settled and stable communities idealised by communitarianism are often the enemies of innovation and experimentation and offer little space for creativity and diversity. Community as a force for conforming can serve to undermine the quest for novel, non-hierarchical modes of policy-making. There is a fundamental difference between restoring communities and transforming them into innovative and democratic institutions (Crawford and Clear 2001). Communities are not the utopias of egalitarianism, which some might wish, but are hierarchical formations, structured upon lines of power, dominance and authority. Communities are intrinsically exclusive – as social inclusion presupposes processes of exclusion – and may solidify and define themselves around notions of 'otherness' potentially infused with racialised overtones. Challenging and disrupting established community order, its assumptions and power relations may be a more fundamental aspect of a progressive politics. As such, nostalgic appeals to community as the basis of moral order may often be incongruous with the radical transformations necessary to realise modern institutions of governance through partnerships.

In short, it is debatable the extent to which the Third Way quest for community is a reworking of tradition or a force for democratic renewal. Rather, it may simply constitute nostalgia disguised as modernisation.

Ambivalent political responses: moral scolding, punitive populism and the rationalistic urge to manage

Finally, there are deep tensions within New Labour's policies regarding the relationship between, on the one hand, developments in community safety and the preventive strategies associated with them and, on the other hand, the growth of 'populist punitiveness' through an increased resort to strategies of penal exclusion (Bottoms 1995: 39–41). These tensions are apparent in the 'tough on crime, tough on the causes of crime' catchphrase and operate at a number of different levels.

First, the (re)moralising urge of communitarianism runs in conflict to the administrative impulse of managerialism. Where the former calls for a new moral crusade upon which to reconstruct civil society, the latter hails administrative efficiencies and cost effectiveness. There are significant tensions between the amoral market place of competition as the dynamic engine of change and the moral authority at the centre of communitarianism: between the instrumental and the moral elements of control. This ambiguity is seen, on the one hand, in the punitive tone and expressive 'moral scolding' which insists upon individual and family responsibility for offending and, on the other hand, in the rationalistic desire to manage crime at a minimal cost (Brownlee 1998). These contrasting visions awkwardly cohabit the Crime and Disorder Act (1998) and associated policy strategies.

Second, the normalisation and de-dramatisation of crime co-exist with the continued demonisation of cultural scapegoats: crime is both an ordinary part of everyday life to be the subject of routine precautions, avoided and prevented as well as a metaphor for urban and civic decline. At one moment the offender is a self-maximising and autonomous rational actor no different in his/her choices from the rest of us, the next minute, the offender is a depraved member of an 'underclass' operating within a wholly different moral frame. The tone shifts from an emphasis upon 'de-differentiation' – namely that crime is a usual and normal aspect of modern life and that criminals are essentially 'like us' – to a pre-occupation with pathological differences and 'otherness'.

David Garland (1996; 1999) relates this duality of 'the commonplace and the catastrophic' to much deeper (structural) interpretations of crime in late modernity, as a product of a decentring of state governance of crime. These two visions Garland refers to as the 'criminology of the self' and the 'criminology of the other' respectively:

> One criminology de-dramatises crime, allays disproportionate fears, and promotes routine preventative action. The other demonises the criminal, arouses popular fears and hostilities, and strives to enlist support for drastic measures of control.
>
> (Garland 1999: 354)

Not only are these antagonistic accounts the product of dilemmas of contemporary state governance, as Garland suggests, but they also find a particular expression in ambiguities within Third Way politics.

This tension helps to explain the moral vacillation in the apparently contradictory processes of 'defining deviancy down' (Moynihan 1993) and 'defining deviancy up' (Krauthammer 1993) which are simultaneously found in the Crime and Disorder Act (1998). In one instance, we see a normalisation of 'crime as everyday life', whereby in response to high crime rates government relaxes notions of deviance and allows previously deviant behaviour to become 'acceptable' or even 'normal', thus limiting the level of demand placed upon criminal justice systems. This is to be found in governmental strategies through the spread of situational crime prevention whereby individuals are increasingly responsible for their own personal safety and the security of their possessions. In another instance, the increasing concern for incivilities, anti-social behaviour, disorder and quasi- or sub-criminal activities constitute an inverse process of 'defining deviancy up'. Here, the previously 'normal' is declared deviant and the deviant is unmasked residing within the normal. Perversely, this can have the consequence of increasing the demand for crime control and judicial interventions. Janus-faced, the Third Way expresses two distinct visions of crime, the criminal and the role of criminal justice.

More fundamentally, these tensions express themselves in ambivalent political responses. Strategies of responsibilisation through appeals to community involvement and plural partnerships beyond the state co-exist with declarations of sovereign authority, notably through punitive sentiments as evidence of the state's commitments and strengths. However, this is also to be found with regard to policing. At one moment, crime rates are portrayed as beyond the competence of the police alone, as under the new rhetoric 'we are all responsible for crime'. In a different moment, however, the government as part of its Crime Reduction Strategy has set targets for the police, notably with regard to domestic burglary, to reduce crime by certain measurable amounts within a certain time-span, as if the police's capacity for action in this field were somehow restored. As Garland argues, state sovereignty over crime is simultaneously denied – as being 'beyond the state' – and symbolically reasserted –

through periodic episodes of hysterical and populist denials of the state's limitations (1996: 462). The limitations of traditional criminal justice – police, prosecution and punishment – are recognised in certain instances only to be discounted or ignored in others. This dualistic denial and recognition produce volatile shifts in the state's presentation of its own capacity for effective action in crime control.

This ambivalence also expresses itself in the uncertain integration of victims within criminal justice (Crawford and Goodey 2000). The victim has become a pivotal figure within contemporary criminal justice and yet victim input remains circumscribed and ambiguous. The recent concern for victims, their rights and needs, has found inconsistent political expression. Victims needs are concurrently embraced and ignored, as illustrated by the integration of victims within the post-sentencing process through victim contact work by the probation service (see Crawford and Enterkin 1999). The interests of victims have simultaneously been used in the service of severity, in the service of offenders and in the service of systems' efficiency (Crawford 2000a: 292). The awkward position of the victim within the complex balance between state/offender and public/private interests expresses itself in the uncertain relation between passion and reason as well as between moral punitiveness and instrumental offender management in Third Way politics.

On Garland's (1996) account, punitive rhetoric and policy are as much a product of problems of state sovereignty and legitimation as they are a rational response to the problems of crime. And yet, he implies that this oscillation and ambivalence are a product of late modern conditions which produce dilemmas for state governance. Whilst this broader canvas is insightful and helps us locate the manner in which similar issues affect different societies it does not accord sufficient attention to the different cultural and political expressions that these contradictions can take. The manner in which ambivalence is played out in the policy field takes on a political form. Hence, these contradictions are also a product of 'political incoherence' (O'Malley 1999), notably, although not exclusively, the 'unholy Trinity' – of appeals to communitarian ideals, governance through partnership and managerialist implementation – at the heart of Third Way politics. As I have argued, it is through the analysis of these more specific aspects of political incoherence that we can identify the sites of contradiction, ambiguity and ambivalence around which the future shape and direction of community safety is likely to unfold.

Notes

1   I borrow this phraseology from Taylor's (1997) article of the same title.
2   An alternative and altogether more cynical interpretation of this ambiguity lies in the unwillingness of central government to be explicitly too prescriptive in order to avoid the counter-accusations from local government, police and other agencies that if central government wish to require them to engage in specified tasks then dedicated funding should be made available, in order to fulfil such a requirement. The Crime and Disorder Act (1998) whilst imposing a statutory duty upon local authori-

ties and the police to establish community safety partnerships did not provide any new or dedicated resources.

3   In the first fourteen months since they came into effect in April 1999, there had been no youth curfews implemented and only eighty ASBOs taken out in England (*The Times* 29 June 2000). This low use rate has been perceived to be problematic by the government, which is strongly encouraging greater usage (SEU 2000: 41). The government now believes that ASBOs should not be viewed as a method of 'last resort', which appears to depart significantly from their initial intentions (Labour Party 1995).

4   The status and role of bodies like the Audit Commission in recent years have become increasingly ambiguous, albeit with considerable influence. Its work often bears little correspondence with traditional depiction of the word audit. Its role frequently appears more consistent with that of a catalyst for organisational change. As Day and Klein (1990) suggest, the Audit Commission is in the position of 'a policeman constantly tempted to turn consultant'.

References

Audit Commission (1996) *Misspent Youth: Young People and Crime*, London: Audit Commission.

—— (1998) *A Fruitful Partnership: Effective Partnership Working*, London: Audit Commission.

—— (1999) *Safety in Numbers: Promoting Community Safety*, London: Audit Commission.

Blair, T. (1995) 'The Rights We Enjoy Reflect the Duties We Owe', *The Spectator* Lecture, 22 March.

—— (1996) *New Britain: My Vision of a Young Country*, London: Fourth Estate.

—— (1998) *The Third Way: New Politics for the New Century*, London: Fabian Society.

Bottoms, A. E. (1995) 'The Philosophy and Politics of Punishment and Sentencing', in C. Clarkson and R. Morgan (eds) *The Politics of Sentencing Reform*, Oxford: Clarendon, 17–49.

Bratton, W. J. (1997) 'Crime is Down in New York City: Blame the Police', in N. Dennis (ed.) *Zero Tolerance: Policing a Free Society*, London: Institute for Economic Affairs, 29–42.

Broadbent, J., Dietrich, M. and Laughlin, R. (1996) 'The Development of Principal-Agent, Contracting and Accountability Relationships in the Public Sector: Conceptual and Cultural Problems', *Critical Perspectives in Accounting*, 7(4): 259–84.

Brownlee, I. (1998) 'New Labour – New Penology?: Punitive Rhetoric and the Limits of Managerialism in Criminal Justice Policy', *Journal of Law and Society*, 25(3): 313–35.

Cabinet Office (1999) *Modernising Government*, Cm 4310, London: HMSO.

Charlesworth, J., Clarke, J. and Cochrane, A. (1996) 'Tangled Webs? Managing Local Mixed Economies of Care', *Public Administration*, 74: 67–88.

Clarke, J. and Newman, J. (1997) *The Managerial State*, London: Sage.

Crawford, A. (1997) *The Local Governance of Crime: Appeals to Community and Partnerships*, Oxford: Clarendon.

—— (1998a) *Crime Prevention and Community Safety: Politics, Policies and Practices*, Harlow: Longman.

—— (1998b) 'Community Safety and the Quest for Security: Holding Back the Dynamics of Social Exclusion', *Policy Studies*, 19(3/4): 237–53.

—— (2000a) 'Salient Themes Towards a Victim Perspective and the Limitations of Restorative Justice', in A. Crawford and J. Goodey (eds) *Integrating a Victim Perspective within Criminal Justice*, Aldershot: Ashgate, 285–304.

—— (2000b) 'Situational Crime Prevention, Urban Governance and Trust Relations', in A. Von Hirsch, D. Garland and A. Wakefield (eds) *Ethical and Social Perspectives on Situational Crime Prevention*, Oxford: Hart Publishing, 193–213.

—— and Clear, T. R. (2001) 'Community Justice: Transforming Communities Through Restorative Justice?', in G. Bazemore and M. Shiff (eds) *Restorative Community Justice: Repairing Harm and Transforming Communities*, Cincinnati: Anderson Publications, 127–49.

—— and Enterkin, J. (1999) *Victim Contact Work and the Probation Service: A Study of Service Delivery and Impact*, Leeds: CCJS Press.

—— and Goodey, J. (2000) (eds) *Integrating a Victim Perspective within Criminal Justice*, Aldershot: Ashgate.

Day, P. and Klein, R. (1990) *Inspecting the Inspectorates*, London: Joseph Rowntree Foundation.

Deakin, N. and Walsh, K. (1996) 'The Enabling State: The Role of Markets and Contracts', *Public Administration*, 74: 33–48.

Dennis, N. (1997) (ed.) *Zero Tolerance: Policing a Free Society*, London: Institute for Economic Affairs.

Downes, D. (1998) 'Toughing it Out: From Labour Opposition to Labour Government', *Policy Studies*, 19(3/4): 191–8.

Downes, D. and Morgan, R. (1997) 'Dumping the Hostages to Fortune?: The Politics of Law and Order in Post-war Britain', in M. Maguire, R. Morgan and R. Reiner (eds) *The Oxford Handbook of Criminology*, Oxford: Clarendon Press, 87–134.

Etzioni, A. (1993) *The Spirit of Community: Rights, Responsibilities and the Communitarian Agenda*, New York: Simon & Schuster.

—— (1997a) *The New Golden Rule: Community and Morality in a Democratic Society*, New York: Harper Collins.

—— (1997b) 'Tony Blair: A communitarian in the making', *The Times*, 21 June.

—— (1997c) 'Community watch', *Guardian*, 28 June.

Garland, D. (1996) 'The Limits of the Sovereign State: Strategies of Crime Control in Contemporary Society', *British Journal of Criminology*, 36(4): 445–71.

—— (1999) 'The Commonplace and the Catastrophic: Interpretations of Crime in Late Modernity', *Theoretical Criminology*, 3(3): 353–64.

Giddens, A. (1991) *The Consequences of Modernity*, Cambridge: Polity Press.

—— (1998) *The Third Way: The Renewal of Social Democracy*, Cambridge: Polity Press.

—— (2000) *The Third Way and Its Critics*, Cambridge: Polity Press.

Hines, J., Holdaway, S., Wiles, P., Davidson, N., Dignan, J., Hammersley, R. and Marsh, P. (1999) *Interim Report on Youth Offending Teams*, London: Home Office.

Home Office (1997) *Getting to Grips with Crime: A New Framework for Local Intervention*, London: Home Office.

—— (1998) *Guidance on Statutory Crime and Disorder Partnerships*, London: Home Office.

Hood, C. (1991) 'A Public Management for all Seasons?', *Public Administration*, 69: 3–19.

—— (1995) ' "The New Public Management" in the 1980's: Variations on a Theme', *Accounting, Organisations and Society*, 20(2/3): 93–110.

Jones, T. and Newburn, T. (1998) *Private Security and Public Policing*, Oxford: Clarendon Press.

Krauthammer, C. (1993) 'Defining Deviancy Up', *The New Republic*, 22 November: 20–5.

Labour Party (1995) *A Quiet Life: Tough Action on Criminal Neighbours*, London: Labour Party.

Leadbeater, C. (1996) *The Self-Policing Society*, London: Demos.

Morgan, J. (1991) *Safer Communities: The Local Delivery of Crime Prevention Through the Partnership Approach*, London: Home Office.

Moss, K. and Pease, K. (1999) 'Crime and Disorder Act 1998: Section 17 a Wolf in Sheep's Clothing?', *Crime Prevention and Community Safety*, 1(4): 15–19.

Moynihan, D. P. (1993) 'Defining Deviancy Down', *American Scholar*, 62, Winter: 17–30.

Newburn, T. (1998) 'Tackling Youth Crime and Reforming Youth Justice: The Origins and Nature of New Labours Policy', *Policy Studies*, 19(3/4): 199–212.

O'Malley, P. (1999) 'Volatile and Contradictory Punishment', *Theoretical Criminology*, 3(2): 175–96.

—— and Palmer, D. (1996) 'Post-Keynesian Policing', *Economy and Society*, 25(2): 137–55.

Osborne, D. and Gaebler, T. (1992) *Reinventing Government: How the Entrepreneurial Spirit is Transforming the Public Sector*, Reading, Massachusetts: Addison-Wesley.

Perri 6 (1997) *Holistic Government*, London: Demos.

Peters, A. A. G. (1986) 'Main Currents in Criminal Law Theory', in J. M. van Dijk, C. Haffmans, F. Ruter and J. Schutte (eds) *Criminal Law in Action: An Overview of Current Issues in Western Societies*, Arnhem: Gouda Quint, 19–36.

Power, M. (1997) *The Audit Society*, Oxford: Oxford University Press.

Raine, J. W. and Willson, M. J. (1997) 'Beyond Managerialism in Criminal Justice', *Howard Journal*, 36(1): 80–95.

Rhodes, R. A. W. (1996) 'The New Governance: Governing without Government', *Political Studies*, 44: 652–67.

—— (1997) *Understanding Governance: Policy Networks, Governance, Reflexivity, and Accountability*, Milton Keynes: Open University Press.

—— (2000) 'The Governance Narrative: Key Findings and Lessons from the ESRC's Whitehall Programme', *Public Administration*, 78(2): 345–63.

Shapland, J. (1988) 'Fiefs and Peasants: Accomplishing Change for Victims in the Criminal Justice System', in M. Maguire and J. Pointing (eds) *Victims of Crime: A New Deal?*, Milton Keynes: Open University Press, 187–94.

—— (2000) 'Victims and Criminal Justice: Creating Responsible Criminal Justice Agencies', in A. Crawford and J. Goodey (eds) *Integrating a Victim Perspective within Criminal Justice*, Aldershot: Ashgate, 147–64.

Simon, J. (1995) 'They Died with Their Boots On: The Boot Camp and the Limits of Modern Penality', *Social Justice*, 22(1): 25–49.

Social Exclusion Unit (1998) *Bringing Britain Together, a National Strategy for Neighbourhood Renewal*, London: Cabinet Office.

—— (2000) *Anti-Social Behaviour*, Report of Policy Action Team 8, National Strategy for Neighbourhood Renewal, London: Cabinet Office.

Straw, J. (1998) 'Building Social Cohesion, Order and Inclusion in a Market Economy', Paper presented to the Nexus Conference on Mapping out the Third Way, 3 July.

Tam, H. (1998) *Communitarianism: A New Agenda for Politics and Citizenship*, Houndmills, Basingstoke: Macmillan.

Taylor, A. (1997) ' "Arm's Length But Hands On". Mapping the New Governance: The Department of National Heritage and Cultural Politics in Britain', *Public Administration*, 75(3): 441–66.

Tilley, N. (1995) *Thinking About Crime Prevention Performance Indicators*, CPU Paper no. 57, London: Home Office.

Warner, N. (1998) 'The Crime and Disorder Bill', presentation to the ESRC Research Seminar on Crime Prevention and Community Safety, King's College, London, 27 March.

Weatheritt, M. (1993) 'Measuring Police Performance: Accounting or Accountability?', in R. Reiner and S. Spencer (eds) *Accountable Policing: Effectiveness, Empowerment and Equity*, London: Institute for Public Policy Research, 24–54.

Wilson, J. Q. and Kelling, G. (1982) 'Broken Windows: The Police and Neighbourhood Safety', *Atlantic Monthly*, March: 29–37.

Young, J. (1992) 'Ten Points of Realism', in J. Young and R. Matthews (eds) *Rethinking Criminology: The Realist Debate*, London: Sage, 24–68.

3 Evaluation and evidence-led crime reduction policy and practice

Nick Tilley

Introduction: the evaluation and evidence-led agenda

Evidence and evaluation for policy and practice are in vogue. The British Prime Minister, Tony Blair, has said that what counts is what works, and that the current Labour government is committed to evidence-led policy. The Crime and Disorder Act (1998) requires partnerships to assemble evidence to determine priorities for their strategies; it also requires them to monitor and evaluate their efforts to tackle local crime and disorder problems. The government's three-year £250 million Crime Reduction Programme, announced in 1998 and begun in 1999, follows from a Home Office report for the Comprehensive Spending review (Goldblatt and Lewis 1998), summarising the evidence on what had been found to work, or to be promising, in reducing crime. Ten per cent of the £250 million is due to be spent on evaluation research. This is a huge investment by the usual standards of social science. Recent reports of Her Majesty's Inspectorate of Constabulary (HMIC) on police work in crime reduction and of the Audit Commission on Local Authority Community Safety work stress the need for evaluation and evidence, but bemoan its typical absence (HMIC 1998; Audit Commission 1999). Moreover, HMIC and the Audit Commission themselves root their inspections in part on evidence from previous evaluation studies, and collect additional evidence on effectiveness and efficiency as a further basis for reports and recommendations.

Traditional patterns of service delivery are no longer to be taken for granted. Evidence-based justifications are required. The probation service is clearly being steered towards a set of interventions for which there is some evidence of effectiveness, and probation services are being asked to measure their own effectiveness (Chapman and Hough 1998). The popularity of problem-oriented policing springs in part from a similar sense that traditional policing will no longer do (Leigh *et al.* 1996; 1998). Evidence is needed about the nature and distribution of the problems currently being faced by the police, and it is then to be collected to see whether efforts to target those problems are effective.

The evaluation agenda includes a strong economic emphasis on value for money (Dhiri and Brand 1999; Stockdale *et al.* 1999). The 'Best Value' movement is about re-examining services to try to get more benefit at less cost, making use of evidence about inputs, outputs and outcomes (Leigh *et al.* 1999). An aspiration of the Crime Reduction Programme is to assemble evidence of what works most cheaply to deliver effective crime reduction. This is a critical agenda: it suggests a move from the use of professional authority or of tradition as a warrant for action. Instead, policy and practice will be dictated by hard evidence about what works and at what cost. The developments in relation to crime reduction are consonant with those presently washing through the criminal justice system, and indeed through much social policy and practice. Health, education, welfare, employment, economic regeneration, housing, and so on, are all being subjected to similar disciplines of evaluation and evidence.

It clearly makes sense for evidence and evaluation to play a part in the development of policy and practice. The issue that is addressed in this chapter, however, is how they should do so. In the first part of this chapter I wish to express doubts about four propositions:

1   that policy and practice can be *led* by evidence;
2   that random controlled trials are the gold standard for all evaluations;
3   that the University of Maryland overview of evaluation studies on crime prevention provides reliable guidance for policy and practice; and
4   that cost-benefit analyses of measures can provide sound guidance for the allocation of resources for crime prevention.

In the second part of the chapter I present what I consider to be a 'realistic' way of taking forward evidence-based policy and practice.

Four doubts

Evidence-led policy and practice

Regardless of its surface appeal, evidence-led policy faces a range of methodological, practical and ideological problems. Together they cast doubt on the project of evidence-led policy and practice.

Methodological issues

All evidence, including that from recorded crime, crime surveys, records of convicted offenders, accounts of emotional responses to crime, etc., is socially constructed (see Bottomley and Pease 1986; Maguire 1997). Data on crime reflect the way they have been assembled. This is not simply a matter of data sometimes being improperly, and hence corrigibly, collected. Rather, data are always a product of the social processes through which they are generated (see Cicourel 1964). Moreover, the range of available evidence, however constructed, is always circumscribed. Clearly, all facts about everything cannot be assembled – data collection is, and has to be, selective (Ragin 1994). Policy that is led by available evidence risks focusing on the easily measurable simply because it is easily measurable.

Evidence does not speak for itself. Reasoning, imagination and values are needed to draw conclusions from it (see Weber 1949). Evidence can be collected and used to test, and potentially to falsify, conjectures about patterns, though even here tested conjectures are not proved – they remain fallible (Popper 1972) and are often disputed. Even in the less contentious world of natural sciences and mathematics, it is only over time that a consensus may emerge (Lakatos 1978).

If we assume that evidence does corroborate conjectures about patterns, this does not mean that these patterns will be sustained over time. The social world is subject to continuous change. One source of change is the understanding of actors in the social world. In the case of crime prevention the preventer adapts to the offender and the offender to the preventer. Each innovates and creates an unstable environment for the other (Ekblom 1997). Policy and practice may need to anticipate events on the basis of informed theory, rather than wait for evidence that patterns are already present (see Foresight Crime Prevention Panel 2000).

Practical issues

Even if the methodological difficulties could be overcome, there are significant practical obstacles to evidence-led policy and practice. No government can be without a policy on crime; no criminal justice system can be suspended pending evidence. Workers within the existing institutions cannot do nothing whilst waiting for evidence to lead them. Much policy and practice has to proceed without a research lead. Policies and practices cannot disregard public opinion (Tilley and Laycock 2000). Politicians need to attend to the views of the electorate, even when those views are not congruent with what the available evidence suggests. Furthermore, elections create a periodic imperative for politicians to show results. This, of course, opens a window for evidence to play a part. It is liable, however, to lead to policies and practices offering relatively quick fixes to take precedence over measures whose effect is only likely to be felt in the longer term.

Established policies and practices will often constitute obstacles to evidence-led changes, especially where there is already a public commitment to them, or where there are vested interests in maintaining them (Weiss 1976).

Ideological problems in evidence-led policy and practice

Crime is a moral issue. Definitions of crime, and policies and practices to respond to it, involve judgements of value. An appeal to evidence can be a way of evading or passing on responsibilities that require those judgements of value. Moreover, it is not only the ends that require ideological debate, so too do the means. Efficacy is not the only criterion for judging the means to attain a given end. The means, too, require that value questions be considered.

This section, it should be stressed, has expressed doubts about evidence-*led* policy and practice – the notion that policies and practices can simply be derived from evidence. It is not intended to cast doubt on the possibility (or desirability) of policies and practices being *informed* by evidence. The distinction may seem a fine (and trite) one, but there are real issues involved. Crime and disorder partnerships can be persuaded to try to assemble and warehouse more and more data in the belief that they will tell them what to do. But the data cannot and will not do so. The notion that evidence can lead policy may also tempt politicians to hide behind evidence where real issues of value and political judgement are at stake.

'Experimental' methods of evaluation

The classic purpose of evaluations is to find out what works and what does not work, so that failures are not reproduced and the need to 'reinvent the wheel' is avoided. The conventional gold standard for evaluation studies to sort the programme wheat from the programme chaff is the randomly controlled trial (RCT), where subjects are allocated blindly and randomly to experimental and control groups.

In RCTs there is usually an experimental group, which is subject to the 'treatment', and a control group, which is not. Both are measured before and after the intervention. Any difference in the change between the experimental and control groups is attributable to the intervention. It is important that the treatment is applied in a standard way so that the experimenter can be certain it was this that had the effect. Of course, in more complex experiments control and experimental groups can proliferate to try to deal with Hawthorne effects, and with the potential independent effects of before measurement and any interaction it might have with treatment. In the medical version of this method of evaluation, a placebo may be given to the control group for the potential effect of treatment *per se*, rather than the specific treatment applied. In social experiments this is more difficult, but rather than no treatment, it may involve an alternative treatment that might otherwise be provided for the subjects. Moreover, there may have to be efforts to keep the experimental and control groups separate to avoid potential contamination.

In this chapter, I wish to use the example of mandatory arrest for domestic violence to reduce repeat incidents as a case study of RCTs for three reasons: first, because the research is well documented; second, because of the high quality of the studies; and finally, because there have been several replications, a welcome but relatively uncommon feature of evaluation studies (Sherman 1992).

Mandatory arrest for domestic violence is probably the most evaluated crime reduction initiative to make use of RCTs. The original Minneapolis Domestic Violence Experiment found arrest (for 'minor assaults which make up the bulk of police calls to domestic violence') the most effective of three standard methods used by the police to reduce domestic violence. The other two responses in the Minneapolis study were counselling or sending assailants away from the home for several hours. In simple misdemeanour domestic assaults, cases were referred at random to one of the three responses. A six-month follow-up checked the frequency and seriousness of any future domestic violence. As ever, implementation and data collection were less than perfect. Yet both official records and victim interviews showed that repeat domestic violence was lowest for those where arrest had been the allocated response. Official records revealed that there had been repeat incidents in 10 per cent of arrest cases, in 19 per cent of the advice cases, and in 24 per cent of the 'send suspect away' cases. On the basis of their findings, and notwithstanding clearly stated caveats, the authors of the report note that: 'the preponderance of evidence in the Minneapolis study strongly suggests that the police should use arrest in most domestic violence cases' (Sherman and Berk 1984).

Domestic violence is of significant social concern and, unsurprisingly, on the basis of the Minneapolis conclusions many US police departments adopted an arrest policy. Sherman (1992) notes that 10 per cent of cities with a population of over 100,000 made arrest the preferred police choice in 1994, 43 per cent in 1986, and 90 per cent in 1988. Further RCTs were conducted in other cities in the US (Sherman 1992) with mixed results: in three cities mandatory arrest increased repeat domestic violence, but in another three cities the level of violence was reduced. This invites the question: why did the impact of mandatory arrest vary? The RCTs themselves can throw little light on this. They were designed to see whether or not the initiatives worked in reducing repeat domestic violence. Collectively they show that mandatory arrest can reduce domestic violence, but it can also increase it. It is shown to be effective, but the problem is that its effects vary.

Following the series of RCTs on mandatory arrest and domestic violence there is some plausible post-hoc speculation to explain the mixed findings and some (non-experimental) evidence is adduced for it. That is, it is believed that arrest may anger unemployed people in marginal communities, whose disposition to violence is thereby increased. In middle-class communities, however, it is believed that it shames people who are employed, and they are then chastened and deterred (Sherman 1992). The structure of these explanations brings out something of the weakness of the RCT method in so far as they highlight the fact that the same measure may work in different ways and thus have different effects according to variations in the circumstances of those involved. The preoccupation of RCTs with net effects obscures this general feature of interventions (see also Pawson and Tilley 1997: 34–46).

RCTs are not always practicable. If areas are the unit of analysis, for example, it may not be possible to find and fund sufficient numbers for random allocation. Random selection of experimental areas is not always politically viable. Isolating/insulating members of experimental and control groups may not be achievable. And so on. In these circumstances, the next best quasi-experimental methods are conventionally preferred. These involve identifying 'matched' control and experimental groups to maximise their comparability.

This approach falls short of the standards of random allocation since there may be significant differences between the experimental and the control groups, which would automatically be eliminated through random allocation.

Ray Pawson and I have looked at the best British study undertaken using this approach (for a detailed discussion see Pawson and Tilley 1994). The study, by Bennett (1991), reports the evaluation of a police patrols initiative aiming to reduce the fear of crime. This initiative was tried because some American evaluation research had found that contact patrols had been associated with a fall in fear of crime. Bennett reports on two experimental sites, in London and in Birmingham, and two composite controls, chosen because of their high crime rates and 'visual indicators' of disorder including graffiti, broken windows, criminal damage and litter. He monitored implementation in the experimental areas by measuring time spent by the police in the area and the contacts made by the police with the public. He found no fall in fear of crime in the experimental areas compared to the control areas. Other output and outcome measures, for example those relating to recent sightings of police, perceptions of the area, and informal social control practices, produced a mixed picture in the two sites. Thus Bennett's is a simple, if expensive, before-and-after experimental/composite control comparison study with programme activity-level monitoring. It is a classic of its type. Unfortunately, at its conclusion we know little of how the programme was delivered or experienced. Encounters are more than just making contact: what is said, who is spoken to, how interaction is managed are important elements of a study, and Bennett's report lacks this kind of information. Our knowledge of the estates is reduced to their comparability in a number of superficial respects. The quality of community life and organisation is not considered (except for an unremarked variation in measurements of 'level of satisfaction' and 'sense of community' in the two experimental sites, not relevant in what were composite controls). There is no explanation for the variations in outcome, nor for the differences between the British and American results. At the end of the initiative we are little the wiser, other than knowing that in these two places the intended fear reduction outcome was not achieved. We could certainly not conclude that in another place police contacts patrol would not lead to a reduction in fear of crime.

The underlying problems here repeat those of the mandatory arrest series of studies. How programmes have effects varies by the circumstances in which they are introduced. This will mean that different outcomes will occur. Sophisticated though they are in technical terms, Bennett's quasi-experimental methods railroad over this.

The University of Maryland overview of crime prevention evaluation studies

The apotheosis of the experimental approach to evaluation is a review of studies of what works in crime prevention conducted for US Congress by the University of Maryland. The findings are posted on the Internet (Sherman *et al.*

1997). Sherman and his associates use a scale from 5 to 1, where, notwithstanding the disastrous effects they may have as evidenced by the mandatory arrest for domestic violence débâcle, the highest score – '5' – is given to RCTs. The next 'best' studies most closely corresponding to RCTs are awarded 4, and so on. The interventions are then classified under four headings: 'what works', 'what doesn't work', 'what's promising' and 'what's unknown'. The result is in my opinion dangerous nonsense.

In recent accounts of this mega overview of evaluations, the Maryland group has used the same headings, but added interesting comments, which seemingly acknowledge some of the problems. For example, under 'what works', they say:

> There are programs that we can be reasonably certain prevent crime or reduce risk factors for crime in the kinds of social context in which they have been evaluated and for which the findings can be generalised to similar settings in other places and times.
>
> (Sherman *et al.* 1998: 6)

Here they recognise that the positive outcomes which programmes bring about are contingent on context, that where programmes are found to have been effective this does not mean that they can be expected to have the same results elsewhere. The effectiveness is dependent on circumstances. The same results will only be brought about in similar settings. This suggests that identifying what is salient in the setting is crucial if transferable lessons are to be achieved. What counts as a 'similar' setting is not self-evident. Here, then,'what works' is adjusted and qualified to become 'what works in (saliently) similar settings'.

Over the issue of 'what doesn't work', however, context-dependency is curiously forgotten. Under the heading 'what doesn't work', the Maryland group says:

> These are programs that we are reasonably confident from available evidence fail to prevent crime or reduce risk factors for crime, using the identical scientific criteria used for deciding what works.
>
> (Sherman *et al.* 1998: 6)

No reference is made here to context-dependence, though the authors give no reason for omitting it. Yet if 'what works' depends on a conducive context, and it is accepted that failure using the same measure might occur in a non-conducive context, it then follows that a trial that has failed may have been undertaken in one of these non-conducive settings. A re-trial in a different setting that is suited to the measure introduced might be followed by a successful outcome. Indeed no number of failures could show that the measure could never be successful. It might simply be that no trial has occurred in a suitable setting.

In general terms with regard to their taxonomy, the Maryland group concedes that:

The weakest aspect of this classification (into 'what works' etc.) is that there is no standard means of establishing external validity: exactly what variations in program content and setting might affect the generalisability of findings from evaluations. In the current state of science, that can be accomplished only by the accumulation of many tests in many settings with all major variations on the program theme. None of the programs reviewed in this report have accumulated such a body of knowledge so far. The conclusions drawn in the report about what works and what doesn't should be read, therefore, as more certain to the extent that all conditions of the programs that were evaluated (e.g. population demographics, program elements, social context) are replicated in other settings. The greater the difference on such dimensions between evaluated programs and other programs using the same name, the less certain the application of this report's conclusions must be.

(Sherman *et al.* 1998: 6)

This is fine as far as it goes, but it begs questions about salience of similarity and difference. It is impossible to replicate 'all conditions'. This would require the same people, same houses, same time, same geography, same age, same external political events, same offender populations, etc. Such a requirement is utopian and therefore absurd. A judgement has to be made about what matters in terms of similarity, both in terms of the intervention measure itself and in terms of the contexts in which it is introduced. The key question, therefore, is: what 'population demographics, program elements, social context', etc. need to be the same, and why? And this is precisely the issue which the experimental approach consistently misses or fudges.

Though the Maryland group do not say so in so many words, once it is conceded that context is crucial for the effects produced, the only conclusion that can be drawn from their review is that there is quite compelling evidence that some measures can be associated with intended outcomes. In relation to any given measure it is necessary to have only one strong study to establish this. Any study which does not find that the intended outcome has followed cannot conclude that the measure cannot produce that outcome. What goes for intended outcomes goes, of course, also for unintended outcomes of interventions. For the same reasons these too will be contextually contingent.

Instead of the bold headings used in the Maryland overview, which proclaim 'what works', 'what doesn't work', 'what's promising' and 'what's unknown', the authors' concessions suggest that more accurate headings would be more circumspect. They might read 'what's been found to work somewhere at some time', 'what's not yet been found to work anywhere, but might do so in the right conditions', 'what seems to work somewhere' and 'what might work somewhere at some time'. Less snappy to be sure, but less misleading, too. The worry is that the Maryland study headlines will be taken at face value and that their proper qualifications will be disregarded

The Maryland group's concessions about the shortcomings of their classifications of evaluations echo weaknesses already mentioned. They accept that past performance is not a good guide to future performance, that performance in one place is not an adequate guide for performance in another place, and the reason for this is that places differ in ways which mean the same measure will work differently in saliently different contexts. This is not a matter that the high-scoring experimental evaluations reviewed have been good at dealing with.

Overviews of evaluations, including Sherman's team's, consistently find inconsistent findings (Poyner 1993; Martinson 1974; Gendreau and Ross 1987). Thus if one takes some examples of frequently advocated crime prevention interventions, contradictory results are the norm. For example, with regard to lighting, Painter (1995) concluded it did help in crime prevention, but Atkins *et al.* (1991) that it did not. With regard to property marking, Laycock (1997) found it did, Knuttson (1984) found it did not. The Kirkholt burglary reduction programme was one of the most successful and influential initiatives in Britain, but efforts to replicate it again produced mixed results (Tilley 1996).

Mixed results are a menace for traditional evaluation, which is concerned with finding whether measures do or do not work and nothing else. They leave the policy-maker in a quandary. Traditional experimental evaluation methods, which consistently produce inconsistent findings, are therefore largely a waste of time and money. Moreover, they are also a travesty of real experimental methods, as used in the natural sciences, where experimental control is seldom effected through random allocation (Tilley 2000).

Those who expect consistent findings misread the logic-in-use of experimental evaluation methods. Experimental methods can only measure the association that did occur between two variables (intervention/outcome) in a specific time and place. There can be no ground from this finding alone for believing that because an association occurred at one place or time it will do so at some future place and time.

Cost-benefit analysis

Cost-benefit analysis tries to standardise inputs and outcomes and to assign them a common currency. In this way it is expected to provide an objective, technical basis for choosing between competing priorities. It assumes that the causal relationship between measures introduced and outcomes achieved can be established and quantified with some confidence. This is clearly not generally the case. For reasons already given, measures produce different outcomes across space and time, and traditional evaluation methods have been unable adequately to capture this.

What count as costs and benefits is not self-evident and what is included may be quite narrowly circumscribed or it may be very wide-ranging. Inputs may include: funds specifically allocated from the public purse for the programme; funds allocated for a variety of purposes including those related to the programme; programme-relevant private sector, individual and household expenditure; resources allocated in kind; and volunteer effort. Benefits may include: savings to the agency responsible for the programme; to insurance companies; to individuals and households; to businesses; to local authorities; and to other national bodies. Some financial benefits may be direct, some may be indirect. Other benefits have to do with quality of life issues. Further benefits still will be reductions in personal harm.

Where the benefits are non-financial the aim is to give them cash equivalent values. The technical and conceptual estimation difficulties are overwhelming. Methods include 'willing to pay estimates' – how much would a person, household or business be prepared to pay to avoid a given harm; and 'willing to accept estimates' – how much would they need to be paid to endure the harm? Both produce arbitrary sums. The first is limited by what people might have and therefore could afford at a given point. The second produces 'infinite amount' answers (for example, when referring to a fatal accident), and this cannot be built into cost-benefit calculations (for useful discussions see Adams 1995; Zimring and Hawkins 1995). As an extreme case, consider murder. In relation to serial killer Harold Shipman's middle-aged and elderly victims, the financial costs of the discovery of their murder will almost certainly have outweighed any savings from their detection. Indeed, given the age of the victims, it may be that in cost-benefit terms their murders saved the public purse! Moreover, the discovery of their murders may well increase the fears that elderly patients have of visiting their general practitioners. Dependency on cost-benefit analysis misses the moral point of attending to murder. There is no means of measuring the value of a prevented homicide or rape. The conventional 'willing to pay' and 'willing to accept' measurements make no sense. Policy ends require discussion and debate about values.

There seems to be no non-arbitrary way of deciding what to include in costs or in benefits or in how to make measurements of non-financial benefits. There are only contestable and modifiable conventions. Moreover, the calculations have to be applied to estimates of net effects which are unstable due to contextual variation and instability. It is difficult not to conclude that cost-benefit calculations are a complex chimera, conjured up by clever people given a superficially sensible but ultimately undoable job.

Whilst it may be possible (and useful) roughly to estimate the financial costs and benefits of past programmes for specific parties, and their net monetary benefits, overall estimates including monetary and non-monetary elements appear unintelligible and arbitrary, and are predictably flawed for predictive purposes. I turn now to an alternative, realistic approach to understanding how evaluation and evidence might inform policy and practice

Realistic evaluation and evidence for policy and practice

Because of the failures of traditional experimental evaluations, Ray Pawson and I have formulated an alternative, which we term 'realistic evaluation' (Pawson and Tilley 1997). At the heart of this approach are precisely those matters where traditional, conventional evaluation has failed. Realistic evaluation is concerned with understanding how programmes and policies bring about different effects in different places and among different people.

Realistic evaluation is rooted in scientific realism. Scientific realism has a distinctive account of causation. Rather than understanding cause in terms of constant conjunctions between observable events (the Humean position assumed in the experimental approach), cause is understood in generative terms. We can think of generative causation in terms of a clock. The hands of a clock move in an orderly way. There is, though, a mechanism that lies behind, or causes the orderly movement of, the clock's hands. We understand the movement of the hands by understanding the (hidden) mechanism lying behind or generating it. For realists science involves explaining regularities by reference to the mechanisms producing them. In social life the signing of a cheque and the transfer of money by the teller to the customer in a bank makes sense in terms of the (unseen) banking system as a whole.

The triggering of mechanisms is not unconditional. It is contingent on an appropriate context. Think of fireworks: the explosions are only triggered when the blue touchpaper is lit if the conditions are right. There must be enough gunpowder, it must be sufficiently compacted, it must be dry enough, etc. Laboratory science comprises the construction of idealised conditions in which conjectured mechanisms will be activated.

A social programme describes an effort to effect a change in some pattern of behaviour. For realists this has to be understood in terms of an alteration in the mechanisms generating behaviour. Either existing mechanisms generating present behaviour have to be disabled or some new causal mechanisms have to be triggered to overcome those that would otherwise operate. The altered behaviour resulting from changes in patterns of mechanisms triggered comprises the programme outcomes.

Ray Pawson and I understand the major mechanisms that programmes introduce or disable to relate to the reasoning and resources of individuals. Reasoning has to do with values, meanings, and estimates of the costs and benefits. Resources have to do with the powers which actors have to choose between varying courses of action. Thus, programmes do not just happen to participants externally, as when one billiard ball strikes another. Rather, it is how human agents engage with programmes that comprises the medium through which they do or do not have their effects. Therefore, evaluation research is concerned with unpicking the ways in which a programme changes the mechanisms triggered to alter the pattern of behaviour within given types of context.

For the realistic evaluator the key evaluation question is: what works for whom in what circumstances, and how? The traditional evaluation question, 'what works?' (which is often assumed to amount to, 'what always works?', because of constant conjunction assumptions) is misconstrued. Programmes do not work unconditionally and useful answers to evaluation questions entail penetrating the contexts for the activation of varying causal mechanisms to produce changed patterns of behaviour. We take evaluation to require a theory to explain or predict how changes introduced by an intervention alter the balance of causal mechanisms at work and lead to a change in behaviour. As already indicated, whether or not an intervention effects such a change, and what change is brought about, will depend on the prior conditions or on context. Some mechanisms may be disabled and some new ones activated as a result of the intervention. The same programme will be encountered by different programme participants in different ways, in accordance with variations in existing bases for their action. A key part of any evaluation will include specification of key subgroups whose members, it is conjectured, will experience and thus respond to the same programme in differing ways.

In regard to replication, what counts as the 'same' programme is also problematic. No two programmes are, or can be, identical in every respect (Tilley 1996). A programme theory is needed to specify what a programme is expected to do in relation to a given target population, to determine what matters from one programme to another for it to count as the same.

Here, we can use prisons as an example. The traditional evaluation agenda asks, 'does prison work?' Yet we know that prisoners and prisons vary, as do the communities in which they are located. We know of various mechanisms that may be triggered by prison – incapacitation, specific deterrence, general deterrence, criminal acculturation, non-criminal capacity building, criminality capacity building, non-criminal opportunity reduction, criminal identity reinforcement, etc. In only one of these mechanisms is the subject relatively passive. Incapacitation happens to individuals; it does not depend much on their agency for its effects (though its crime preventive impact depends on an estimate of their exercise of agency were they not incarcerated). The other mechanisms depend on alterations in choices available for agents, their apparent consequences and the meanings attached to them by those agents. If we treat all prisons and prisoners alike, and all social conditions in which prisons are lodged as the same, we will miss that variation. If we take as our example groups of prisoners, where net nil effects are found this could reflect less the causal impotence of prison (or a particular regime) than its capacity to generate countervailing causal forces working their way through to have competing impacts on differing inmates.

Many crime prevention measures provide no physical obstacle to crime at all. CCTV, lighting improvements, alarms, drugs counselling, employment opportunity creation, etc., all depend on mechanisms affecting choices if they are to have their effects. Even where programme participants are relatively passive, mechanism questions arise, but are less concerned with choices. Drugs, surgery, dietary modifications, for example, involve the operation of biochemical mechanisms. The same basic question still needs to be asked: how, for whom, and in what contexts will these generate what effects?

Realistic evaluation calls for the formulation, test and refinement of 'context-mechanism-outcome pattern configurations' (CMOCs, or 'seemocks'). Seemocks comprise models explaining how measures bring about outcomes in specified sorts of social conditions. They are middle-range theories (Merton

1968) in three senses. First, they go beyond the descriptive particulars of specific interventions at particular places and times, but they do not provide universal truths for all places and times. Second, they do not provide general theories of the phenomena being examined. In the case of prisons, they do not provide a general theory of the prison or of criminal careers, though they may draw on and inform general theories. Third, they will pay less attention to broader conditions for social action, and focus more on the locally variable within that relatively stable set of background circumstances. What is primarily at issue in the theory is that which is variable within social formations and in the relatively short term. In relation to prison, this might include, for example, attributes of inmates, rates of imprisonment, rates of unemployment outside prison, the level and content of educational provision within prison, the regime provided within prison, density of prison occupation, prison lay-out, etc. Seemocks specify what interventions within relatively variable local contextual conditions trigger which mechanisms with what outcomes, though at their best they will also make explicit the broader structural arrangements that are taken for granted but crucial for the potential causal efficacy of the measures which are introduced.

Doing realistic evaluation

The realistic evaluator's starting point is to construct the seemock theory or theories in relation to a programme, after which the next task is to design a study that will test the seemocks. There are various sources of theory in relation to a programme. A good starting point will be the architects of the programme. How do they expect the measures they are planning to change behaviour? Whose behaviour do they expect to change and whose to remain the same? What unintended changes might be sparked amongst those touched by the programme, and how? Practitioners, too, will have ideas about how the programme is working for whom and why. They will also have an idea about those for whom the programme is not working and why this is the case. Practitioners are not, of course, best asked baldly about their implicit theories, but can usually speak with conviction about cases encountered, and it will be for the researcher to build a theory out of this and then to check that the practitioner goes along with it. In the event, the theory is often co-produced by a succession of practitioners' tales; the realistic evaluator formalises the theory reflecting the underlying context, mechanism, outcome elements. The practitioner theory, like that of the policy-maker, may well be mistaken, of course. The job of the realistic evaluator in designing the research is to devise methods to test it. Other sources of theory include social science literature, previous evaluation studies, common sense, and so forth. A range of theories can be developed.

Practitioner and policy-maker theory will often need to be supplemented by accounts of unintended consequences and unacknowledged conditions, beyond the practical consciousness of those implicated in programmes. The formalised and supplemented middle-range realist theories can then be worked through to identify appropriate comparison groups within the programme, where detailed outcome patterns variations would be expected. The upshot will be a tested theory or series of theories that provides an improved grasp of what worked how and with whom within the programme.

Policy and practice in the sight of realism

The evaluation agenda sketched out requires that programmes be unpicked, unpacked and evaluated in terms of sets of variable outcomes. The result will rarely be that programmes have had and can have no impact along the intended lines, or that programmes do have and will always have their planned effects. Programmes, people and social settings are simply not like that.

If the evaluation enterprise is deemed to be about finding out about what works and spreading it, practitioners may be encouraged to adopt a recipe book approach, assuming that measures can be pulled off the 'works' shelf. Because of contextual variability and fluidity, however, this is unlikely to maximise efficiency and effectiveness. Ideally, practitioners need to understand seemocks and be able to think through their own problem situations in terms of the scope there is to trigger change mechanisms using available intervention measures. They need then to refine practice through monitoring what is produced. They need to be (evidence-based) theory learners, users, refiners and developers, not mechanical deliverers of standard programmes implemented with integrity. That is, they need to be reflective, evidence-based practitioners.

The rationale for recipe books is that some people can produce palatable meals more easily with them than without them. Consider the person who 'knows what they like' but has never cooked. He knows that he likes gin, sugar, garlic, aniseed, mushrooms, smoked salmon, custard, ice cream, black sausage and rice. So he mixes them up and puts them in the oven. That person would be better off with a recipe book. Recipe books are better than nothing. Moreover, there are better and worse recipe books. Talented cooks, however, make rather little use of them. The popular British television programme, *Ready, Steady, Cook*, is about guests coming to the show with sets of ingredients, each of which they presumably like, and presenting them to the professional chef who conjures up a tasty meal from them. The chef knows enough about the principles of cooking and the attributes of the ingredients, and has enough evidence of what kinds of things work in cooking, to be creative in an informed way.

Some current developments appear to treat occupational groups like cooks 'who know what they like' but produce 'dogs' dinners' as a consequence. Hence teachers have pre-programmed and standardised literacy and numeracy hours; and probation services are being channelled into delivering accredited programmes with detailed instructions about what is to be done and when. Probation and community safety workers are to be trained (rather than educated) into 'occupational standards', so that they have 'core competences' to deliver standard 'approved services', in the light of the 'skills maps' which describe what they are expected to do. In the worst cases the recipe books will reflect the prejudices of a central authority rather than the practitioner. In the best cases they may reflect evidence about what has been shown to work in some context for some subjects. Where untutored, counterproductive discretion is used then recipe books will be useful and damage will be reduced by requiring their employment. Where situations are relatively stable (as in the kitchen), many benefits may follow from the creation of recipe books and requirements that they be followed. McDonald's illustrates well the profit to be made by standardisation. The company's Hamburger University is presumably a model that others in the business of vocational training for standardised service delivery should follow.

Enforcing the adequate may dispense with the truly awful. It will also inhibit the brilliant. McDonald's may serve up something better than a dog's dinner, but it will be worse than the fashionable London restaurant the River Café. Enforcing the adequate is in effect to engage in mediocratisation. Evaluators steering us towards it belong to a new class of evidence-based mediocrats.

In the light of some experience of crime reduction efforts in Britain, there are examples of dogs' dinners (Tilley *et al.* 1999). There are also calls for recipe books. One role for evaluators might be to contribute to recipe books (and to help eliminate recipes that don't work). Another is to help identify CMOCs that policy-makers and practitioners can use intelligently to determine what evidence suggests would make sense in differing conditions. Reflective practice requires the intelligent deployment of principles or theories, which have been refined through a series of evaluation studies. The elements of theory that will be transferable/applicable relate to causal mechanisms which may be triggered and/or inhibited in specified types of contexts to effect changes in behavioural regularities in the intended direction. Evidence is assembled to arbitrate between/refine theories for practitioners to apply reflectively.

There are real risks of standardisation and mediocratisation in crime reduction and in evaluation studies designed to inform standardising and mediocratising processes. The apparently competent may turn out to be dangerously incompetent. One example of the dangers of crass mediocratisation in crime prevention comes from just that use of mandatory arrest for domestic violence as a means to reduce repeat incidents produced in the experiments discussed earlier in this chapter. Indeed, on the basis of the Minneapolis experiment and the six subsequent studies, Sherman (1992) has concluded that mandatory arrest laws should be repealed, and there should be 'structured police discretion'. The mandatory arrest for domestic violence research seems to suggest that informed discretion is better than either ignorant discretion or substitution of rule-book recipes for it.

Conclusion

Evidence is useful for policy and practice: for informing decisions about priorities and for identifying promising responses to deal with problems. Most social scientists will welcome the present government's expressed commitment to see more use made of evidence. The evidence-*led* agenda, however, promises too strong a role for evidence. Evidence is useful, of course, for checking ideas, but it is good ideas that have survived critical scrutiny that are needed for effective policy and practice. The orthodox experimental paradigm for evaluation asks the wrong question and comes out with misleading and inconsistent answers. Evaluation studies need to be realistic if they are to be informative. Such studies require theoretical sensitivity as well as technical skills. The lessons they will most usefully generate are not crass and unconditional suggestions that measures will or will not work. What they will do is help develop tested theory of what works for whom, in what circumstances, and this should help practitioners and policy-makers think through their responses to issues and problems with a better chance of producing their intended outcomes.

Even with this realistic understanding, however, there are crucial value questions at stake in policy and practice, and in the theories behind them, that cannot be sidestepped by reference simply to the authority of empirical social science.

References

Adams, J. (1995) *Risk*, London: UCL Press.

Atkins, S., Husain, S. and Storey, A. (1991) *The Influence of Street Lighting on Crime*, Crime Prevention Unit Paper no. 28, London: Home Office.

Audit Commission (1999) *Safety in Numbers: Promoting Community Safety*, London: Audit Commission.

Bennett, T. (1991) 'The Effectiveness of a Police-initiated Fear-reducing Strategy', *British Journal of Criminology*, 31: 1–14.

Bottomley, K. and Pease, K. (1986) *Crime and Punishment: Interpreting the Data*, Milton Keynes: Open University Press.

Chapman, T. and Hough, M. (1998) *Evidence Based Practice: A Guide to Effective Practice*, London: Home Office.

Cicourel, A. (1964) *Method and Measurement in Sociology*, New York: Free Press.

Dhiri, S. and Brand, S. (1999) *Analysis of Costs and Benefits: Guidance for Evaluators*, Crime Reduction Programme, Guidance Notes 1, London: Home Office.

Ekblom, Paul (1997) 'Gearing Up Against Crime: A Dynamic Framework to Help Designers Keep Up with the Adaptive Criminal in a Changing World', *International Journal of Risk, Security and Crime Prevention*, 2: 249–65.

Foresight Crime Prevention Panel (2000) *Just Around the Corner: A Consultation Document*, London: Department of Trade and Industry.

Gendreau, P. and Ross, R. (1987) 'The Revivification of Rehabilitation', *Justice Quarterly*, 4: 349–408.

Goldblatt, P. and Lewis, C. (1998) (eds) *Reducing Offending: An Assessment of the Research Evidence on Ways of Dealing with Offending Behaviour*, Home Office Research Study no. 187, London: Home Office.

Gould, S. J. (1981) *The Mismeasure of Man*, New York: Norton.

HMIC (1998) *Beating Crime*, London: Home Office.

Knuttson, J. (1984) *Operation Identification: A Way to Prevent Burglaries?* Report no. 14, Stockholm: National Swedish Council for Crime Prevention.

Lakatos, I. (1978) *The Methodology of Scientific Research Programmes*, Cambridge: Cambridge University Press.

Laycock, G. (1997) 'Operation Identification, or the Power of Publicity', in R. Clarke (ed.) *Situational Crime Prevention: Successful Case Studies*, New York: Harrow and Heston.

Leigh, A., Mundy, G. and Tuffin, R. (1999) *Best Value Policing: Making Preparations*, Crime Prevention and Detection Series Paper 116, London: Home Office.

——, Read. T. and Tilley, N. (1996) *Problem-oriented Policing: Brit Pop*, Crime Prevention and Detection Series Paper 75, London: Home Office.

——, Read. T. and Tilley, N. (1998) *Brit Pop II: Problem-oriented Policing in Practice*, Police Research Series Paper 93, London: Home Office.

Maguire, M. (1997) 'Crime Statistics, Patterns and Trends: Changing Perceptions and their Implications', in M. Maguire, R. Morgan and R. Reiner (eds) *The Oxford Handbook of Criminology*, 2nd edition, Oxford: Oxford University Press.

Martinson, R. (1974) 'What Works? Questions and Answers About Prison Reform', *Public Interest*, 35: 22–45.

Merton, R. (1968) *Social Theory and Social Structure*, New York: Free Press.

Painter, K. (1995) *An Evaluation of the Impact of Street Lighting on Crime, Fear of Crime and Quality of Life*, unpublished Ph.D. thesis, Cambridge University.

Pawson, R. and Tilley, N. (1994) 'What Works in Evaluation Research?' *British Journal of Criminology* 34: 291–306.

—— (1997) *Realistic Evaluation*, London: Sage.

Popper, K. (1972) *Objective Knowledge*, Oxford: Clarendon Press.

Poyner, B. (1993) 'What Works in Crime Prevention: An Overview of Evaluations', in R. Clarke (ed.) *Crime Prevention Studies*, vol. 1, Monsey, NY: Criminal Justice Press.

Ragin, C. (1994) *Constructing Social Research*, Thousand Oaks, CA: Pine Forge Press.

Sherman, L. (1992) *Policing Domestic Violence*, New York: Free Press.

—— and Berk, R. (1984) *The Minneapolis Domestic Violence Experiment*, The Police Foundation.

——, Gottfredson, D., MacKenzie, D., Eck, J., Reuter, P. and Bushway, S. (1997) *Preventing Crime: What Works, What Doesn't, What's Promising: A Report to the United States Congress*. Online. Available: http://www.ncjrs.org/works/index.htm

—— (1998) *Preventing Crime: What Works, What Doesn't, What's Promising*, National Institute of Justice: Research in Brief, Office of Justice Programs, US Department of Justice.

Stockdale, J., Whitehead, C. and Gresham, P. (1999) *Applying Economic Analysis to Policing Activity*, Crime Prevention and Detection Series Paper 103, London: Home Office.

Tilley, N. (1996) 'Demonstration, Exemplification, Duplication and Replication in Evaluation Research', *Evaluation*, 2: 35–50.

—— (2000) 'Experimentation and Criminal Justice in the United Kingdom', *Crime and Delinquency*, 46(2): 194–213.

—— and Laycock, N. (2000) 'Joining Up Research, Policy and Practice About Crime', *Policy Studies*, 21(3): 213–27.

——, Pease, K., Hough, M. and Brown, R. (1999) *Burglary Prevention: Early Lessons from the Crime Reduction Programme*, Crime Reduction Research Series Paper 1, London: Home Office.

Weber, M. (1949) *The Methodology of the Social Sciences*, New York: Free Press.

Weiss, C. (1976) 'Using Research in the Policy Process', *Policy Studies Journal*, 4: 224–8.

Zimring, F. and Hawkins, G. (1995) *Incapacitation*, New York: Oxford University Press.

4 Crime, community safety and toleration

Lynn Hancock and Roger Matthews

Introduction

The recently published Home Office Statement of Purpose informs us that its aim is:

> To build a safe, just and tolerant society, in which the rights and responsibilities of individuals, families and communities are balanced, and the protection and security of the public are maintained.
>
> (Home Office 1998)

This claim appears at first sight to be eminently commendable and there are few in Britain who, if asked, would not identify with some if not all of these objectives. However, as has been pointed out, rather than strive to develop a more tolerant society, recent British government policies have been associated with the 'regimentation of opinion, moral closure, the repression of dissent and institutional intolerance' (Hughes 1998). In contrast to the stated aim of promoting greater levels of tolerance government policy has expressed a profound intolerance for a range of activities including noisy neighbours, squeegee merchants, youths hanging around the streets as well as other forms of 'anti-social' behaviour (Muncie 1999). Significantly, most of the activities which have become the object of official intolerance in recent years are, in themselves, relatively innocuous. Nevertheless, we are reminded that we are now engaged in a 'war against crime' and a 'war against drugs', although it is not clear whether these are two fronts of the same war or two different wars. Either way, the language of war presents offenders as the enemy to be defeated or dominated, rather than helped or tolerated. At the same time the emphasis on zero tolerance, or selective intolerance as it has been more accurately described, has been actively pursued by different agencies and given considerable official support. Being 'tough on crime and the causes of crime' means, according to the Home Secretary Jack Straw, the instigation of 'tough and consistent prison sentences for serious criminals', and he insists that the 'purpose of our criminal justice system is to catch and punish offenders not to make excuses for them' (Straw 1999). Within this punitive paradigm, the focus is largely on punishment, incapacitation, longer prison sentences and generally getting tough on offenders. There is little attention given to disadvantage, mitigation, rehabilitation or toleration.

Government-sponsored campaigns to inform on drug dealers, welfare scroungers and other 'anti-social' groups are designed to encourage citizens to display increasing intolerance towards certain forms of activity and these have run alongside anti-sexist and anti-racist campaigns which have called for greater intolerance of what are increasingly deemed to be unacceptable acts and attitudes. Thus it is apparent that the government is formally calling for greater tolerance while simultaneously pursuing a strategy of selective intolerance. The implicit message which is conveyed in recent policy developments in the field of 'law and order' would seem to be that greater intolerance is the route to a safer and more just society.

How can we make sense of this apparent contradiction? We could simply dismiss it as an example of hypocrisy or as a consequence of the inevitable gap between rhetoric and reality, or the mismatch between intentions and outcomes. Or more cynically we could see it as a product of the 'New Managerialism' which, while espousing the virtues of cost effectiveness, spends valuable time producing mission statements and statements of purpose that are either bland, vague or in some cases totally vacuous. However, rather than just dismiss this statement of purpose or engage in deep cynicism (although this does have a certain attraction), our intention is to show that embedded in the Home Office's Statement of Purpose are some important issues centred around the notion of tolerance and that these are linked to an unresolved political tension between liberalism and communitarianism.

Consequently, this chapter has two main aims. First, to articulate the notion of toleration, which we believe to be a much misunderstood concept, and at the same time to examine its largely unacknowledged role as centrally organising concept of sociological investigation. Second, we aim to examine both the liberal and the communitarian approaches to toleration and attempt to show that the tension which is evident in current crime control and community safety policy arises from an uneasy mix of these two political doctrines.

What is toleration?

'Toleration' is a term, which like 'community', is virtually devoid of any negative associations. Tolerance suggests respect for others, a recognition of individual rights, as well as an acceptance of individual difference and social diversity. It is, however, not an expression of benevolence, but rather it embodies a sense of disapproval and implies a degree of suffering or sufferance (Yovel 1998). The working definition of 'tolerance' which is widely used is: 'The deliberate choice not to interfere with conduct or beliefs, with which one disapproves'. In this way we might distinguish tolerance from indifference and from those situations where there may be no real choice over whether to take action or not. Thus in examining the exercise of toleration we need to know something about the reasons for intervention and non-intervention (Horton and Nicholson 1992).

Public tolerance is not the same thing as public opinion. Public opinion, as expressed in public attitude surveys, asks people what they would advocate whereas the notion of toleration is concerned with what people will accept or be willing to endorse under certain circumstances. For example, a public opinion survey may characteristically ask what length of sentence members of the public would advocate for a certain type of crime whereas what respondents might be willing to live with or tolerate may be considerably different (Turner *et al.* 1997). Thus the term toleration is much broader than public opinion and not only involves some consideration of spontaneously expressed viewpoints, but invites a more detailed consideration of the range and depth of public attitudes.

The notion of toleration, although mainly discussed and refined by political philosophers, is central to the understanding of crime, law and punishment. The distinction between crime and incivilities, law and norms, as well as the application of different sanctions, is conditioned by the prevailing forms of toleration. Although it is the case that in relation to certain activities such as rape, murder and robbery there may be a relatively high degree of consensus that these offences should not be tolerated, the situation becomes more complicated when we consider forms of social disorder or non-criminal activity (Burney 1999), since those committing lesser transgressions may well claim some 'right' to engage in these activities (e.g., to buy or sell sex, to play music, to 'hang around' on the street), and this right is itself associated with notions of freedom and autonomy (Mendus 1989; Newey 1999). Inasmuch as the concept of toleration has featured in the criminological literature it is often presented as a uni-dimensional expression of free-floating benevolence. However, a review of the relevant literature suggests that it has a number of important attributes.

First, the notion of tolerance is profoundly social and arises out of social interaction and in turn serves to regulate that interaction. It involves an expression of power in that it suggests the ability to limit or influence the activity of others, and like the concept of power as Michel Foucault (1979) has shown, it is a *relational* concept. Just as people do not simply 'hold' or 'exercise' power over others, so toleration implies a degree of reciprocity and mutual recognition. Second, toleration is tied to the *material* conditions of existence in that the decisions over the expression of tolerance are conditioned by the structural location and situational pressures of those expressing tolerance. Thus the class, gender or ethnic position of those involved in this relation will deeply influence the nature of tolerance involved and how it is expressed. Third, it is *purposeful* and *intentional*. The expression of toleration is a rational and conscious act even if it is expressed through inaction. As sociologists have consistently pointed out, refraining from engaging in an act is no less meaningful than the decision to engage in one. It is also no less real in its consequences. Fourth, like concepts such as 'trust' or 'stigma' the notion of toleration will normally exhibit a number of different dimensions, which may not in themselves appear as complementary or consistent. As a *multi-dimensional* concept it will contain ambiguities and uncertainties. Thus, any investigation of toleration will require a multifaceted form of enquiry which will also need to be able to distinguish between the object of toleration and the mode of expression.

Finally, toleration is an intrinsically *moral* concept. It implies exercising judgement, taking responsibility and making choices between that which is acceptable and unacceptable. It is the case that we may tolerate things which we believe to be wrong, but this does not preclude the fact that our decision to tolerate involves an element of moral choice (Bauman 1995).

The centrality of toleration to criminological investigation

A number of well-known criminological terms have all been associated with the expression of intolerance. These include 'shaming', 'censure', 'stigmatisation' and 'labelling', and each of these concepts have been influential in criminology in different periods (Goffman 1963; Schur 1971; Sumner 1990). Their relation to the term toleration, which is arguably a more generic concept, is often alluded to but rarely explained. At a more general level the concept of toleration is directly and indirectly associated with a number of central concepts in criminology such as fairness, culpability, equity and responsibility which inform the meta-theories of crime and justice in both everyday life and among criminal justice agencies.

Over the past few years a number of criminological texts have touched in various ways upon the issue of toleration. In particular, those which have explored issues connected with punishment and sentencing have addressed the relation between changing penal practices and climates of public opinion in different periods. These investigations have been encouraged by a sense that there is considerable agreement within and across advanced western societies in relation to the appropriate forms and levels of punishment (Doob and Roberts 1988; Garland 1990; Young and Brown 1993).

Among these contributors a number have drawn on Norbert Elias' (1994) work on the 'civilising process'. Elias' focus is on how people have internalised social constraint, become more self-disciplined and learned to manage their feelings in a more discreet way. As a result of growing social interdependency coupled with the formation of a centralised state authority which claimed a monopoly on the legitimate use of violence, people in Europe have, he argues, become less tolerant of overt demonstrations of violence. It has been claimed that Elias' work provides a non-economistic account of changing attitudes towards public demonstrations of violence. In particular, his approach has been used as a basis for explaining the demise of public executions and the development of the modern prison (Franke 1992; Spierenburg 1984). Elias' approach, however, while containing suggestive observations on changing forms of toleration historically, has been charged with vagueness, evolutionism and a one-dimensional understanding of social change (van Krieken 1989). Most damaging for the Elisian approach is the claim that it is unable to effectively account for the reversals and ambiguities which have been identified in the deployment of punishment historically and that it is not very useful in explaining a number of contemporary developments, such as the decline of the rehabilitative ideal, the emergence of the 'new penology' and the 'new correctionalism' with its return to boot camps as well as the use of chain gangs alongside the development of other 'decivilising' processes (Pratt 1998; Vaughan 2000).

A more focused and grounded approach which has linked the issue of toleration to expressions of punitiveness has been presented by Leslie Wilkins and Ken Pease (1987) who have suggested that one of the cultural determinants of society's penal climate is its relative egalitarianism. That is, they claim that the greater the society's tolerance of inequality, the more extreme the scale of punishment is likely to be. Just as those at the top are seen to receive disproportionate rewards for their achievement so those at the bottom end of the social scale who 'fail' are punished particularly severely. Thus, countries that have a highly individualistic and competitive ethos, they argue, and in which there is a high degree of inequality will tend to be comparatively severe in the use punishment. Mobilising solid comparative evidence, however, to test this hypothesis is difficult given the limited nature of the available data (Pease 1994). The United States is the usual point of reference in debates over relative punitiveness, particularly since currently it has in excess of two million people incarcerated. However, while there is evidence that the US tends to impose longer sentences for a range of crimes, the use of incarceration itself is not, in general, too dissimilar from European countries (Langham and Farrington 1998). Variations between European countries provide only limited support for the hypotheses, while it is clear that the use of imprisonment, for example, in different countries is also likely to be conditioned by other factors such as the availability of non-custodial sanctions and the degree of social and political stability. Nevertheless, it remains a relevant and plausible hypothesis.

One of the few attempts to analyse explicitly the role of tolerance in shaping systems of punishment was the study by David Downes (1988) of the different use of sanctions in England and Wales and in the Netherlands. Downes saw the different approaches to the use of imprisonment and alternatives to custody in these two countries as a function of 'contrasts in tolerance'. He attributes the relatively low use of incarceration in the post-war period in the Netherlands to a greater level of tolerance than existed in England and Wales, although he points out that Dutch tolerance does not involve a 'blanket acceptance of all manner of behaviour and opinion'. Rather, it is a selective strategy based on a 'politics of accommodation' which relies less on scapegoating and the exclusion of deviants and instead provides a more integrative approach. Herman Franke (1990) in a critical review of Downes' *Contrasts in Tolerance*, emphasises that tolerance is not of one piece and therefore it is inappropriate to talk about a 'culture of tolerance'. Instead, there is a need, he argues, to examine the history, the political context, the composition and orientation of criminal justice agencies as well as the role of the media in influencing the exercise of tolerance.

In relation to the construction of crime it has been pointed out by radical realists that public attitudes, informal normative structures and sanctions are a critical dimension of the 'square of crime' (Lea 1992; Matthews and Young 1992). While it is the case that victims as primary definers play a critical role in transforming incidents or 'problematic situations' into potential 'crimes' the decision to report will not only be conditioned by the gravity of the offence, the willingness of the police to take it seriously or their ability to do something about it, but will also be dependent on the level and nature of public tolerance. The recent shift, for example, in attitudes towards interpersonal violence in which child abuse, domestic violence, bullying and the like have been 'redis-covered' reflects a changing framework of social attitudes which will affect individual decisions to report incidents (Pahl 1985; Saraga, 1996). It will also affect the sanctions imposed and the severity with which different kinds of offences are viewed. Thus, as Steven Box and Chris Hale (1986) have pointed out, it is essential when looking at the problem of crime to understand the social and cultural processes through which different types of activity become problematic. It is also necessary to understand why it is felt that certain activi-ties can no longer be adequately dealt with informally and why the sanctions which were previously deployed to control certain deviant activities are no longer seen as being adequate. The importance of this point is that we should not simply see the growing public intolerance of certain types of incivilities or crimes as a consequence of the growth in crime, but rather regard both the growth of crime and the changing attitudes to punishment as two sides of the same process. This relation provides a useful corrective to those criminologists who see shifts in public tolerance purely as a *reaction* to higher levels of crime. Thus we might explain the steady increase in crime over the past two decades and the intensification and extension of punishment as a product of the twin effects of shifts in the nature of toleration. By the same token there is a need to identify those activities which have been effectively decriminalised over time or which have slipped down the 'law and order' agenda.

This two-way development is evident in the Crime and Disorder Act (1998) which on one side transforms a number of incivilities into criminal offences and simultaneously involves the intensification of the sanctions relating to each of these activities. In a similar vein, we have seen in recent years on both sides of the Atlantic how the 'war against drugs' has resulted in the criminalisation of a range of previously tolerated drug-taking activity and the widespread use of formal sanctions, particularly imprisonment (Tonry 1995). In this process the concern across the political spectrum associated with widespread illicit drug use can effectively be translated into forms of selective enforcement. Thus although shifts in the nature of public toleration play a critical role in this process, and may be fuelled by media campaigns, this growing intolerance may be formally expressed through criminal justice agencies which have their own interests and organisational constraints. Of central importance, therefore, is the relation between informal and formal processes of regulation as well as the role of medi-ating institutions in shaping the nature and expression of toleration.

If we are correct in our claim that toleration is germane to the whole criminological enterprise, then why should it be that criminologists have historically been reticent to engage with this concept? We can suggest three main reasons. First, the issue of toleration is seen to be located in political philosophy which is a discipline that remains relatively unexplored by criminologists. Although it is the case that much of the more interesting criminological work in recent years has been that which has vicariously lifted ideas and materials from other disciplines – particularly sociology, urban studies and cultural studies – successful forays into the world of political philosophy have been less frequent. Second, toleration does not lend itself easily to direct measurement, since its exercise involves inaction as well as action. Since toleration is also a relational, complex and multi-faced activity its study requires a more imaginative and sophisticated form of analysis than is normally undertaken by criminologists. Third, an examination of toleration is likely to draw researchers into the perplexing areas of norm creation, systems of classification, and probably the area in which they feel most uncomfortable – morality (Bauman 1995; Cohen 1979).

The growing interest in public tolerance

Despite the reluctance to engage directly with the notion of toleration a number of criminologists have begun to address the question of public attitudes (Hough and Roberts 1999; Mirrlees-Black *et al.* 1996). Policy-makers and funders who sense it is necessary to take some account of public attitudes are increasingly turning to public attitude surveys. These surveys, however, are fraught with methodological problems and are able at best to provide a 'snapshot' of public opinion and at worst provide a distorted one-dimensional picture of what members of the public actually think (Herbst 1998; Norris 1999). This shift in interest has been largely a consequence of external developments rather than arising from pressures within the discipline itself. Among the major developments which have taken place in recent years are the changing role of the national state, globalisation, increased political apathy and cynicism, growing public insecurity, the fragmentation of communities and the breakdown of regulatory institutions, as well as growing anxieties about the direction of political leadership.

We are currently witnessing a significant change in the organisation and role of the national state. This involves a process in which decision-making is simultaneously becoming more global and international and more local. As a consequence, the sovereign state has spread the responsibility for crime control and community safety onto a range of statuary, private and voluntary agencies while sending out the message that the state alone is not, and cannot, be responsible for preventing and controlling crime (Garland 1996; Jessop 1994). There has also been a growing involvement of citizens in crime prevention and crime control. This, however, is not just a process of the state and other agencies pressurising local communities to take responsibility for their own security; but also represents a new social movement in which local social networks attempt to actively defend their communities from the effects of globalisation. The net result is that a significant proportion of citizens are involved, albeit in some cases on a token level, in crime prevention and community safety programmes through neighbourhood watch, tenants associations, block watch, citizen patrols, local support groups and other community-based organisations. An indication of this can be found in David Bayley's (1994) findings, that in New York organised self-protection activities on the part of citizens have mushroomed with over 151,000 people involved in crime prevention programmes in 1985. This involvement reflects a deeply felt need to supplement the usual police protection in the context of growing concerns about public security. Similar trends can be found in Britain. There are now over 150,000 neighbourhood watch schemes operating in England and Wales covering approximately 10 million households, although the involvement of these members may in some cases be fairly token. There are a growing number of tenants organisations, community liaison groups, citizen patrols and the like who are involved in crime control and improving public security (Hancock 2001). The growing involvement of local community groups has, however, been met with ambivalence by the state authorities, since the attempts to encourage 'active citizens' has been tempered by the spectre of vigilantism (Johnston 1996).

The devolving of responsibilities to local authorities following the publication of the Morgan Report in 1991 has given crime prevention and crime control a more differentiated and local focus. One consequence of this strategy, however, is that it has promoted interest in the experiences and attitudes of local populations. It also creates new demands and expectations from local residents which need to be accommodated. There is the prospect that within this emerging set of relations changes are likely to occur in the prioritisation of crime and disorder and that the newly established community safety groups will reflect local priorities and concerns as well as shifts in toleration.

Communities, however, have become more fragmented as a result of economic restructuring. As the routines and habits of everyday life are undermined through the introduction of new forms of flexible accumulation the basic trust in the security of the world has been thrown into disarray (see Young in this volume). In these conditions the willingness of citizens to tolerate difficult and deviant activities is likely to be curtailed, and creates a climate which encourages forms of scapegoating, particularly in the form of racism (Cohen 1998). It is often as the conditions for the expression of intolerance grow that official calls for greater tolerance arise.

The development of globalisation and the advent of the 'information society' has at the same time increased the complexity of decision-making and the plurality of values and interests which have to be taken into account such that the actors shaping our political life are themselves diminishing in stature. The lack of any clear profile amongst different political parties is associated with growing political apathy and cynicism. There is a consequential legitimation deficit and it becomes increasingly difficult to mobilise the population behind governmental policies. At this juncture there is seen to be a need to reinvigorate flagging institutions and to increase confidence, particularly in the criminal justice process which plays an increasingly important practical and symbolic role in late modernity (Hirst 1997).

The combined effect of these related processes has been to increase interest in public attitudes and changing forms of toleration. However, as yet the investigation and understanding of how these attitudes are formed and transformed remains underdeveloped.

Why tolerate?

It is clear that whatever one's beliefs are that one cannot express intolerance towards everything one dislikes or disapproves of. Toleration, therefore, is necessarily selective. The critical issues are how toleration is constructed, changed and expressed. Strategic decisions are often made in relation to pragmatic and moral considerations. The problem of analysis is that pragmatism and moralism tend to be interconnected. The main pragmatic consideration, often suggested by utilitarians, is that the benefits of toleration may outweigh the harms. Toleration may also enable us to mitigate or avoid damaging social conflict. The difficult question is, however, how do we make a distinction between acts which should be prevented and punished and those that should be permitted and tolerated. Harm itself is not a sufficient criterion of intolerance since the notion of harm is open to wide interpretation and comes in a multitude of different forms, while the decision about whether and how to respond will be conditioned by a range of other moral and practical considerations.

Primary amongst these considerations is the relation between the activities to be tolerated and the level of social support which is available. According to Richard Taub and his colleagues (Taub *et al.* 1984) in their study of community transition in Chicago, the exercise of tolerance is conditioned by the quality and the quantity of local amenities. The factors, they suggest, that will influence the capacity of different individuals and groups to tolerate different activities will include the organisation and density of housing, the seriousness of other local problems and the range and quality of amenities. It is also suggested that the level of tolerance is not just a function of the level of absolute deprivation in an area but often a consequence of relative deprivation. That is, intolerance is seen to arise from the gap between what people have got and what they expect (Campbell 1991). The focus on relative deprivation may go some way to explain the apparent paradox which has been reported that it is those groups located near the top as well as those at the bottom of the social scale who exhibit the greatest level of punitiveness (Brillon 1988).

In everyday discussions of toleration reference is often made to 'thresholds' and to 'the limits of tolerance', which suggests that there are critical points in the exercise of tolerance at which a qualitative change occurs. In this point of transition it would seem that activities which were once tolerated take on a different significance. The implications of this observation are that it is not only the number of incidents which is important but the point at which a threshold of toleration is crossed. Thus it may be the case that seven or eight prostitutes working in a certain locality may be acceptable and although local residents may not particularly approve of the activity they are willing to tolerate it. However, at a certain point the visibility of, say, twelve women regularly working on the streets transforms the nature of the activity such that it is seen to 'swamp' or change the neighbourhood in a way that local residents are no longer willing to tolerate, and they call on the authorities to do something about it. This scenario appears by and large to have occurred in various parts of Britain during the 1980s, and although the relevant authorities were slow to respond to growing public pressure many residents groups took it upon themselves to deal with the problem (Matthews 1993). The other important implications of this observation are that firstly we need to give greater attention to the *impact* of crime and disorder in different areas and that, second, we need to identify the *thresholds* of tolerance. In this way we might become less concerned with the rise and fall of recorded offences – or with strategies which simply aim to reduce crime and disorder or other problems by an arbitrary amount – and instead develop a greater regional and local sensitivity to variations in the thresholds of toleration.

Liberalism and communitarianism

The articulation and defence of toleration has historically been associated with the classic liberal theorists such as Locke and Hobbes and more recently the writings of Rawls (1971) and Dworkin (1977). In essence, the standard liberal defence of toleration is centred around the notion of respect for other persons and the defence of individual liberty. This is normally expressed in terms of the protection of rights. In this process the state is seen as a neutral arbiter between competing moralities. Therefore, in principle the state should not prescribe any particular moral or religious view but allow equal recognition to all citizens. The emphasis on respect for other persons is based upon the principle which maintains that citizens should be able to make choices about how they live and be able to act as autonomous and rational agents. Thus for liberals there is a private sphere of individual autonomy which the state should not interfere with unless an individual inflicts harm on another individual. The protection of a separate private sphere is seen to be a necessary condition for the maintenance of individual freedom.

This familiar liberal position has been the object of a sustained critique by communitarian thinkers who have taken issue with the individualistic premise of the position as well as the preoccupation with rights and the associated conceptions of liberty, freedom and justice. This communitarian critique has gained some ascendancy since the election of New Labour in 1997, and the government's thinking has been greatly influenced by the work of Amitai Etzioni (1993; 1997). This critique has direct implications for the status of the theory and practice of toleration since the distancing from liberalism suggests by implication a rejection of, or at least a shift away from, the liberal defence of toleration.

In contrast to liberalism the communitarian emphasises the primacy of the community, claiming that the self is built up intersubjectively. Communities, therefore, are more than a collection of autonomous individuals and they represent more than the sum of their parts. Communitarians have taken issue with the liberal emphasis on individual rights. Some have argued that a rights-based policy is ultimately unsustainable since claims about competing rights are themselves difficult to resolve, and that these policies find themselves in the awkward position of deciding which rights to defend and which to prioritise over others, since the exercise of one person's rights often involves the infringement of the rights of others. Some communitarians accept that there are certain basic rights which should be defended such as the right to a fair trial, the right to be presumed innocent until proven guilty, and so forth, but most would endorse Etzioni's contention that liberals tend to place too much emphasis on individual rights and not enough on social obligations and duties. Communitarians also take issue with the liberal conception of freedom as a state of non-interference of the solitary individual. For the communitarian freedom is a social achievement through the guarantee of protection. It is not a state of chance but a process in which each citizen is equally protected by law (Braithwaite and Pettit 1990). The emphasis on equality draws attention to the importance of treating both the offender and the victim equally and in ways which are constructive but not overly intrusive (Walzer 1983).

One of the few criminologists who has examined the notion of tolerance from a communitarian perspective is John Braithwaite. In his influential study, 'Crime, Shame and Reintegration' (1989), he provides an explicit critique of liberal notions of toleration and argues that liberal tolerance can be counterproductive. For example, when parents allow their children to freely use illicit drugs, or engage in various forms of anti-social or undesirable behaviour without receiving any sanction, it can lead to the escalation and intensification of these problems. Braithwaite's argument is reminiscent in certain respects of Herbert Marcuse's (1965) critique of 'pure tolerance', which he suggests can turn into 'repressive tolerance' when it does not address or remove social inequalities, but instead implicitly endorses and perpetuates them.

In contrast to liberalism, Braithwaite argues that: 'Low crime societies are societies where people do not mind their own business, where tolerance of deviance has definite limits, where communities prefer to handle their own crime problems rather than hand them over to professionals' (1989: 8) Moralising control through informal networks, he argues, is likely to be more effective than formal forms of 'repressive' social control which denies human dignity, limits autonomy and serves to confirm deviance as a master status. The aim for Braithwaite is to mobilise shaming strategies not simply in order to stigmatise deviants but instead to reintegrate them whenever possible back into the community. The important point here is that greater intolerance does not necessarily lead to greater punitiveness.

In opposition to the atomistic vision of order which is evident in strands of liberalism, it is argued by communitarians that the community structure itself shapes local crime rates by defining what is acceptable behaviour and by establishing normative structures which guide both the definitions of 'problematic situations' and how they are categorised. A communitarian notion of toleration is bound up with the defence of the community and the decision of whether to exercise tolerance or not will be conditioned by how valuable the community under threat is. Therefore, actions which may appear to be fairly innocuous can have a cumulative impact on the community and consequently can become the object of intolerance. However, in promoting intolerance the communitarian has to give due consideration to the level of harm inflicted as well as the capacity of the community to absorb or deflect these 'anti-social' activities as well as considering the consequences of stigmatising or marginalising the offender since this may cumulatively weaken the community. It is also necessary for the communitarian to distinguish between interventions which are practically designed to improve community safety and those interventions which are more symbolic and are designed to regenerate moral obligations between citizens (Crisp 1992; Gutman 1985).

In general, the communitarian critique can be seen as providing a corrective to certain liberal conceptions of the autonomous self-propelling individual, although liberalism has not been without its defenders (Kymlicka 1989). As Allen Buchanan (1989) has pointed out, this ongoing debate between liberalism and communitarianism has operated on a number of different levels and that in trying to think through these important issues it is useful to distinguish between radical, moderate and cautious communitarians. It is only in its radical version that communitarianism rejects outright the significance of individual rights and the liberal conception of freedom. In its more moderate version it concedes the importance of certain rights, but denies the priority which the liberal attributes to them. In its more cautious variant it urges those who value community not to abandon the framework of individual rights, but rather to appreciate the role which individual rights can play in protecting communities under certain historical conditions. In opposition to the radical communitarian he argues that the defence of individual rights of association, to pursue religious beliefs and the right to political participation need to be defended and that:

> Given the apparent diversity of the conditions of human flourishing, the pronouncement that the best life for all (or even most humans) requires participation in the most inclusive forms of political organisation is sheer dogmatism in the absence of a well-defended, highly particularistic, and absolutist theory of objective good.
>
> (Buchanan 1989: 859)

In the absence of such a point of reference individual rights allow individuals who are dissatisfied with current forms of community or who find existing communities unduly restrictive or oppressive to develop alternatives. Closing such a possibility raises for the liberal the spectre of totalitarianism. Moreover, as Axel Honneth (1995) has suggested, while it may be the case

that self-confidence and self-identity are built up intersubjectively, the establishment of legal rights is important in recognising the dignity, autonomy and
capacity of persons to act as morally responsible legal agents. He also argues
that crime itself can be seen as a struggle of interests or as a clash of identities. Crime involves not only a material loss or a physical violation but an
attack upon individual identity. If crime only involved a material or physical
deficit it would not be so socially important. It is precisely because it involves
issues of recognition and identity that it takes on such a degree of significance, particularly in a period in which social recognition and identity
formation are becoming increasingly problematic (Fraser 1997).

A major problem with the communitarian position in terms of crime prevention and community safety is that it is notoriously difficult to establish
community strategies to reduce crime in high crime areas and probably even
more difficult to sustain involvement in low crime areas. Further, social control
tends to be maintained in the more affluent suburban communities by social
avoidance, privatisation, low levels of interaction and through 'moral minimalism' (Hope 1995). This notion of moral minimalism is reminiscent of Iris
Young's (1990) depiction of modern urban communities as being composed of
lightly engaged strangers. This state of affairs raises particular problems for
communitarianism since it would appear that there is a growing emphasis upon
difference and diversity within contemporary urban environments rather than
on close-knit communities. Where new collectivities arise there is little
evidence that they approximate to the notion of the ideal community. In fact,
the individualism/community opposition is becoming less tenable and masks
rather than elucidates the nature of modern urban groupings. Rather than
seeing the individualism/community opposition as exhaustive, Iris Young sees
them as mutually sustaining:

> Too often contemporary discussion of these issues sets up an exhaustive
> dichotomy between individualism and community. Community appears in
> the oppositions individualism/community, separated self/shared self,
> private/public. But like most such terms, individualism and community
> have a common logic underlying their polarity, which makes it possible for
> them to define each other negatively. Each entails a denial of difference
> and a desire to bring multiplicity and heterogeneity into unity, though in
> opposing ways. Liberal individualism denies difference by positing the self
> as a solid, self-sufficient unity, not defined by anything or anyone other
> than itself. Its formalistic ethic of rights also denies difference by bringing
> all such separated individuals under a common measure of rights.
> Proponents of community, on the other hand, deny difference by positing
> fusion rather than separation as the social ideal. They perceive the social
> subject as a relation of unity or mutually composed by identification and
> symmetry among individuals within a totality. Communitarianism repre-
> sents an urge to see persons in unity with one another in a shared whole.
>
> (Young 1990: 229)

It is the ideal of community, she argues, which by encouraging a sense of mutual identification with some persons serves to problematise difference. The fear of difference can promote racism and classism in society and fosters forms of exclusion and marginalisation, while simultaneously suppressing diversity.

Rather than seeing a movement towards the ideal of 'community' we appear to be witnessing the emergence of new groupings and forms of neo-tribalism centred around temporary forms of solidarity and political organisation which challenge rather than endorse the legitimacy of traditional moralities (Maffesoli 1996; Sennett 1991). In these 'tribes' membership is easily revocable and is not tied to long-term obligations. Their existence is transient and always in flux. In these transient urban networks the very notion of 'community' is becoming increasingly problematic. In the context of increasing contingency, ambivalence and fragmentation the search for 'community' appears more hopeless and unrealistic. The identification of consensus becomes more elusive and the ability to mobilise universal truths in order to sanction, humiliate or stigmatise becomes increasingly difficult. The construction of order begins to look more artificial and fragile. The protection of the 'community' as a geographically-bounded space of local networks, which is increasingly invoked by policy-makers as a justification for cracking down on various forms of anti-social behaviour, appears to coincide with the transformation and dissolution of these local networks.

Alongside the reorganisation and differentiation of communities the communitarians face a related problem. This is the demise of regulatory and socialising institutions. In much communitarian writing there is to be found a backward looking and often romantic vision of these institutions – the family, the school, the police, the prison and indeed the state. It is no accident, however, that they have repeatedly been referred to by commentators from across the political spectrum, as being in a state of 'crisis'. The implications of this assessment is that the pivotal traditional mechanisms through which social order and discipline are normally maintained are in disarray.

It is in this context that the repeated references to the relation between single parent households and delinquency should be seen. The suggestion that these parents are often irresponsible and feckless combined with calls for making parents take more responsibility for their children, overlooks the reality that such families lack resources to impose 'discipline' on children who live in a world in which there is great uncertainty about what constitutes an appropriate form of discipline. Therefore, attempts to salvage the 'cornflake' family are unlikely to work in the longer term and instead of perpetuating a backward-looking view of the role of weak and outdated institutions, the critical political question is how to establish the appropriate socialising and disciplinary mechanisms in a post-Fordist and postmodern urban environment characterised by new forms of individualism and collectivism.

The paradox of the dominant forms of political thinking on both sides of the Atlantic is that they are guided by principles which are simultaneously wildly utopian and nostalgic and appear increasingly out of touch with the changing realities of urban life, while espousing a mixture of opportunistic and pragmatic policies couched in the language of managerialism.

There is a lingering problem about the scope, legitimacy and accountability of state institutions which classic liberalism finds difficult to address because it was designed to protect society *from* the state, rather than deal with the problems of liberty in a state and civil society dominated by large hierarchical institutions (Hirst 1997). Thus the attempts of liberalism to shape and develop state power and improve accountability have been largely ineffective. The weakness of communitarianism, on the other hand, in this respect and its failure to confront and reform institutions derives from its desire to urge a consensus on a deeply divided society with plural and competing values.

By contrast to those 'moral communitarians' who see the solution to problems of crime and community safety through the creation of informal control mechanisms and particularly through shaming, Tim Hope (1995) has argued there are two dimensions along which crime control strategies work in communities:

> The first is a 'horizontal' dimension of social relations among individuals and groups sharing a common residential space. This dimension refers to the often complex expressions of affection, loyalty, reciprocity, or dominance amongst residents, whether expressed through informal relationships or organised activities. Second, there is a 'vertical' dimension of relations that connect local institutions to sources of power and resources in the wider civil society of the locality is acknowledged to be a part.
>
> (Hope 1995: 24)

Although these two dimensions are related it is the case that:

> While the principal mechanisms for maintaining local order may be expressed primarily through the horizontal dimension, the strength of the expression – and hence its effectiveness in controlling crime – derives, in large part, from the vertical connections that residents of localities have to extracommunal resources.
>
> (Hope 1995: 24)

Although research has shown that community organising in some locations can make a difference (Sampson *et al.* 1997), the ability of residential communities to withstand the impact of different forms of crime and incivilities will depend in large part on the available resources and their access to support networks (Cullen 1994; Matthews 1992).

If it is the case that the cautious communitarian can establish some degree of compromise with the liberals over rights, there still remains a major split between those communitarians who prioritise the community and community controls and those liberals who see crime control and community safety as an individual responsibility within a market-driven framework. This tension is located at the heart of current government thinking on 'law and order'. In the post-welfarist society, the emphasis on individual self-help and 'freedom' consists in extracting oneself from the supposed restraints and debilitating consequences of welfare. Government policy encourages the individualisation and commodification of security, offering only minimum guarantees, above which individuals are encouraged to take responsibility for themselves. This neo-liberal notion of 'freedom' and responsibility, in turn, influences notions of personal morality and the dependent subject of welfarism is replaced by the juridical subject of neo-liberalism (Pratt 1996). It is in this context that we can begin to make sense of the contradictory policy initiatives which on one side establish agencies to reduce social exclusion, while at the same time implement a reduction in welfare payments to marginalised populations: and how at one moment the government is advocating minimum mandatory sentences for burglary, drug dealing and violence, while at another it is generously funding programmes of restorative justice and community programmes for disaffected youth.

The tension between market-based policies and more socially-oriented policies creates further difficulties for 'balancing' communitarian approaches with liberalism. Most communitarians have a commitment to distributive justice but often defer to market mechanisms for the overall allocation of resources. This has resulted in a growing divide between the rich and the poor as well as growing regional disparities. As inequality increases, the basis of the communitarian vision begins to collapse since it undermines the realisation of both social and distributive justice, while creating new conflicts and antagonisms (Walzer 1983). The major difficulty for policy-makers is the formulation of realistic criteria by which the balance between rights and duties could be struck. Despite the proliferation of official pronouncements, reports and glossy publications there are no identifiable criteria of how and where to intervene, when to express intolerance, how to balance up social protection and individual rights and how to decide on the appropriate response (see Braithwaite and Pettit 1990) .

Some recognition of these difficulties has been expressed by Anthony Giddens (1998) in his elaboration of a 'Third Way', which constitutes an attempt to move beyond neo-liberalism and old-style statism and collectivism. Although he recognises that the ideal of 'community' is no longer a realisable objective and that the modern world is characterised by diversity, increasing 'ontological insecurity' and rising crime, his policy programme involves a mixture of public order and community policing as well as the development of local multi-agency interventions incorporating a range of state and non-state agencies, with a particular focus on the expansion of the voluntary sector. In these proposals he seems to be unaware of the fact that this is precisely the mixture of strategies which has been employed over the last decade or so under both New Labour and previous conservative governments and that it is precisely the effectiveness of this combination of strategies which is currently in question (see Crawford in this volume).

Thus although it may be possible to develop a theoretical compromise by adopting a more cautious form of communitarianism the danger is that in the absence of any clear principles or criteria for intervention, government policy is seen as either oscillating uncontrollably between a free-market mechanism and the promotion of idealised communities or alternatively falling between these two objectives. Ultimately, however, it has been suggested that the difficulty of working out such a conceptual and political compromise has been that much more difficult because the social relations and social structures around which these divisions have been historically articulated are themselves in a process of transformation and reconstruction. Thus, it would appear that this long-standing political antagonism between liberalism and communitarianism is being overtaken by events and that there is a growing sense in which classical liberalism is unable to defend individual liberty against the growing power of an unchecked corporate and managerial elite; while old-style communitarianism seeks to restore ailing institutions by trying to change people's values in an attempt to avoid engaging in major organisational and structural reforms. Paradoxically, however, the current drive towards 'modernisation' encourages greater diversity and flexibility, the fragmentation of traditional communities, new forms of social exclusion, the problematisation of identities, the rise of neo-tribalism and creates a growing lack of moral consensus in a world in which ever greater percentages of the population are becoming 'problems' (Bauman 1995; Young 1999).

Conclusion

In general, a number of social and political commentators seem to agree that toleration is an important element in the functioning of liberal democracies. But debates continue about where to draw the line between tolerance and intolerance and how such 'moral' decisions are linked to images of the 'good society'. Increasingly, criminologists have become aware that toleration plays an important, if not pivotal, role in the construction of crime and in influencing crime control policies. As we move into a situation in which the public are an increasingly important point of reference in providing information, co-operation and legitimacy within a restructured system of regulation a greater awareness of what the public want and what they are willing to accept has gained greater prominence. Alongside these organisational imperatives there have been growing demands for security from different social groups and a greater willingness to participate, at some level, in the development of community safety.

These developments have opened the door to greater community involvement in decision-making and to the introduction of new forms of accountability. The shifting responsibility for crime control and community safety to local authorities has been identified as a 'sea change' or a 'watershed' in policy development in Britain, introducing new forms of governance (Crawford 1997). There is now a clear sense of the limits of the nation-state and that there is no way back to the centralised forms of regulation which characterised previous periods. The watch words are now diversity, flexibility, cost-effectiveness and risk management.

Within this changing framework the relation between tolerance, forms of punishment, the distribution of justice and security become more problematic. There is an issue at one level of how to balance tolerance and intolerance, rights and obligations, as well as guilt and justice (Cohen 1979). There are no clear principles which tell us how such a balance is to be struck. At a second, and related, level there is an issue of how to identify, analyse and express forms of toleration.

The pursuit of tolerance and intolerance is not mutually exclusive. There is also nothing intrinsically negative or undesirable about intolerance. Intolerance can be instructive and constructive, just as the application of tolerance can be damaging and repressive in certain situations. In fact, to argue for tolerance in the abstract can be vacuous and counterproductive. If it is the case, however, that the aim of government policy is to argue for a different balance between tolerance and intolerance or for an increase in specific forms of toleration then a number of material, relational and social issues need to be addressed. On one level material inequalities and deprivations need to be reduced. This is an issue of distributive justice. At another level issues of recognition, solidarity and identity require serious consideration. These issues are bound up with notions of social justice. The spheres of distributional and social justice are directly and indirectly linked and are conceptually connected through notions of 'fairness' in the distribution of rewards and deserts. These notions, in turn, will influence the expression of toleration.

It has also been suggested that seeing the business of crime control and community safety through an examination of toleration could provide a very different vantage point for analysing and evaluating policy developments. However, the mechanisms for investigating and channelling public attitudes remain underdeveloped. The current preoccupation with the relatively arbitrary reductions in officially recorded crime rates and the emphasis on developing policy through the cumulative production of 'evidence' constructed through a series of uncoordinated, patchy and idiosyncratic forms of research stands in contrast to the suggestion that crime and crime control policies are profoundly influenced by shifts in public tolerance, however restricted its expression might be.

The approach of the present British Labour government, we have argued, involves an uneasy and unresolved mix of liberal and communitarian ideas on toleration, rights and justice. These two philosophies were always in themselves problematic, but it has been suggested that the changing problem of security facing different social groups and the tranformation of 'communities' has rendered these modes of thinking even more problematic. The current impasse will require some serious rethinking. It is a problem which involves three aspects, first, a change in the nature of risks and hazards which individuals and groups face; second, a change in the social relations, social networks and associated identities; and third, it involves the changing nature of the socialising and regulatory mechanisms which are in place to shape and control these developments. The interrelated nature of these problems makes the possibility of a 'quick fix' resolution increasingly untenable and calls instead for a fundamental re-examination of crime and control and this in turn, we have suggested, will involve the mobilisation of certain basic organising and sensitising concepts such as toleration.

References

Bauman, Z. (1995) *Life in Fragments: Essays in Postmodern Morality*, Oxford: Blackwell.

Bayley, D. (1994) *Police for the Future*, New York: Oxford University Press.

Box, S. and Hale, C. (1986) 'Unemployment, Crime and Imprisonment: The Enduring Problem of Prison Overcrowding', in R. Matthews and J. Young (eds) *Confronting Crime*, London: Sage.

Braithwaite, J. (1989) *Crime, Shame and Reintegration*, Cambridge: Cambridge University Press.

—— and Pettit, P. (1990) *Not Just Deserts: A Republican Theory of Criminal Justice*, Oxford: Clarendon.

Brillon, Y. (1988) 'Punitiveness, Status and Ideology in Three Canadian Provinces', in N. Walker and M. Hough (eds) *Public Attitudes to Sentencing*, Aldershot: Gower.

Buchanan, A. (1989) 'Assessing the Communitarian Critique of Liberalism', *Ethics*, 99 (July): 852–82.

Burney, E. (1999) *Crime and Banishment*, Winchester: Waterside Press.

Campbell, A. (1991) *The Sense of Well Being in America*, New York: McGraw Hill.

Cohen, M. (1998) *Culture of Intolerance*, New Haven: Yale University Press.

Cohen, S. (1979) 'Guilt Justice and Tolerance: Some Old Concepts for a New Criminology', in D. Downes and P. Rock (eds) *Deviant Interpretations*, Oxford: Martin Robertson.

Crawford, A. (1997) *The Local Governance of Crime: Appeals to Community and Partnerships*, Oxford: Clarendon.

—— (1998) *Crime Prevention and Community Safety*, London: Longman.

Crisp, R. (1992) 'Communitarianism and Toleration', in J. Horton and P. Nicholson (eds) *Toleration: Philosophy and Practice*, Aldershot: Avebury.

Cullen, F. (1994) 'Social Support as an Organising Concept for Criminology', *Justice Quarterly*, 11(4): 527–59.

Dennis, N. (1997) (ed.) *Zero Tolerance: Policing in a Free Society*, London: Institute of Economic Affairs.

Doob, A. and Roberts, J. (1988) 'Public Punitiveness and Public Knowledge of the Facts: Some Canadian Surveys', in N. Walker and M. Hough (eds) *Public Attitudes to Sentencing*, Aldershot: Gower.

Downes, D. (1988) *Contrasts in Tolerance: Post-war Penal Policy in the Netherlands and in England and Wales*, Oxford: Clarendon.

Dworkin, R. (1977) *Taking Rights Seriously*, Cambridge, Mass: Harvard University Press.

Elias, N. (1994) *The Civilising Process*, Oxford: Basil Blackwell.

Etzioni, A. (1993)*The Spirit of Community*, New York: Crown Publishers.

—— (1997) *The New Golden Rule*, London: Profile Books.

Foucault, M. (1979) *History of Sexuality: Volume 1*, Allen Lane: Penguin.

Franke, H. (1990) 'Dutch Tolerance: Facts and Fables', *British Journal of Criminology*, 30(1): 81–94.

—— (1992) 'The Rise and Decline of Solitary Confinement', *British Journal of Criminology*, 32(2): 125–43.

Fraser, N. (1997) *Justice Interruptus: Critical Reflections on the Post-Socialist Condition*, New York: Routledge.

Garland, D. (1990) *Punishment and Modern Society*, Chicago: University of Chicago Press.

—— (1996) 'The Limits of the Sovereign State: Strategies of Control in Contemporary Society', *British Journal of Criminology*, 36(4): 445–71.

Giddens, A. (1998) *The Third Way*, Cambridge: Polity Press.

Goffman, E. (1963) *Stigma: Notes on the Management of a Spoiled Identity*, Englewood Cliffs, NJ: Prentice Hall.

Gutman, A. (1985) 'Communitarian Critics of Liberalism', *Philosophy and Public Affairs*, 14(3): 308–22.

Hancock, L. (2001) *Community, Crime and Disorder: Responses to Change in Urban Neighbourhoods*, London: Palgrave.

Harrison, R. (1992) 'Tolerating the Offensive', in J. Horton and P. Nicholson (eds) *Toleration: Philosophy and Practice*, Aldershot: Avebury.

Herbst, S. (1998) *Reading Public Opinion*, Chicago: University of Chicago Press.

Hirst, P. (1997) *From Statism to Pluralism*, London: UCL Press.

Home Office (1998) *Annual Report*, Cm. 3908, London: HMSO.

Honneth, A. (1995) *The Struggle for Recognition*, Cambridge: Polity Press.

Hope, T. (1995) 'Community Crime Prevention', in M. Tonry and D. Farrington (eds) *Building a Safer Society: Strategic Approaches to Crime Prevention*, volume 19, Chicago: University of Chicago Press.

Horton, J. and Nicholson, P. (1992) (eds) *Toleration: Philosophy and Practice*, Aldershot: Avebury.

Hough, M. and Roberts, J. (1999) 'Sentencing Trends in Britain: Public Knowledge and Public Opinion', *Punishment and Society*, 1(1): 11–27.

Hughes, G. (1998) *Understanding Crime Prevention*, Buckingham: Open University Press.

Jessop, B. (1994) 'Post-Fordism and the State', in A. Amin (ed.) *Post-Fordism: A Reader*, Oxford: Blackwell.

Johnston, L. (1996) 'What is Vigilantism?', *British Journal of Criminology*, 36(2): 220–36.

Kymlicka, W. (1989) *Liberalism, Community and Culture*, Milton Keynes: Open University Press.

Langham, P. and Farrington, D. (1998) *Crime and Justice in the United States and in England and Wales, 1981–96*, Bureau of Justice Statistics, Washington DC: US Department of Justice.

Lea, J. (1992) 'The Analysis of Crime', in J. Young and R. Matthews (eds) *Rethinking Criminology: The Realist Debate*, London: Sage.

McIntyre (1981) *After Virtue*, London: Duckworth.

Maffesoli, M. (1996) *The Time of the Tribes: The Decline of Individualism in Mass Society*, London: Sage.

Marcuse, H. (1965) 'Repressive Tolerance', in R. P. Wolff, B. M. Moore Jr. and H. Marcuse (eds) *A Critique of Pure Tolerance*, Boston: Beacon Press.

Matthews, R. (1992) 'Replacing Broken Windows: Crime Incivilities and Urban Change', in R. Matthews and J. Young (eds) *Issues in Realist Criminology*, London: Sage.

—— (1993) *Kerb-Crawling, Prostitution and Multi-Agency Policing*, Paper 43 Crime Prevention Unit Series, London: Home Office.

—— and Young, J. (1992) 'Reflections on Realism', in J. Young and R. Matthews (eds) *Rethinking Criminology: The Realist Debate*, London: Sage.

Mendus, S. (1989) *Toleration and the Limits of Liberalism*, London: Macmillan.

Mirrlees-Black, C., Mayhew, P. and Percy, A. (1996) *The 1996 British Crime Survey, England and Wales*, London: Home Office.

Moynihan, D. (1993) 'Defining Deviance Down', *American Scholar*, 62 (Winter): 17–30.

Muncie, J. (1999) 'Institutional Intolerance: Youth Justice and the 1998 Crime and Disorder Act', *Critical Social Policy*, 19(2): 147–75.

Newey, G. (1999) *Virtue, Reason and Toleration: The Place of Toleration in Ethical and Political Theory*, Edinburgh: Edinburgh University Press.

Norris, P. (1999) *Critical Citizens: Global Support for Democratic Governance*, New York: Oxford University Press.

Offe, C. (1996) *Modernity and the State: East, West*, Cambridge: Polity Press.

Pahl, J. (1985) *Private Violence and Public Policy*, London: Routledge and Kegan Paul.

Pease, K. (1994) 'Cross-national Imprisonment Rates', in R. King and M. Maguire (eds) *Prisons in Context*, Oxford: Clarendon.

Podolefsky, A. and Dubow, F. (1981) *Strategies for Community Crime Prevention: Collective Responses to Crime in Urban America*, Springfield, Illinois: Charles C. Thomas.

Pratt, J. (1996) 'Reflections on Recent Trends in the Punishment of Persistence', *Crime, Law and Social Change*, 25: 243–64.

—— (1998) 'Towards the Decivilising of Punishment', *Social and Legal Studies*, 7(4): 487–515.

Rawls, J. (1971) *A Theory of Justice*, Cambridge, Mass: Harvard University Press.

Sampson, R. J., Raudenbush, S. W. and Earles, F. (1997) 'Neighborhoods and Violent Crime: A Multilevel Study of Collective Efficacy', *Science* 277 (August): 918–24.

Sandal, M. (1982) *Liberalism and the Limits of Justice*, Cambridge: Cambridge University Press.

Saraga, E. (1996) 'Dangerous Places: The Family as a Site of Crime', in J. Muncie and E. McLaughlin (eds) *The Problem of Crime*, London: Sage.

Schur, E. (1971) *Labelling Deviant Behaviour*, New York: Harper and Row.

Sennett, R. (1991) *The Conscience of the Eye*, New York: Alfred A. Knopf.

Skogan, W. G. (1988) 'Community Organizations and Crime', in M. Tonry and N. Morris (eds) *Crime and Justice a Review of Research*, volume 10, Chicago: University of Chicago Press.

Spierenburg, P. (1984) *The Spectacle of Suffering*, Cambridge: Cambridge University Press.

Straw, J. (1999) Foreword to the 'Government's Crime Reduction Strategy', London: Home Office.

Sumner, C. (1990) *Censure, Politics and Criminal Justice*, Milton Keynes: Open University Press.

Taub, R., Taylor, D. and Dunham, J. (1984) *Paths of Neighbourhood Change: Race and Crime in Urban America*, Chicago: University of Chicago Press.

Tonry, M. (1995) *Malign Neglect: Race Crime and Punishment in America*, New York: Oxford University Press.

Turner, M. and Cullen, F., Sundt, J. and Applegate, B. (1997) 'Public Support for Community Based Sanctions', *The Prison Journal*, 77(1): 6–26.

Van Krieken, R. (1989) 'Violence, Self Discipline and Modernity: Beyond the Civilising Process', *Sociological Review*, 37: 193–218.

Vaughan, B. (2000) 'The Civilising Process and the Janus Face of Modern Punishment', *Theoretical Criminology*, 4(1): 71–93.

Walzer, M. (1983) *Spheres of Justice: A Defence of Pluralism and Equality*, New York: Basic Books.

Wilkins, L. and Pease, K. (1987) 'Public Demand for Punishment', *International Journal of Sociology and Social Policy* 7(3): 16–29.

Young, I. (1990) 'The Ideal of Community and the Politics of Difference', in L. Nicholson (ed.) *Feminism/Postmodernism*, New York: Routledge.

Young, J. (1999) *The Exclusive Society*, London: Sage.

Young, W. and Brown, M. (1993) 'Cross National Comparisons of Imprisonment', in M. Tonry (ed.) *Crime and Justice: A Review of Research*, volume 17, Chicago: University of Chicago Press.

Yovel, Y. (1998) 'Tolerance as Grace and as Rightful Recognition', *Social Research*, 65(4): 897–921.

5 'Broken Windows' and the culture wars

A response to selected critiques

George L. Kelling

Introduction

Since the publication of my article, 'Broken Windows: The Police and Neighborhood Safety', in the journal *Atlantic Monthly* in 1982, it has caused considerable consternation in much sociological, legal and criminological literature.[1] Its main ideas, however, are widely accepted by policy-makers in most cities in the United States. These include most police and criminal justice agencies, neighbourhood organisations and local political leaders – regardless of their ethnicity, race or political orientation. Intellectually and politically, 'Broken Windows' grew out of the centre right. Professor James Q. Wilson, a well-known neo-conservative, co-authored the original 'Broken Windows' article. New York's Mayor Rudolph Giuliani, also centre right, and Commissioner William Bratton gave 'Broken Windows' unprecedented publicity when it was implemented as policy and practice in New York City. The Manhattan Institute, a thriving conservative New York urban think-tank, is one of its strongest intellectual strongholds. This chapter argues that the middle/left liberal criminological establishment has been held captive for decades by the radical individualism of the far left. The consequence has been that liberals, traditionally champions of cities, have abandoned them. The stridency of the far-left attack on 'Broken Windows', indeed its nastiness, signifies its desperation. It also signifies the intellectual stinginess of the near left, as it attempts to reposition itself in relation to the issue of disorder.

'Broken Windows'

'Broken Windows' is a metaphor. It argues that just as a broken window left untended is a sign that nobody cares and leads to more damage, so disorder left untended also signifies that nobody cares and leads to fear of crime, more serious crime and urban flight and decay. The original article, and subsequent writings, have put forward the following points:

- incivilities, disorderly behaviour and conditions, and minor offences can cumulatively be as significant to citizens as felonies like rape, robbery, burglary and assault;

- such problems increase the fear of crime;
- citizens act on these fears – they move, take protective measures and in other ways shape their lives on the basis of their fears;
- citizens want something to be done about disorder;
- disorder and fear are sequentially linked to serious crime and urban decay;
- nevertheless, the effects of disorder on a neighbourhood vary considerably: some neighbourhoods have the capacity to tolerate and absorb a significant amount of disorder while others are highly vulnerable to lower levels of disorder;
- *intervening to restore order* is a means of interrupting or reversing the downward spiral into crime and urban decay in vulnerable communities, while *managing disorder* can prevent this spiral from starting in more resilient ones; and
- police order maintenance activities are, by their very nature, highly discretionary.

Each of these points is to be found in the original 'Broken Windows' article. To be sure, some are spelled out in more detail than others, but all are there. Moreover, each is discussed in considerable detail in *Fixing Broken Windows: Restoring Order and Reducing Crime in Our Communities* (1996), written with Catherine Coles after I was involved in implementing police order maintenance activities in the New York City subway system.

And, lest I be misunderstood, I do not suggest that 'Broken Windows' should go unquestioned. On the contrary, the original formulation about the causal links between disorder, fear and crime was put forward as a hypothesis and invited questioning and research. To date, the research on these linkages has been mixed. On the one hand, Skogan's (1990) research is highly supportive, on the other hand, Harcourt (1998), using Skogan's data, draws different conclusions. My own belief, based on my experiences and reading of the research, is that the original formulation will withstand research, although it will be refined (e.g., only specific categories and subcategories of crime are linked to disorder). And finally, I am not unaware of the potential abuses that can result from police order maintenance activities. I am keenly aware of them and wrote about them, and their history, at length in *Fixing Broken Windows*. I am so concerned about doing police order maintenance properly, that immediately after completing *Fixing Broken Windows*, I authored *Broken Windows and Police Discretion*, which identifies a model for guiding police discretion in the conduct of order maintenance (Kelling 1999).

For me, the sources of the ideas in 'Broken Windows', aside from some literature, include observing foot patrol officers, interviewing citizens, citizen surveys, observing neighbourhoods and communities, meeting formally and informally with citizen groups (especially in inner cities), and problem-solving activities (disorder in the New York City subway and 'squeegeeing' on New York City streets). These ideas took form within the context of community policing as it evolved in the United States during the mid- and late 1980s and, for me at least, are inseparable from this context.

Professor Wilson and I continue to be pleasantly surprised by the original article's 'legs'. It has been reprinted often, is available on the Internet, has been reported by *Atlantic Monthly* as one of its most popular articles, has been translated into several languages, has engendered countless 'Broken Windows' police programmes, and has been applied to probation, education, health and other professional endeavours. Most visibly, it has been associated with the historic reductions in crime in New York City. Both Mayor 'Rudy' Giuliani and his first Police Commissioner, William Bratton, are outspoken advocates of a 'Broken Windows' approach to policing. *Fixing Broken Windows* is now being translated into Polish, Portuguese and Spanish.

The original article also spawned immediate and often vitriolic attacks. The National Institute of Justice (the research arm of the US Department of Justice) issued a request for a proposal the same year that 'Broken Windows' was published to test the article's thesis that crime was linked to disorder. After the research was designed, the US Attorney General quashed it as being too controversial. Professor Samuel Walker published the first academic critique in 1984. Others followed. Former Kansas City, Missouri and San Jose, California Police Chief Joseph McNamara has been the most vitriolic practitioner opposing 'Broken Windows', primarily on radio and television talk shows and in newspaper op-ed editorials (McNamara 1997). Among other allegations, 'Broken Windows' supposedly gives rise to racism, 'wars' on the poor, police brutality and criminalises the homeless. At least one author has labelled James Q. Wilson and myself as racists – 'aversive' racists at that (Stewart 1998).[2] These critiques have not exactly been in lightweight journals. They include the Yale and University of Michigan law journals, both representing prestigious law schools in the US (Harcourt 1998; Stewart 1998).

On reflection, the academic and professional assaults are not surprising. Certainly Professor Wilson foresaw them. By the early 1980s, his neo-conservatism had already alienated many criminologists and he predicted that merely by writing with him I would fall under academic suspicion.[3] Professor Wilson's reputation notwithstanding, 'Broken Windows' is controversial in at least two overlapping yet distinct respects. First, it directly challenges the reigning 'root causes' of criminal justice ideology – not surprising given the traditional liberalism of sociology/criminology. Second, it runs head-on into the 'culture war' raging over the competing demands of individual rights and community interests.

Criminal justice

The reigning criminal justice ideology in the US is a direct outgrowth of President Lyndon Johnson's 1960s crime commission and its 1967 report, *The Challenge of Crime in a Free Society*. A conceptual offshoot of the 'War on Poverty', *Challenge* emphasises the tragic consequences of racism, poverty and social injustice and links them to crime, social disorder and violence

(President's Commission, 1967). These broad social problems are the 'root causes' of crime. Not surprisingly, their amelioration is fundamental to preventing crime and violence. Police, prosecutors, corrections and criminal courts comprise a criminal justice *system* whose purpose is to process offenders – murderers, rapists, robbers, burglars and others who commit serious offences. Minor offences and 'victimless' crimes should be actually or virtually decriminalised to end the 'overreach' of the criminal law.

The most obvious policy implications of the report are, of course, that basic structural changes are required in American society to reduce crime: wealth redistributed, racism ended and social injustices rectified. Beyond this, the report has two major sets of recommendations. First, the relationship between criminal justice agencies and minorities must be improved, partially by ensuring that minorities are represented among police, prosecutors, corrections and courts. Second, the criminal justice system should be improved through enhanced planning, technology and modernised administrative processes (recruitment, training, supervision, etc.).

It is impossible to exaggerate to non-Americans the extent to which these ideas permeate criminology, criminal justice academic programmes and criminal justice practice in the US. 'Root causes' became conventional wisdom, in popular as well as professional culture. At its extreme, the premise is stretched to a syllogism: crime is caused by poverty, racism and social injustice; police can do nothing about these problems; ergo, police can do little, if anything, about crime. The business of justice agencies is processing cases. To the extent that, say, police can have an impact on crime, it is by being the front end of the 'system': arresting serious offenders and forwarding them for processing.

One can be concerned about the problems of poverty, racism and social injustice and still be unhappy with this formulation. Indeed, one can find much in *The Challenge of Crime in a Free Society* with which to agree: its calls for lawfulness in the justice process; the urgency with which it calls for improving the relationship between criminal justice agencies and minority communities; and its mandate that minorities must be recruited, hired and promoted in criminal justice. In each of these areas, the document was genuinely and appropriately revolutionary (President's Commission, 1967).

As a primer of crime control, however, the President's report was a disaster. The 'root causes' assumption has never stood up to rigorous analysis. Crime varies too much by time, demography, economy, region and country to be attributed to such structural characteristics. Moreover, the 'system' metaphor is so entrenched and self-apparently 'true' that it thwarts careful scrutiny about how agencies actually function. The reality that criminal justice agencies, almost literally, never talk to each other and often work at cross-purposes is obfuscated by the power of the metaphor. The idea that such agencies could *plan together* was, at best, ahead of its time and remains optimistic today – although there now are some wonderful examples of what can result when they do (Kennedy 1997). Also, the report looked solely to government to solve the crime problem by declaring a 'war on crime' – akin and complementary to the

United States' other domestic war, the 'war on poverty'. The private sector, funding and sponsoring by far the largest crime control capacity in the United States, is completely disregarded in the report. Likewise, citizens and community organisations are relegated to consumers of professional crime control agents: they are to be good observers, reporters and witnesses – and to increase their financial support of criminal justice agencies. Finally, most of the 'system improvement' agenda – improved recruiting, training, supervision, co-ordination and technology – has been on the table since the 1920s in the US. Regardless, 'root causes' ideology largely held crime prevention hostage until well into the 1990s in the US.

The culture wars

Professor Francis Fukuyama has labelled the social revolution that characterised the US during the 1960s and 1970s as 'The Great Disruption' (Fukuyama 1999). Between 1960 and 1990, profound changes in values, beliefs and philosophies swirled through, not just the US, but through every western country with enormous social and cultural impact. Fundamental to these changes was a shift in the balance between individual rights and community interests. James Q. Wilson summarised this issue:

> The competing demands of liberty and community constitute a fundamental cleavage that divides contemporary political philosophers and has produced among the public at large the American culture war. The defenders of liberty envisage a world of autonomous individuals who freely choose their destinies and whose liberties are essential to personal development and social democracy. The advocates of community rejoin that no one is truly autonomous, that liberty can only exist in an environment of reasonable order, and that personal development requires familial and neighborhood support.
>
> (Wilson 1999: xii)

This shift towards unfettered individualism affected every facet of personal and public life: the family, church, education, sex roles, medicine, housing, mental illness, law, commerce, drug policy, and so on. But nowhere are these competing demands – between individual rights and community interests – more discernible than in matters of criminal justice policy. Regarding 'serious' crime – murder, rape, assault, robbery and burglary – criminologists/sociologists have quarrels, however, a broad consensus exists that these crimes need to be taken seriously. While issues like sentencing, the death penalty, the transfer of juveniles to adult court, and others are debated heatedly, at least agreement exists that felonies should be taken seriously.

For minor offences – begging, prostitution, public drinking, graffiti, and so on – the cleavage is yawning. The far left – including a good share of sociologists, criminologists and civil rights lawyers and advocates – not only does not want anything done about such offences, it views perpetrators of minor offences as victims of a corrupt/unjust society who are 'enriching' society with their messages. Thus, begging is elevated to the status of a political message about the inequitable distribution of wealth; graffiti is the 'folk art' of disenfranchised youth who have no other means to express their beliefs; and 'squeegeeing' (the unsolicited washing of car windows) is the 'work' of unemployed and homeless youth. And, of course, schizophrenics are not ill: they are heralds of society's pathology. Liberal enlightenment in this world means that, short of violence – and even this may be questionable – there are no outrages that are not 'understandable' and deserving of toleration given society's inequities and pathology. 'Tolerating the intolerable' in America's great cities is the acid test of one's true commitment to civil rights and social justice (Myerson 1998; Podhoretz 1999). Every 'in your face' indignity is someone's constitutional 'right' and must be endured.

Some background about 'Broken Windows'

The ideas in 'Broken Windows' originated during an era when policing was undergoing serious examination in the US – the depths of which may not be easy for non-Americans to comprehend. By the late 1970s, the impact of preventive patrol and rapid response to calls for service, the then-core capacities of police, seemed negligible (Kelling et al., 1974; Kansas City Police Department 1977). The Supreme Court had moved to bring criminal investigation under control earlier and a 1975 study of detectives by the Rand Corporation suggested that secretaries could have done most of their work (Chaiken 1975). Nothing seemed to work, disorderly conditions were rife and crime was skyrocketing.

As befuddled by these circumstances during the mid-1970s as most others, I started to look outside of policing's then-conventional wisdom about how crime could be controlled. In policing itself, I wondered about the potential of foot patrol and looked for a location to study it. While police held foot patrol in disdain, citizens and politicians pushed hard for its implementation (The Newark Foot Patrol Experiment 1981). Outside of policing, I became aware of the inchoate movement among citizens to organise themselves into neighbourhood crime control groups and I wondered about their potentials. Based on my exploratory work on foot patrol in Boston, Massachusetts and Newark, New Jersey I also started to speculate about the possibility of new measures of police performance – specifically, what I called 'quality of life' measures (Kelling 1978). In a 1978 article inspired by a rereading of Jane Jacobs' *The Death and Life of Great American Cities* and a rereading of Egon Bittner's classic work (1967) on order maintenance, I wrote for the first time about minor offences and disorderly behaviour and conditions:

> [O]rder maintenance in the normal work-a-day world ... is what people miss on the streets of United States cities (and this is the central theme of this paper): a police presence which operates to insure that the norms,

rules, and regulations of civil contact between people are facilitated and, when these social control functions break down, to assist restoration of street equilibrium.

(Kelling 1978: 111)[4]

Most recently, in *Fixing Broken Windows*(1996), Catherine Coles and I traced the evolution of 'Broken Windows' forward from the findings of foot patrol research, through the *Atlantic Monthly* article, and finally to its implementation, first, in the New York City subway system and, later, in New York City itself under Mayor Rudolph Giuliani and Commissioner William Bratton (1996).

There was an important 'wrinkle', however, in the evolution and implementation of 'Broken Windows'. It first appeared during the early 1990s attempts to reduce disorder in the New York City subway and later became an integral part of police order maintenance activities there. At the time of writing, it is at the core of the political struggles in New York City. Liberals, incensed at Giuliani's reputation for reducing crime avidly attempted to neutralise it as an issue when it appeared that he would be Hillary Clinton's opponent in New York State's 2000 senatorial race (not that they will be any less incensed now that he has decided not to run).[5] It has become clearer since the publication of *Fixing Broken Windows* (1996) that this wrinkle deserves some systematic discussion.

On reflection, it was a credit to Bratton that when he was chief of the New York City Transit Police Department he both closely monitored his tactical implementations and, when progress was noted, immediately provided feedback throughout the department.[6] For him, systematic feedback was a means of ensuring accountability, adjusting tactics to changing conditions, providing a vision of the 'business' of the transit police and communicating with line personnel about their achievements. Early in the Department's attempts to reduce fare beating in the subway, crime analysts noted that in some stations many who were arrested for fare beating either were carrying illegal weapons, mostly guns, or had warrants out for serious felonies.[7] The significance of this was not lost on either Bratton or his emerging tactical strategist Jack Maple. Not all fare beaters were serious criminals or gun carriers, but a significant percentage was.

Until this time, the primary means of confiscating weapons on US streets had been through traffic stops and vehicle searches – some of dubious legitimacy. Such practices go back to the 1950s when police in cities like Chicago routinely stopped cars for traffic offences and searched them for guns. At times these searches were legitimate: officers had good reason to suspect that guns were in the cars. At other times, the searches were a tacit *quid pro quo*: 'you let me search your car and I will not give you a ticket'. At yet other times, they were illegal: police simply stopped and searched cars with youths, often minority youths not committing any traffic offence. Such stops were a pretext to give officers the opportunity to search cars. If guns were found, it was not unusual for the person to be arrested and jailed, the gun confiscated and the matter dropped. Often police would not bother to appear at the hearing the next morning and the matter would be dismissed. From the point of view of most police the matter had been handled: a gun was confiscated and the person spent the night in jail (Kelling 1999).

Bratton, however, saw the matter differently in the subway and, later, city-wide:

> An unanticipated by-product of the sweeps came when we checked the identification and warrant status of everybody we were arresting. During the early stages of the initiative, we found that one out of every seven people arrested for fare evasion was wanted on an outstanding warrant for a previous crime. One out of every twenty-one was carrying some type of weapon, whether a box cutter, a knife, or a gun. As so often happens in policing, we had focused on one problem to the exclusion of others. Now we were beginning to understand the linkage between disorder and more serious crimes.
>
> (Bratton 1998: 154)

Discovering that such a high percentage of fare beaters was carrying weapons was one of those 'eureka moments'. And, in Jack Maple's fertile street-smart mind, arresting someone with a weapon provided additional possibilities. Did the person have more guns? Where did he get the gun? Who else had guns and was carrying them? As Bratton put it when referring to the impact this had on the subway: 'After a while, the bad guys wised up and began to leave their weapons at home' (Bratton 1998: 154).

The true potential of this finding, however, was only to become apparent after Bratton became Commissioner in New York City. With over 2,000 murders a year, most of them committed with handguns, New York City was in the midst of a bloodbath during the late 1980s and early 1990s. And New York City wasn't alone: name the American city and violence was spinning out of control. Something had to be done about gun carrying, but just what basically stymied police, policy analysts and researchers. Research had been largely fruitless. Sherman, Shaw and Rogan, for example, published the 'Kansas City Gun Experiment' in 1995. Funded by the National Institute of Justice, this study did little more than refine and endorse conventional police practice: use of traffic stops to search cars when officers felt their safety was threatened; asking citizens to submit to voluntary searches of their cars; looking into stopped vehicles for weapons; and other forms of consent searches including, for example, glove compartments (Sherman et al., 1995). In the meantime, criminological pundits were loudly proclaiming that we had not seen the worst violence yet: a second 'baby boom' cohort would soon turn loose a new generation of predators.

But in this context, Bratton and Maple saw *investigative* opportunities in police order maintenance activities – specifically about the issue of gun carrying. Despite the epidemic of gun violence, Jack Maple notes the NYPD's lackadaisical attitude about confiscating guns:

Taking guns off the street didn't seem to interest the [detective] squads at all. During the previous year patrol made almost 9,000 arrests for crimes in which a firearm was confiscated, but the entire Detective Bureau developed only four confidential informants to help identify gun sellers and took, as a result, fewer than fifty additional guns off the street.

(Maple 1999: 26)

But Maple was not just concerned about special or detective units. 'All ... arrests made must be viewed as opportunities to do more debriefings' (Maple 1999: 26). Based on the subway experience this principle, of course, included arrests for minor offences. Someone arrested for public urination? Question him. Does he have a weapon? Where did he get it? Does he know someone who carries a weapon? Where did that person get the weapon? For Maple, quality of life arrests were a potential treasure trove, not just for guns, but for other forms of contraband as well.

And this, of course, brings us to a critical issue, both about the whole idea of 'Broken Windows' and the current political and professional controversies in New York City. An important serendipitous finding – that many fare beaters were felons carrying weapons – added a new dimension to the 'Broken Windows' idea. Probably I should not have been surprised. Street cops probably could have told me about this all along and they might have, however, it just never registered. Nonetheless, police leaders expanded order maintenance. Heretofore, police saw it as a means to reduce citizen fear of crime and prevent crime by restoring order, empowering citizens and maintaining neighbourhood/community standards. Now, police understood it to be an investigatory tool as well, not the least for getting weapons off the street.

In the context of the national furore over gun-related violence and 2,200 murders a year in New York City – most of them with handguns – this was a big-time finding. It was highly dramatised in 1996 after a man brutally assaulted three women near Central Park. He was identified when fingerprints at the scene of the assault matched those taken earlier when he was arrested for fare beating. Maintaining order gained new meaning for line cops: it was not just a matter of dealing with obstreperous citizens and unpleasant conditions; it was an opportunity to apprehend some serious offenders. Like traffic enforcement earlier, where stops had potential beyond maintaining safe and orderly automobile and pedestrian movement, order maintenance put police into contact with serious trouble-makers and gave them opportunities to check for weapons, drugs and other contraband. But like traffic stops as well, it opened new possibilities of excesses in the name of contraband reduction, especially guns.

In the New York City context of the early 1990s, it was a small step from order maintenance activities as part of routine police activities to 'stop and frisk' by special anti-crime units attempting to reduce gun carrying. Guns were a major problem; disorderly behaviour, like traffic offences before them, provided the legal basis to stop persons on the street. The focus, however, shifted from a wide range of order maintenance activities to a concentration on arrest and its threat to allow officers to search and interrogate citizens, especially youths.

Also complicating the picture during the late 1990s was the emergence of the phrase 'zero tolerance' and its use as a substitute term for 'Broken Windows'. I will not go into length about the phrase here. I never used it, and view the phrase as a political sound-bite, not a viable set of policies. On the surface, the phrase is antithetical to the highly discretionary activities that 'Broken Windows' implies and which Coles and I made explicit in *Fixing Broken Windows*. Unfortunately, zero tolerance as a phrase is so entrenched in some countries that it is futile to attempt to do other than make people aware of its problems. I have often suggested that both the far left and far right love the term: for the far left it demonstrates that 'Broken Windows' is fascist; for the far right it justifies 'head knocking' by police.

A final point to be made about the evolution of 'Broken Windows' during the 1990s: I have little quarrel with, nor am bothered by the investigatory use of 'Broken Windows' as part of routine policing functioning. When people break the law, they open themselves up to such questioning. It is the use of order maintenance by *special* units for investigatory purposes that I find worrisome. While one can develop justifications for their limited use, they tend to be elitist, have little touch with neighbourhoods and communities, develop a life and agenda of their own, demoralise beat officers, and tend to get into trouble. 'Sweeps' by special units was always inconsistent with 'Broken Windows' as I have conceived of it. I have been explicit about this, especially in *Fixing Broken Windows*. At best, in my judgement, special units should have limited life, be as decentralised as possible, and should be brought in to support neighbourhood patrol officers. But this is a complicated issue in need of much study.[8]

The response to 'Broken Windows'

As I write this chapter, demonstrators are protesting about a series of police shootings of civilians: most notably, the Diallo incident in New York City. In this case an unarmed African immigrant was shot and killed in a high crime area by four police officers who fired their weapons forty-one times and hit Diallo nineteen times. A mixed race jury found the officers innocent of any criminal act.[9] At a demonstration at Rutgers, one of my faculty colleagues – not a criminal justice colleague – waved *Fixing Broken Windows* in front of the audience claiming that it is New York Mayor Giuliani's blueprint for policing in NYC and, as such, responsible for the killing of Diallo. Likewise, at Harvard, a leaflet announcing a protest there began with 'Protest Harvard University Research Fellow George Kelling: architect of racist "zero tolerance" police policies' – again, laying Diallo's death at my feet.

I mention this to make a point. My view of these demonstrators is considerably different than my view of some of my 'academic' critics. The demonstrators' activities are patently political. I wish that speakers, especially academics, would accurately reflect my points of view, however, I do not kid myself. The far left's animosity towards Giuliani is so rabid, and their anti-police feelings so passionate, that one would hardly hope for a careful reading of the text. Moreover, I had no right to be surprised. I had entered the political arena by authoring an op-ed piece in the *Wall Street Journal* about the incident.

Nor do I expect much quarter from civil rights and advocacy lawyers in the central arena in which 'Broken Windows' and order maintenance issues are being fought: the courts. It is in the nature of the advocacy process, really an extension of political processes, that briefs and writs will contain misrepresentations like 'criminalising the poor' and 'police harassment of minorities' in litigation when discussing order maintenance and 'Broken Windows'.

I had expected something else, however, from academic critics writing in, say, prestigious academic journals like *The American Sociological Review*. Before I say what I expected in academic circles, let me indicate what I had not expected. I had not expected that people would agree with me or would not see potentially negative consequences of 'Broken Windows' policies. My hope, instead, was for 'second order agreement'. By second order agreement, I mean that people who disagree put forward opposing points of view accurately, if not convincingly.[10] Most academic critiques of 'Broken Windows', even the best, have not been characterised by such intellectual forthrightness nor, I would add, honesty.

I have responded to many of the more outrageous misrepresentations ('aversive racist', etc.; see Kelling 1998). Moreover, I have ignored many criminological ditherings (Foucault and techniques of punishment, and whether or not 'Broken Windows' constitutes a legitimate 'theory'). My interest here is in what is happening in liberal/left criminology and why 'Broken Windows' sticks in their craw as much as it does.

The fact is that liberals lost cities – politically and intellectually. In the post-1960s era, liberals, including most American criminologists, simply walked away from disorder, fear of crime and serious crime and their impact on neighbourhoods and communities. Early twentieth-century Progressives/liberals were the great defenders of public spaces and neighbourhood interests. They mapped an agenda of what was wrong with cities and took concrete steps to remedy the wrongs. Now, political conservatives reign in most American cities.[11]

Hunter University Professor Fred Siegel has written about the transformation of liberals:

> Beginning roughly a quarter-century ago, the work of the Progressives and their New Deal Successors was undone. In a great but now all too obviously failed experiment, the Progressive ideals of integration and uplift that had served the city so well were largely abandoned as repressive mechanisms of middle-class social control. In the great wave of moral deregulation that began in the mid-1960s, the poor and the insane were freed from the fetters of middle-class mores. The 'revolution' achieved some important gains: it freed people unjustly imprisoned in mental hospitals, made the police a bit less highhanded, and gave welfare recipients the dignity afforded by due

process rights. But like every revolution, it had its victims. In the new climate in which drug use was redefined as a 'victimless crime' and purity of legal procedure took precedence over the safety of the community, people who had once been shackled by the inequities of the law found themselves trapped by a pervasive lawlessness. Delivered into the tender mercies of the streets, the most vulnerable among us have suffered immeasurably.

(Siegel 1992: 37)

Nowhere did liberals lose touch as badly as in crime control policy. The liberal crime control agenda, stuck as it was in 'root causes', was completely overwhelmed by conservatives, especially in sentencing policy. 'Truth in sentencing' and 'three strikes and you're out' carried the day in policy innovations. The major political crime control battles raged over gun control (liberals for, conservatives against), capital punishment (conservatives for, liberals against) and drug legalisation (a funny mix on each side) – all largely symbolic issues that said little or nothing about what could be done *today* to prevent crime. In the meantime, neighbourhood residents could tell you that the kids who were stealing hubcaps from cars would soon be stealing the cars if something wasn't done pretty soon. They could tell you as well that if you made the cars theft-proof, some of the youths would find a way to steal them anyway – and they did. They simply hijacked them at gunpoint, increasing the danger. Police and criminal justice agencies in Newark, New Jersey, for example, became such a joke that kids would steal cars and, to provoke police who were forbidden to chase them, bump into police cars to 'air-bag' them in the hope that police would get angry enough to get into 'hot pursuits'. It *was* a game: even if they were arrested, nothing would happen. In a world without meaningful sanctions for minor offences, some youths – not most, but a lot – spun out of control and by the time they were entering their late teens were starting to accumulate felony records. And then it was too late. 'Three strikes you're out' and 'truth in sentencing' ended the joke, but only after innumerable minor offences and many other serious crimes. Now, liberals like to castigate conservatives and 'authoritarian elements' for the tragically high imprisonment rate in the US, but liberals should be looking to themselves as well to attribute blame.

Regarding police, the liberal agenda paid little attention to their crime control potentials – after all, since crime was linked to structural features of our society what could police do except process offenders? Community policing, at least in its early days in the 1980s, was widely viewed as 'soft' policing – providing services and seeking community approval – to such an extent that it was widely rejected by most practising police officers. Generally, criminological liberals lauded community policing because it was 'nice' policing characterised by great concern for establishing good relationships to communities and neighbourhoods. Community policing might enhance criminal investigation as a consequence of its access to information; however, the inherent aggressiveness of community policing was largely lost on most criminologists. Traditional policing was inherently passive and non-intrusive: patrol, wait for a crime to happen, and then respond. The response might appear forceful – fast car, lights, siren – however, its premises and execution were reactive. Community policing was far more intrusive and aggressive than traditional policing. More crimes came under the purview of police (minor offences as well as serious), their source of authority was broadened to include civil as well as criminal authority, and police got out of their cars to 're-police' public spaces, streets and neighbourhoods. Nonetheless, until very recently, the agenda of most criminologists for police was limited to civilian review, corruption control and reduction of abuse – all focusing on what police should not do rather than what they should do. Even problem solving, an enormously powerful, and inherently aggressive, tool first articulated by Herman Goldstein, took on an ideological edge as well. For example, in New York City the resolution of 'squeegeeing' – extortion of money from automobile drivers under the guise of washing car windows at busy intersections – was not a problem-solving exercise according to some of its advocates, because it did not deal with the 'root causes' of squeegeeing.[12] And, of course, all of this came to a head when Giuliani and Bratton mobilised the NYPD around very specific crime control goals and succeeded beyond anyone's dreams. They not only reduced crime, they 'called their shots' and explicitly challenged the premises of root cause criminology. Liberals fumed: this is not community policing; police are 'cooking the books'; the crime reductions are the result of structural changes – demography, the economy, changing drug use patterns; and finally, well, the NYPD might be reducing crime, but at the unacceptable cost of high-handed 'stop and frisk' practices and the abuse of citizens, especially minorities. Never mind that in New York City murders are down 1,600 a year and robberies 60,000; that civilian deaths from police shootings are down from 41 in 1990 to 11 in 1999; or, that allegations of abuse of force are down by over 1,000, during a time when 8,000 officers were added to the NYPD.

In fact, liberals ceded crime control as an issue to conservatives. The radical left notion that order maintenance is really racism, cultural imperialism, 'criminalisation of the poor', ignores the plain reality that liberals refuse to acknowledge: poor and minority neighbourhoods are being ravaged by disorderly persons and conditions and the refusal of officials to take neighbourhood priorities seriously.

It is in this context that I will briefly address two critiques of 'Broken Windows'. One, 'Replacing "Broken Windows": Crime, Incivilities and Urban change' by Roger Matthews (1992), is written from a British point of view.[13] It is well known in both Britain and the US and has shaped many commentaries on 'Broken Windows'.[14] The second is 'Systematic Social Observation of Public Spaces: A New Look at Disorder in Urban Neighborhoods,' by Robert J. Sampson and Stephen W. Raudenbush. The most recent critique, it was published in the prestigious *American Sociological Review*. Both are important articles by established social scientists. I have no doubt that the latter article will become as influential as the first. It already has been put forward in the

National Institute of Justice Journal as a response to 'Broken Windows' (*National Institute of Justice Journal*, April 2000).

For Matthews, 'Broken Windows' is the focal point of the debate between new realists and radical realists with 'Broken Windows' an example of new realism. Within this context, Matthews raises three issues: 'The first involves the degree to which crime and incivilities are inextricably linked. The second is whether 'Broken Windows' – either metaphorically or literally – have the same effect in different areas; and the third involves the accuracy of the developmental sequence which is suggested' (Matthews 1992: 22). Matthews properly suggests that these issues are more than theoretical; they have 'a direct bearing on the formulation of policy' (*ibid.*).

The discussion that Matthews presents during roughly the first half of the article is a welcome one, sober and straightforward, based upon an examination of both US and British research conducted since 'Broken Windows' first appeared in 1982. Regarding Matthews' first and third issues, Wilson and I were well aware that we were hypothesising about the relationship among disorder, fear, serious crime and urban decay. We believed strong sequential linkages existed; however, we presented the article as exploratory in nature. The second issue that Matthews raises – whether 'Broken Windows' have the same impact in different neighbourhoods – is a non-issue. Wilson and I argued explicitly that disorder is less likely 'in places where people are confident they can regulate public behaviour by informal controls' (Wilson and Kelling 1982: 33).

Matthews' discussion goes distinctly awry, however, once he gets into the area of the 'problems of policing disorder' (1992: 34). He writes: '[Wilson and Kelling] unequivocally endorse the use of extra-legal methods and the need to 'kick-ass' to keep people in order. Significantly, the asses of the people they want kicked are winos, street prostitutes, panhandlers, and juveniles' (1992: 35). First, *extra-legal* is not synonymous with *illegal*.[15] Throughout all my writings, lectures and consultations, I have encouraged police only to invoke the law (cite or arrest) as a last resort, and to use extra-legal means – counselling, education, cajoling, persuasion, warning, etc. – as much as possible to solve problems. But, more to the real point, the article simply does not include an *unequivocal endorsement* to kick the asses, as Matthews writes, of winos, street prostitutes and others. To be sure, Wilson and I describe an officer who himself says, when describing the problems of dealing with gangs in public housing, 'We kick ass', yet any fair reading of this section of the paper would understand that we are raising the same complex issues about which Matthews and others are rightly worried. These include the endorsement by a troubled community of illegal police means to help solve its problems, the lack of consensus in many communities, the role of due process when responding to neighbourhood problems, the possible over-reliance on police to keep order and other such complex issues. 'Unequivocally endorse' is nothing less than a misrepresentation of our argument – and a gross one at that. To the contrary, we 'hedge' throughout the article, struggling with the complexity and subtleties of the issues we are raising. For example, in response to police deployment issues, we first call for experimentation. Then we add: 'The second answer is also a hedge – many aspects of order-maintenance in neighborhoods can probably best be handled in ways that involve the police minimally, if at all' (Wilson and Kelling 1982: 36).

Notwithstanding the substance of 'Broken Windows', or its cautious exploratory tone, Matthews' critique degrades from an interesting discussion of valid substantive and policy issues about which there is ample opportunity for honest disagreement, into a diatribe that has little to do with 'Broken Windows' theses, tone, or spirit. Examples abound. Matthews writes: 'When the public report these problems [rowdy youths, etc.] to the police, it is often not because they want a heavy-handed, truncheon-wielding army of police offi-cers descending on their neighborhood' (1992: 37) Who suggested a heavy-handed, truncheon-wielding army? This is absolutely out of the spirit of what was written. Matthews goes on: 'Wilson's and Kelling's contention is that the police are the key to controlling disorder' (*ibid.*: 38) In fact, as the quote from 'Broken Windows' above demonstrates, we say the opposite. Nonetheless, continuing in this line, Matthews avers:

> Wilson and Kelling express little interest in developing mechanisms and agencies which may empower the poor and the powerless, and they seem even less interested in directing resources towards the disadvantaged and marginalised. Instead, their main concern is to remove these undesirables from respectable areas, and since they do not want to do very much about their condition, they will, presumably, be deflected towards those poorer areas which already have more than their fair share of social problems. In their diatribe against decriminalisation and decarceration, they seem to be suggesting that 'if only we got really tough' on these people and put them in prison for longer, then urban decline in respectable areas could be prevented.
>
> (Matthews 1992: 41)

A diatribe against decriminalisation and decarceration? Put them in prison longer? While some might extend the logic of 'Broken Windows' in this fashion, it is by no means an inevitable logical extension. In fact, much in 'Broken Windows' suggests that we would find such an extension inappropriate. Regardless, Matthews carries *his* logic further:

> [T]hey advocate more 'get tough' policies, greater use of imprisonment, and the extension of selective incapacitation. At the same time, they want, not only more legal sanctions, but also endorse the use of extra-legal tactics by the police and seem to suggest that the appropriate response to intimida-tion and harassment on the street is more intimidation and harassment by the police.
>
> (Matthews 1992: 43)

Imprisonment? Selective incapacitation? I can only assume that we are not talking about 'Broken Windows', but about James Q. Wilson's *other* writings: what started as a discussion of the 'Broken Windows' idea has become a critique of Wilson's position on other criminal justice policy issues. The issue here, of course, is how independently discrete an article should be viewed within the context of a scholar's total work. Matthews could argue that it is fair to critique 'Broken Windows' within the context of Wilson's (or my) total position. Clearly, when I write that 'Broken Windows' should be viewed within the context of my writings about community policing generally, I am inviting analysis within this larger context. Yet, scholarship requires acknowledgement of this fact and proper citation – both of which are lacking in Matthews' paper. Matthews' justification of such a broad view argues that 'Broken Windows' comes complete with all the conceptual baggage he delineates above (1992: 43). This is mistaken; *Wilson and I bring conceptual baggage.* 'Broken Windows' says what it says and deserves to be treated as such. Beyond this, its premises and implications are certainly fair game, in so far as they are accurately represented. It is not too much to ask that when scholars move from critiquing the 'Broken Windows' ideas to critiquing either Wilson's or my other work they are explicit about it.

Taking another cut at the same issue, it can be argued that one of the problems of 'Broken Windows' is that extremists of one ilk or another rely on it to justify harsh police or other governmental action against 'problem' populations. Matthews is rightly concerned about this possibility. Moreover, Matthews can properly claim that he and others were attempting to fashion a centre social democratic position during the late 1980s when his article probably was being conceptualised. Clearly one can go from the basic arguments of 'Broken Windows' – disorder matters, people want something done about it, it is linked to serious crime and urban decay – to oppressive policies and regimes. But, this is not inevitable, either logically or in reality: Wilson and I did not do so in the article (in fact we worried about it in the article). The very policies that Matthews finds so promising for dealing with troubled communities – multi-agency approaches, the development of 'intermediary agencies' (park keepers), improved building design, improved housing policies, and others – are entirely congruent with, and can be deduced from, the original 'Broken Windows' piece and were discussed in *Fixing Broken Windows* (1996) at considerable length. In fact, his 'centre' left and my 'center' right have more in common with each other than with each of their extremes. Failing to acknowledge this overlap restrains both policy and scholarly development.

The second article, 'Systematic Social Observations of Public Spaces: A New Look at Disorder in Public Spaces,' was a lead article in the November 1999 *American Journal of Sociology* – *the* place for any sociologist, criminological or otherwise to be published, at least in the US. Aside from *AJS* reviewers, criminological heavy-hitters like Albert J. Reiss, Jr., John Laub and others are mentioned as sources of inspiration and as reviewers. In contrast to Matthews' article, which is a state-of-the-art 'think piece', Sampson and Raudenbush report on research that is well-funded by the John D. and Catherine T. MacArthur Foundation and the National Institute of Justice.

Sampson and Raudenbush's (1999) basic argument goes something like this: first, disorder is conceptualised as an integral aspect of crime; second, the same factors that produce disorder produce more serious crime; third, 'both crime and disorder are rooted in neighbourhood structural characteristics such as concentrated disadvantage and neighbourhood social processes such as lowered collective efficacy' (Sampson and Raudenbush 1999: 2).

The publication of the article was announced by a press release that opens with: 'Does disorder lead to crime? The "Broken Windows" thesis holds that' (Sampson and Raudenbush 1999: 1). Thus it is clear that for good or ill the authors are 'spinning off' 'Broken Windows'. Although I had heard rumours that such an article was being published, I first became aware of it when a reporter faxed me a copy of the press release on 14 December. Sure enough, the reporter got the message and queried me about 'Broken Windows' being disproved. Nonetheless, it is an important article.

'Collective efficacy' is the authors' 'big idea'. Collective efficacy is defined as 'the linkage of cohesion and mutual trust with shared expectations for intervening in support of neighbourhood social control' (Sampson and Raudenbush 1999: 612). It is an apt and useful phrase that captures a point that advocates of community policing and, later, community justice have been making since the 1980s: for disorder, fear and crime to be managed in neighbourhoods, the inherent strengths of neighbourhoods must be active and/or mobilised. It probably is a good thing that criminologists/sociologists are recognising it too. (By the way, it is a point that Wilson and I made in 1982 in the original 'Broken Windows' article and Coles and I discussed in great detail in *Fixing Broken Windows* in 1996, although this is not acknowledged by Sampson and Raudenbush.)

A variety of issues could be raised about 'A New Look'. I will raise three. The first is methodological. The second is interpretative: how the authors present some of their findings. The final is political: how Sampson and Raudenbush represent 'Broken Windows'.

The methodological issue concerns sampling – the underpinning of good research and analysis (this does not mean that there are not other methodological problems – there are). The observations that make up the main database of the project, and are put forward as methodological advances, are measures of disorder videotaped between 7 a.m. and 7 p.m. The limitations of such a time sample are casually dismissed in a footnote: 'Although it would be desirable to assess disorder during the night-time hours, a pretest confirmed that this was not feasible with current videotaping technology (or with the naked eye).' Drunks leaving a bar and creating neighbourhood problems at closing time cannot be seen with contemporary videotaping technology or the naked eye? Drug dealers and prostitutes at 6 a.m. on a street corner near an expressway exit soliciting the 'on the way to work' trade cannot be observed? Drunken youths blaring a 'boom box' in a neighbourhood park at 1 a.m. are not observable? This sampling methodology appears to be determined by the 'law of the instrument' rather than the nature of the phenomenon to be studied.

Consequently, it is not surprising that the indicators of *physical* disorder wildly diverge from disorderly *behaviour* (pages 617 and 618). Signs of physical disorder are in the many thousands while disorderly behaviours, aside from loitering, are in the 10s, 20s and 30s. But the deck is stacked: physical disorder is a continuous event. Graffiti, save cleaning or painting it over, is always available for observation. Likewise, garbage and beer bottles, unless picked up, are *there*. They *exist in space*. Disorderly behaviour, however, is highly ephemeral and time-sensitive; it exists in *time and space* – occurring more or less often depending on a wide range of situational variables. In the random method chosen to look for disorder in 'A New Look', disorderly conditions will always be observable, while disorderly behaviour may or may not be. The authors claim to resolve this issue by using statistical techniques, however, looking at the right times might have been more appropriate. Looking for disorderly behaviour between 7 a.m. and 7 p.m. is like looking for lost keys under a lamp-post – not because that's where they were lost, but because that's where the light is good.

It is interesting to contrast Sampson and Raudenbush's approach with the sophisticated sampling and measurement methodology of Anthony Braga and his colleagues (Braga 1999). While they also used videotape technologies to measure disorderly conditions, they understood both that disorderly behaviour was time sensitive and that measurement techniques could affect the behaviour of disorderly persons, especially those breaking the law. Consequently, rather than being driven by their technology, they used a different method to measure disorderly behaviour. The idea that a SUV (sports utility vehicle) cruising slowly down Chicago streets with two video cameras pointed out the side windows, the core of Sampson and Raudenbush's SSO (social science observation), would go unnoticed by street people like prostitutes and drug dealers and not influence their behaviour defies experience and logic. To give just one example, drug dealers hire kids to watch for unusual happenings in neighbourhoods (e.g., police attempting to record their drug dealing behaviour).

Second, a variety of interpretative issues could be raised, but let me address just one: the handling of robbery. The authors rely heavily on homicide data 'arguably one of the best measures of violence'. Arguably indeed. Murder is a reliable measure because it certainly is the most accurately *reported to* police and *recorded by* police. But this does not mean that it is necessarily a more valid measure, especially given its relative rarity. Nonetheless, Sampson and Raudenbush conclude in their press release: 'The results therefore support the inference that public disorder and most predatory crimes share similar features and a consequently explained by the same constructs at the neighbourhood level, especially the concentration of disadvantage and lowered collective efficacy' (page 4). Ignored in the press release is the following from the article itself:

The exception to the emerging conclusion that disorder is spuriously related to predatory crime is robbery. ... Areas with greater cues of disorder appear to be more attractive targets for robbery offenders, perhaps because disorder increases the potential pool of victims without full recourse to police protection, such as those involved in drug trafficking and prostitution.

(Sampson and Raudenbush 1999: 630)

In plain language, this means that robbery is related to disorder. The authors, however, are dismissive of what might be one of their most interesting findings: 'Only for robbery does the estimated effect of disorder remain large' (page 629). *Only* for robbery? Isn't robbery a serious problem?[16] Since the only other violent crime analysed is homicide, the rarity of which almost precludes a statistical link to disorder, this is a rather cavalier dismissal. And, by the way, where is aggravated assault in this analysis? If one is to make claims about measures of violence, ignoring aggravated assault is a glaring omission

To be fair, 'A New Look' raises an important issue that is obscured by the need to put 'disadvantage and collective efficacy' in the best light and to diminish 'Broken Windows'. In respects, the 'Broken Windows' formulation – disorder to fear to serious crime to urban decay – *is* oversimplified. Clearly, whatever causal sequencing is ultimately developed, 'serious crime' is an over-simplified aggregation of a complex range of offences, some of which are forms of debt settlement, others predatory, while others are situational. For example, I would be hard pressed to say that all categories of robbery are sequentially linked to disorder. The estranged lover who demands back rent from his former roommate at gunpoint is probably not much affected by disorderly behaviour or conditions. Plenty of other examples could be given from each legal category of offence. My guess is that the main contribution of Sampson and Raudenbush here is that while they do not disaggregate the crime data themselves, their preliminary results on homicide and robbery suggest that future analyses require disaggregation to establish sequencing, precursors, or causes.

The final issue has to do with how Sampson and Raudenbush portray 'Broken Windows'. Throughout the article, the authors exaggerate differences between their findings and 'Broken Windows', ignore similarities and limit their presentation of 'Broken Windows' policies to their construct: 'strong "Broken Windows"'– whatever that may be.

Apparently by 'strong version' they mean something like the following: 'What we would claim, however, is that the current fascination in policy circles (see Kelling and Coles 1996; Kelling 1998) on cleaning up disorder through law enforcement techniques appears simplistic and largely misplaced, at least in terms of directly fighting crime' (1999: 638). Note the citations: they suggest that Kelling and Coles either reflect or contribute to such a narrow approach. This is a deliberate misrepresentation. *Fixing Broken Windows* argues for a subtle and nuanced approach to dealing with neighbourhood problems. Both 'Broken

Windows' and *Fixing Broken Windows* are extremely cautious about the potentials of police to control crime on their own. *Fixing Broken Windows*, for example, while maintaining that police had an impact on crime in New York City during Giuliani's and Bratton's administration, further argued that it was only understandable in the context of the efforts of business improvement districts (BIDs), the transportation authority, neighbourhood groups, the evolution of a community court and other community efforts (Kelling and Coles 1996: Chapter 4). *Fixing Broken Windows* argues for services, collaborations, involvement with citizens, problem solving, involvement of the faith community and private business and provides examples of all. (I suppose this was acknowledged to me in a note that Sampson attached to a copy of the article in which he indicates, 'The results are complex and we think the "softer" version of "Broken Windows" is more compatible with the data' [personal communication, undated.]) 'Softer' version? I think I know what this means: it is a contrast to the 'tough' version of 'Broken Windows' – nothing more than Sampson and Raudenbush's construct in the first place. To be sure, neither Wilson nor Coles and I back away from law enforcement, but *Fixing Broken Windows* is very explicit in its rejection of highhanded police tactics. Anyone who has read it is well aware of this.

Reading Sampson and Raudenbush carefully, it is clear that their article is misleading; 'Broken Windows' is inexcusably misrepresented. Moreover, the idea, professed in their article, that: 'This article is part of a larger effort to build a *social* science of ecological assessment' (Sampson and Raudenbush 1999: 639) is pretentious. As a matter of fact, police researchers have been struggling with measurement problems in neighbourhoods for decades. Sampson and Raudenbush simply failed to learn from them – as is evident when their research is compared with that of Braga (1999) and his colleagues. Sampson and Raudenbush's acceptance of the limitations of their sampling design in the name of 'advanced systematic social observation' reflects a stunning lack of 'street smarts'.

It does not take much imagination to understand, however, what is going on here. The article was written and disseminated to gain maximum attention: it disproves 'Broken Windows'; it is a major methodological breakthrough. The dawning has taken place and left-centre criminologists and sociologists are aware that ignoring disorder and minor offences is simply unsustainable. Their quandary appears to be how to say something that protects root causes and yet does not acknowledge that conservatives were correct, both when they argued that minor offences mattered and that, if police and criminal justice agencies were to take citizens' concerns seriously, and do something realistic about them, serious crime could be reduced short of solving all of society's problems. This does not mean that police can do it alone or that poverty, racism, social injustice and family breakdown (the equivalent of 'root causes' for the political right) should not be addressed. They should be in their own right. But crime prevention should not be held hostage to solving these problems.

Conclusion

The last decade of the 1990s proved to be a pivotal one for criminology and criminal justice. The liberal 'rediscovery' of disorder and its consequences in neighbourhoods represents a significant shift in criminological thinking. I have no quarrel with liberals who want to 'spiff up' the idea a bit to make it more palatable. This is exactly what the liberal *New Yorker* journalist Malcolm Gladwell is doing in *The Tipping Point*, a trade book now approaching the best-seller list in the US (Gladwell 2000). He argues that, in many respects, liberals were right all along adding, provocatively, that Mayor Giuliani is really a liberal when it comes to crime. Conservatives, he maintains, view character as the source of crime. Liberals, on the other hand, maintain that social context explains crime. Their mistake is that they view context too broadly: poverty, *et al.* What is important is the *immediate* context. While Gladwell specifically uses 'Broken Windows' as a prime example, context is a core concept in both situational crime prevention (Cornish and Clarke 1986) and routine activity analysis (Felson and Cohen 1980) as well. This explains, for Gladwell, why circumstances changed so dramatically in New York's subway: a small change in the context, eradicated graffiti and ended fare beating, achieved a tipping point that altered how people, including those disposed to crime, behaved in the subway. But Gladwell makes his own points positively; he has no need to diminish the insights of others – even conservatives.

My quarrel instead is with 'scholarly' works that deliberately attempt to 'spin-off' of 'Broken Windows', distort it, and in so doing, denigrate it, and then use the distortion to enhance their own work. The shame is that just as the importance of Gladwell's 'tipping points' is not diminished by his forthright recounting of 'Broken Windows' in New York's subway, Sampson and Raudenbush's 'collective efficacy' would not have been diminished by a similarly straightforward presentation of 'Broken Windows'. Their work is important in its own right; they don't have to devalue it by misrepresenting other points of view. My own guess is that their views will converge very nicely with 'Broken Windows' as research progresses. (Putting aside the problems of sampling and homicide data, it would be fascinating to disaggregate robberies to see if types of robberies are related to types or levels of disorder.)

If the issue of the accurate representation of 'Broken Windows' was a mere academic quibble, I would have been loath to respond to either of the above articles. History has a way of sorting these things out. But the debate is not academic; it is about crime control now. Political tracts are fine in the current policy debate, but they should not be confused with scholarly work. Finally, if Wilson and I had 'only' been right about the link between disorder and robbery, I still would be delighted.

I would like to thank Catherine M. Coles, William Sousa and Michael Wagers for their comments on drafts of this chapter. I would also like to thank Marissa Potchak for her research assistance.

Notes

1 The full explication of 'Broken Windows' is found in the original article, cited above, and in George L. Kelling and Catherine M. Coles (1996) *Fixing Broken Windows: Restoring Order and Reducing Crime in Our Communities*, New York: The Free Press, and in George L. Kelling, *'Broken Windows' and Police Discretion*, National Institute of Justice Research Report, NCJ178259, October 1999.

2 Gary Stewart, 'Black Codes and Broken Windows: The Legacy of Racial Hegemony in Anti-Gang Civil Injunctions', *The Yale Law Journal*, vol. 107, no. 7, May 1998, pp. 2249–79. An 'aversive' racist, according to the author, is a smart racist. One can tell that someone is a racist when he or she doesn't talk about race.

3 In a somewhat amusing example of attempts to redeem me from this encumbrance, one doctoral student (not from Rutgers) has indicated to me that he is working on a paper in which he conducts a contextual analysis of the original 'Broken Windows'. He has identified what parts of the paper are the 'good' parts – and I authored them – and what are the 'bad' parts – and they are authored by Wilson. However, I was not a stranger to such 'suspicion'. The Kansas City Preventive Patrol Experiment (Kelling *et al.* 1974) had already put me at odds with most of the police establishment during the 1970s. Moreover, the sociological/criminological establishment, for example Albert Reiss Jr., had attacked the Kansas City study even before its publication (personal experience and communications).

4 While this paper is relatively obscure, it represents for me an initial foray into what later crystallised as community policing: seeking local legitimacy; the local configuration of problems; the need for decentralised decision-making; the links between order maintenance and crime control; the role of citizens in crime control, etc.

5 Giuliani withdrew from the race in late May 2000 as a result of the discovery that he was suffering from prostate cancer.

6 For those who don't know the history, Bratton was chief of the transit police from April 1990 to 1992. He then returned to Boston. In 1994 he returned to NYC as Commissioner under Giuliani. Later, during Bratton's administration, the transit police were absorbed by the NYPD.

7 Fare beating was an unusually serious problem. Up to 250,000 people a day were not paying their fare. This not only created an extraordinary sense of the subway being a lawless place out of control, but the loss of income threatened the entire infrastructure of the subway. Transit officials estimated losses at over $100 million a year.

8 The use of laws against disorderly behaviour has also been an important means of controlling gang behaviour – right now, a dangerous mix of drugs, drug selling, 'turf' and guns. Such matters have appeared in the US Supreme Court on at least one occasion (Chicago *v.* Morales) and are bound to occur in the future. While the Supreme Court invalidated one Chicago law that gave the police broad discretionary authority to order gangs to 'move on', the Court literally invited Chicago to redraft a somewhat more limited ordinance.

9 For a detailed discussion of this event, and the reasons he believes that it was not an example of police abuse, see, James Fyfe (2000) 'Reflections on the Diallo Case'.

10 This phrase, for me at least, has its origins with Mark H. Moore, my colleague in the Kennedy School of Government at Harvard University.

11 I write political conservatives rather than Republicans because mayors like Daley in Chicago and John Norquist in Milwaukee are not Republicans, but are conservative nonetheless. Norquist, for example, has taken an extremely strong stance against the use of federal funds in cities – once a funding mainstay of the liberal urban alliance (Norquist 1999).

12 I became aware of this when I attended a panel on problem-solving at a meeting of the American Society of Criminology. When I approached a presenter after the session to discuss with her some points about my squeegeeing problem-solving process in New York City – which eradicated squeegeeing in three weeks once it was implemented – it was summarily dismissed because I resorted to law enforcement to solve the problem, rather than solve the problem that led to young men becoming squeegee merchants.

13 The most recent British critique of 'Broken Windows' is Benjamin Bowling (1999) 'The Rise and Fall of New York Murder: Zero Tolerance or Crack's Decline', *British Journal of Criminology*, vol. 39, no. 4 (Autumn), pp. 531–54. Basically, the article reviews the homicide declines in New York City, restates the arguments of the last half decade about the cause of those declines and dismisses 'Broken Windows' in terms so similar to Matthews (1992) that one wonders if Bowling has limited his familiarity to 'Broken Windows' to Matthews' account of it. What is inexcusable about Bowling's article is that he not only misrepresents 'Broken Windows' – for example, 'Their [Wilson and Kelling's] main policy recommendation to the police is to "kick ass"' (548) – he had *Fixing Broken Windows* available to him. But this is another story.

14 In fact, I have listened to many speakers who rely on it and practically could have told them the chapter and verse of 'Replacing' they were using as they critiqued 'Broken Windows'.

15 This may well be an example of 'two peoples separated by a common language' (English and Americans). If it is, it makes the point of how careful scholars must be to understand the nuances of languages across cultures, especially technical terms like 'extra-legal'.

16 Interestingly, the experience in New York's subway mirrors Sampson and Raudenbush's finding (although not their interpretation of it): when order was restored, robberies declined dramatically.

References

Bittner, E. (1967) 'The Police on Skid Row: A Study of Peacekeeping', *American Sociological Review*, 32: 699–715.

Bowling, B. (1999) 'The Rise and Fall of New York Murder: Zero Tolerance or Crack's Decline', *British Journal of Criminology*, 39(4): 531–54.

Braga, A. (1999) 'Problem-oriented Policing in Violent Crime Places: A Randomized Controlled Experiment', *Criminology*, 37(3): 541–80.

Bratton, W. (1998) *Turnaround*, New York: Random House.

Chaiken, J. (1975) *The Criminal Investigation Process: Volume II. Survey of Municipal and County Police Departments*, The Rand Corporation, R-1777-DOJ.

Chicago *v*. Morales, 1998 (97–1121), 177 Ill. 2d 440 687 N.E. 2d53.

Cornish, D. B. and Clarke, R. V. (1986) *Situational Prevention, Displacement of Crime and Rational Choice Theory*, London: HMSO, 1–16.

Felson, M. and Cohen, L. (1980) 'Human Ecology and Crime: A Routine Activity Approach', *Human Ecology*, 8(4): 389–406.

Fukuyama, F. (1999) *The Great Disruption: Human Nature and the Reconstitution of Social Order*, New York: Basic Books.

Fyfe, J. (2000) 'Reflections on the Diallo Case', *Subject to Debate. A Newsletter of the Police Executive Research Forum*, 14: 4.

Gladwell, M. (2000) *The Tipping Point: How Little Things Can Make a Big Difference*, Boston: Little, Brown, and Company.

Harcourt, B. E. (1998) 'Reflecting on the Subject: A Critique of the Social Influence Conception of Deterrence, the Broken Windows Theory, and Order-Maintenance Policing New York Style', *Michigan Law Review*, 97(2): 290–389.

Jacobs, J. (1961) *The Death and Life of Great American Cities*, New York: Vintage.

Kansas City Police Department (1977) *Response Time Analysis: Volume II – Part I Crime Analysis*, Kansas City, MO.

Kelling, G. L. (1978) 'Police Field Services and Crime: The Presumed Effects of a Capacity', *Crime and Delinquency – Hackensack, NJ*, 24(2): 173–84.

—— (1998) 'Crime Control, the Police, and Culture Wars: Broken Windows and Cultural Pluralism', in *Perspectives on Crime and Justice: 1997–1998 Lecture Series*, volume II, US Department of Justice, Office of Justice Programs, National Institute of Justice.

—— (1999) *Broken Windows and Police Discretion*, National Institute of Justice Research Report, NCJ178259.

—— and Coles, C. M. (1996) *Fixing Broken Windows: Restoring Order and Reducing Crime in Our Communities*, New York: The Free Press.

——, Pate, T., Dieckman, D. and Brown, C. E. (1974) *The Kansas City Preventive Patrol Experiment*, Washington, DC: Police Foundation.

Kennedy, D. M. (1997) 'Pulling Levers: Chronic Offenders, High-Crime Settings, and a Theory of Prevention', *Valparaiso Law Review*, 31: 449–84.

McNamara, J. D. (1997) 'Brutality in the Name of Public Safety', *Los Angeles Times*, August: M 1 and 3.

Maple, J. (1999) *The Crime Fighter: Putting the Bad Guys Out of Business*, New York: Doubleday.

Matthews, R. (1992) 'Replacing "Broken Windows": Crime, Incivilities and Urban Change', in R. Matthews and J. Young (eds) *Issues in Realist Criminology*, London: Sage Publications, 19–50.

Myerson, H. (1998) 'Why Liberalism Fled the City …', *The American Prospect*, March–April: 46–52.

The Newark Foot Patrol Experiment (1981) Washington, DC: Police Foundation.

Norquist, J. (1999) *The Wealth of Cities: Revitalizing the Centers of American Life*, New York: Perseus Books.

Podhoretz, N. (1999) 'My New York', *National Review*, June: 35–41.

President's Commission on Law Enforcement and Administration of Justice (1967) *The Challenge of Crime in a Free Society*, Washington, DC: US Government Printing Office.

Sampson, R. J. and Raudenbush, S. (undated) 'A New Look at Crime and Disorder in Urban Neighborhoods', Press Release. p. 1.

—— (1999) 'Systematic Social Observations of Public Spaces: A New Look at Disorder in Urban Neighborhoods', *American Journal of Sociology*, 105(3): 603–51.

Sherman, L. W., Shaw, J. W. and Rogan, D. F. (1995) *The Kansas City Gun Experiment*, National Institute of Justice, Research in Brief, US Department of Justice, Washington DC.

Siegel, F. (1992) 'Reclaiming Our Public Spaces', *The City Journal*, Spring: 37.

Skogan, W. G. (1990) *Disorder and Decline: Crime and the Spiral of Urban Decay in American Neighborhoods*, New York: Free Press.

Stewart, G. (1998) 'Black Codes and Broken Windows: The Legacy of Racial Hegemony in Anti-Gang Civil Injunctions', *The Yale Law Journal*, 107(7): 2249–79.

Walker, S. (1984) '"Broken Windows" and Fractured History: The Use and Misuse of History in Recent Patrol Analysis', *Justice Quarterly*, 1(1): 75–90.

Wilson, J. Q. (1999) Foreword in George L. Kelling and Catherine M. Coles, *Fixing Broken Windows: Restoring Order and Reducing Crime in Our Communities*, New York: The Free Press.

—— and Kelling, G. L. (1982) 'Broken Windows: The Police and Neighborhood Safety', *Atlantic Monthly*, March: 29–38.

6 Ethnic minorities and community safety

Marian FitzGerald

Introduction

The 1999 Macpherson report into the murder of the black London teenager Stephen Lawrence set the tone and the content of the British government's commitments to ethnic minority communities on issues of crime and community safety. These commitments were unprecedented in that not only were they explicit and high profile but they were also attached to a wide-ranging programme of action. This chapter examines what has been achieved to date with regard to two key issues addressed by the programme of action – stop and search and racist incidents. I raise a number of questions which will need to be resolved if the government is to meet these specific commitments in the context of its commitments to community safety more widely.

In March 1999, the Home Office, the Lord Chancellor's Department and the Attorney General published a Strategic Plan for 1999 to 2002, along with a Business Plan for its implementation in the first year. The plans represented a 'new approach in working together', and the Foreword from the three ministers invokes a protean notion of 'community'. One of the priorities they identified was 'improving the confidence of the community as a whole, but especially the ethnic minority communities, in the criminal justice system' (Home Office 1999a). That is, the priority is based on the notion of a single community, but there is a further assumption that – within a minority section of this community – there is also a multiplicity of communities.

The context in which the government made this commitment was strongly influenced by the report of the inquiry into the death of the black teenager, Stephen Lawrence. Shortly after coming to office in 1997, the Home Secretary appointed the senior judge Sir William Macpherson of Cluny to 'inquire into the matters arising from the death of Stephen Lawrence on 22 April 1993 to date, in order particularly to identify the lessons to be learned for the investigation and prosecution of racially motivated crimes' (Macpherson 1999: 6).

Three members were appointed to assist Sir William – a black bishop, the retired deputy chief constable of a provincial force and the chair of the Jewish Council for Social Responsibility. Late in 1997 they began a series of public hearings which continued until the summer of 1998. These were largely concerned with the murder itself and its investigation. Part two of the inquiry began in the autumn of 1998, when they turned their attention to the investigation and prosecution of racially motivated crimes. Eschewing 'a narrow interpretation of our terms of reference', they chose at this stage to broaden their focus to what they perceived to be the central problem, 'the lack of trust which exists between the police and the minority ethnic communities' (Macpherson 1999: 311).

The report was eventually published in February 1999; and its overall conclusion was that 'the investigation was marred by a combination of professional incompetence, institutional racism and a failure of leadership by senior officers'. It defined the problem of 'institutional racism' as:

> The collective failure of an organisation to provide an appropriate and professional service to people because of their colour, culture or ethnic origin. It can be seen or detected in processes, attitudes and behaviour which amount to discrimination through unwitting prejudice, ignorance, thoughtlessness, and racist stereotyping which disadvantage minority ethnic people.
>
> (Macpherson 1999: 321)

The problem was not peculiar to the Metropolitan Police Service (MPS), it affected all police services; and other institutions and organisations could not be complacent: 'Collective failure is apparent in many of them, including the Criminal Justice system' (*ibid.*: 321). The report made seventy recommendations, all of which were accepted by the government, albeit a small number were accepted only in principle or subject to 'further consideration'; and a month after the report appeared, the Home Secretary published his Action Plan for implementing them (Home Office 1999b). The process was to be overseen by a steering group personally chaired by the Home Secretary. The success of the Action Plan was to be measured 'using existing indicators in 1999/2000', but 'more comprehensive indicators' would be put in place from 2000 onwards (Home Office 1999b: 3).

Even though the main body of the report was taken up with the first part of the inquiry and part two was covered in just six of its 300-plus pages, most of its recommendations related to part two. They were addressed to a range of agencies in addition to the police, including government departments and local authorities. Those addressed to the police included a number which focused on stop and search and racist incidents. Police performance in both areas featured strongly in the report's description of the 'central problem' of ethnic minorities' lack of trust in the police. For many years they have also served as a dual focus of research into issues concerning ethnic minorities in Britain as victims and as suspects of crime.

The data available on both stop and search and racist incidents are of particular symbolic importance in showing the extent to which the government is meeting its stated commitment to ethnic minorities. Setting the figures in context, though, and examining the trends they show highlights a number of largely unacknowledged tensions between these commitments and other government priorities.

At the time of writing, published statistics for all forces were available only up to the end of the financial year 1998–99. This means that the last two years in these series effectively reflect, first, the situation inherited by the government on coming to office; and second, the year of the Macpherson Inquiry. The figures were published in the now annual Home Office publications on 'race and the criminal justice system'. These were originally instigated under s95 of the 1991 Criminal Justice Act and are commonly referred to as 's95 publications'.

In addition to these national figures, the Performance and Information Bureau of the MPS provided me with statistics *ad hoc* on both stop and search and racist incidents for the year 1999–2000. These shed further light on developments in London in the year following the Macpherson report. While London may not be typical of other areas, it is the force most directly affected by the inquiry; and, as this chapter highlights, it has a major influence on the national statistics for both searches and racist incidents.

Stop and search

Statistical sources

Although police stops have long been a major source of tension between black people and the police, it was not until 1993 that any obligation was placed on forces systematically to monitor the issue. The 1984 Police and Criminal Evidence Act (PACE) had already required all police forces to provide the Home Office with raw figures on searches undertaken following a stop under s1 of the Act; and London had consistently accounted for nearly half of the national total. Since concerns about the searching of black people in the capital predated PACE (not least as an important factor in triggering the Brixton riots of 1981), the MPS had already kept an ethnic breakdown of the figures for some years. Numerous studies, however, supported widespread anecdotal evidence that recording across all forty-three police forces in England and Wales was very unreliable (Brown 1997).

At first, the police inspectorate (HMIC) simply asked forces to monitor which of their records related to white people and which to a generic category of ethnic minorities – even though the existing research suggested that this would mask the extent of searches on black people relative to whites. Three years later, though, the Home Office asked for the non-white category to be broken down into 'black', 'Asian' or 'other' minorities (FitzGerald and Sibbitt 1997). The first published Home Office figures covered the financial year 1996 to 1997, and they compared the numbers of recorded searches with the 1991 Census population figures for each police force. The 1997 figures confirmed that, on this yardstick, black people were significantly more likely to be searched by the police than white people but there was no comparable over-representation of Asians. This pattern was repeated again the following year – that is, the year which ended just as the Macpherson Inquiry got underway.

Recent trends

Figures for the year during which the Macpherson Inquiry was conducted, however, showed a fall of 15 per cent in the number of black people searched in England and Wales, with a more modest drop (6 per cent) for Asians. Read superficially, the figures might imply that the inquiry was already proving effective in reducing the level of searches on black people relative to whites. In fact, the national figures give a misleading picture of trends for two inter-related reasons.

The first is that the different minority populations are not distributed evenly. Nearly two-thirds of all black people (62 per cent) live in London and the next largest black community is in the West Midlands which accounts for a further 9 per cent. The Asian population is more dispersed; but again the main areas of settlement are London and the West Midlands, which account respectively for 35 and 16 per cent of the population. By contrast, only 17 per cent of the white population lives in these two conurbations put together. What happens in these two force areas, therefore, will significantly affect any presumed 'national' picture for both the black and the Asian group; and it may distort their national showing relative to the white population. In effect, national trends for black people are largely determined by what happens in London.

The second reason why the national figures are misleading is that there is wide variation in the recorded use of the power by different forces. The Home Office 's95' figures (Home Office 1999b) gave a national figure of twenty-two PACE searches per thousand population in 1997 and 1998; but the figures for individual forces ranged from four to just under a hundred. For London the number was fifty-one per thousand; but in the West Midlands it was only nineteen. In the year of the Macpherson Inquiry, the national average remained the same; but the London figure fell to forty-five per thousand and that in the West Midlands to eleven. Yet there was almost no change in the proportion of searches on black people in either area. In London the proportion of black people searched fell by one percentage point (from 26 to 25 per cent); but in the West Midlands it rose from 14 to 15 per cent, with a higher rise for Asians (from 17 to 20 per cent).

The apparent fall in the proportion of searches on black people during the year of the inquiry, therefore, did not represent any marked drop in searches on black people *per se*. It was largely due to the fall in searches on all groups in London. Meanwhile, the rise in the proportion of black people searched in the West Midlands had no effective impact on the national figures, despite the relatively large number of black people in the area. This was because the fall occurred in a force which contributed relatively little to the national total in the first place.

Developments in London

On closer inspection, the figures for London show that this fall during the year of the Macpherson Inquiry was especially precipitate in the early part of 1999 – the point at which the report was awaited. At the same time there was a significant increase in recorded crime in London; and sections of the media were sympathetic to claims by some police officers that the two phenomena were associated.

Anticipating the wider criticisms the inquiry was likely to level at them, the MPS had begun to try to seize the initiative. Its new approach to tackling racist incidents is described in the next section; but it had also recognised stop and search as a key issue on which action was needed. At the beginning of 1998, therefore, it designated five pilot sites (later increased to seven) to try out a new approach to stop and search. The initiative largely consisted of intensified scrutiny of two things: officers' performance within and across the pilot sites; and statistical data. Its stated aims were to ensure that the power was used both more effectively and fairly. Progress was to be closely monitored throughout and the results were to be evaluated at the end of the first year.

In the course of this monitoring and evaluation it became apparent that the data already held by the MPS were a potentially rich source of new insights into the pattern of searches and the factors which drove these. Research into the impact of the pilots required more detailed analyses of these data than had ever previously been undertaken, and it generated further information *ad hoc* to complement these analyses (FitzGerald 1999a; 1999b).

Effectiveness

The interim evaluation report in the summer of 1999 showed a marked improvement in the arrest rate from searches – which has conventionally been used as the key measure of success. However, it also showed that this success should not be taken entirely at face value. Although the MPS was known to record a higher proportion of its searches than other forces (FitzGerald and Hale, forthcoming), it became apparent that many searches in London were still going unrecorded. Where searches resulted in an arrest, officers might simply not bother to complete a record for the search in addition to doing the paperwork for the arrest. Once the search figures were put under the twin spotlights of the pilots and the Macpherson Inquiry, this provided a major incentive to rectify these omissions. Thus the apparent improvement in the arrest rate gave the impression that the power was being targeted more effectively; yet much of it was probably due simply to improved statistical housekeeping.

The focus on the improved arrest rate distracted attention from a development which was arguably far more important in terms of effectiveness. It was taking place in the context of a major fall in searches overall which had set in as the Macpherson Inquiry started. The fall in searches became more precipitate as the inquiry moved into phase two and dropped more sharply still in anticipation of the report. While the burst of statistical housekeeping referred to above meant

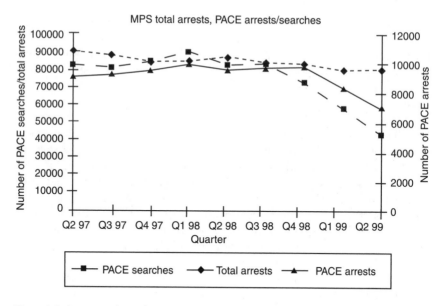

Figure 6.1 Arrests and searches: London 1997–1999

Source: MPS Performance Information Bureau (PIB)

that the number of arrests attributed to searches held up for a while, by the last quarter of 1998 they too started to plummet. While the improved arrest rate was being represented as a success, in practice searches were now contributing far less to arrests overall (see Figure 6.1).

It cannot be assumed, however, that the fall in arrests from searches had any serious consequences for community safety. The largest proportion of arrests from searches was for drugs; and data from the pilot sites confirmed that by far the majority of these drugs arrests were for personal possession of small amounts of cannabis. Cannabis use is not believed to be causally associated with other types of offending; nor does it appear to be a matter of public concern – except inasmuch as the fact that it is illegal may serve to legitimate potentially discriminatory police searches (Young 1994; Runciman 2000). The second largest category of searches was for stolen property; and a fall here also seemed unlikely to have any significant impact on the crime figures. Burglary is by far the largest category of property crime, but only a small minority of burglaries are cleared up through arrests of any sort and only a small minority of these would have been the result of a search (see FitzGerald and Sibbitt 1997: 70).

On the other hand, searches for offensive weapons and firearms or for going equipped to steal or burgle together accounted for under 15 per cent of search arrests early in 1998. Their relative insignificance in the context of searches overall meant that their potential importance in the context of community safety was largely overlooked. Yet searches for offensive weapons and firearms or for going equipped to steal or burgle consistently produced the majority of all arrests for these preparatory offences. So, while the decrease in searches generally might have little influence on levels of crime overall, the fall in arrests in these particular categories might nonetheless have a disproportionate impact.

The claims of a link between the rise in crime and the fall in searches overall, seemed almost certain to be spurious; although they were as difficult to disprove as to prove using the administrative statistics available. Academic analysis, however, did find a completely counter-intuitive statistical relationship between the sudden fall in searches and the marked rise in crime which followed in the early months of 1999 (Penzer 1999). The explanations for this finding are likely to be complex. It cannot be taken to imply that the fall in searches *per se* caused a rise in crime or even that the rise in crime was directly linked to the fall in searches for offensive weapons, firearms and going equipped. However, other research has found an association between a sudden fall in the use of searches and a rise in crime (NACRO 1997). The findings from the MPS study suggest that it is worth undertaking further work to explore the reasons for this pattern; and this might usefully focus on the preventive effect of the power – both direct and indirect.

The issue of disproportionality

In addition to confirming existing concerns about drugs searches, the MPS study systematically confirmed other well-rehearsed complaints about the way the power was used. It also revealed new ones, though, and it began to set the question of 'disproportionality' in a different light. The final report (FitzGerald 1999b) showed that there was more support in principle for the power as a means to improve community safety than might have been expected. The support came from all ethnic groups, including from young people who had themselves been searched. However, there was widespread dissatisfaction with the gratuitously abrasive way it was applied by many police officers.

The report also highlighted considerable variability in the extent to which the targeting of searches was directly related to patterns of crime and it showed that searches seemed to be used on occasion beyond what was legitimate in terms of PACE. Of particular interest in the context of this chapter, however, was the way in which officers themselves often rationalised this by invoking considerations of community safety. Thus searches were seen as an effective way of gaining intelligence on people who were 'known' to the police; and the power was also used to break up and move on groups of youths whose very presence constituted a nuisance or a perceived threat to others. Yet these purported benefits to some sections of the community were having a negative effect on those sections of the community who were on the receiving end of the searches. In the case of people already known to the police, they constitute a form of harassment. At the same time, the use of the power as a means of social control was arguably criminalising people who were not previously known to the police but who were arrested for possession of cannabis where searches were used as a means of social control on groups of young people.

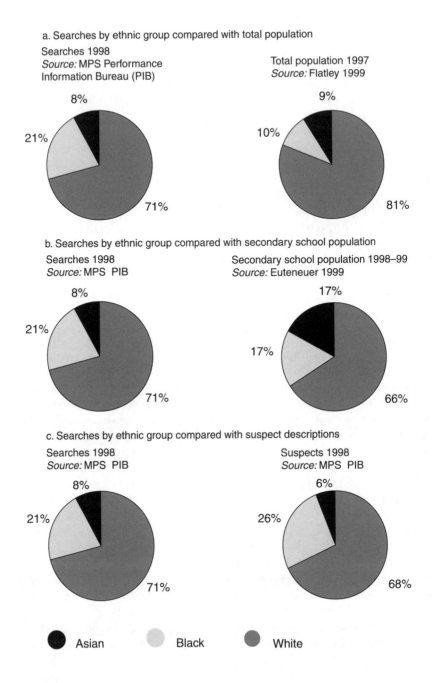

Figure 6.2 Searches, population and suspects: London 1998–1999

With regard to the ethnic patterns in the search figures, the study exposed numerous complexities in interpreting local statistics. It established that comparisons with the local population in general were irrelevant and potentially misleading for many reasons, not least because of the non-resident population represented in the search figures. In some areas people from outside the area accounted for the majority of those people searched; but there were further ethnic variations within this. The two main influences on the ethnic patterns in the search figures, though, appeared to be age and the extent to which different groups featured among the suspects described in crime reports. This is illustrated by Figure 6.2 which compares the pattern of searches on different ethnic groups in London with: (a) the population at large; (b) the population of secondary school age; and (c) the descriptions of suspects of crime.

Figure 6.2a shows the basis on which 'disproportionality' has usually been calculated. It confirms the extent to which, measured in this way, black people are over-represented in the search figures in relation to their presence in the population at large. Yet Figure 6.2b shows that this 'over-representation' reduces considerably when age is taken into account since there are important variations in the age structures of the different ethnic groups. This is especially relevant in the context of community safety. For the young and the old may be thought of as different communities of interest whose conflicting needs may sometimes be difficult to reconcile. In many areas white people will constitute a much higher than average proportion of the old population while ethnic minorities constitute a much higher than average proportion of the youth population than is apparent from figures for the population as a whole. In over half of the thirty-two London boroughs, ethnic minorities account for 45 per cent or more of the school age population; and in some they constitute a majority of the young people in the area (FitzGerald 2000). This not only highlights the importance of controlling for age with some precision when making inter-ethnic comparisons. It also flags up the danger of racialising what are essentially age-related differences by the uncritical use of crude ethnic statistics.

In fact, the closest match for the ethnic composition of the search figures in Figure 6.2 is with descriptions given to the police of suspects of crime (6.2c). Importantly, the study also showed that black people were no more likely than white people to be stopped by police officers acting entirely on their own discretion. It established that black people who were searched were as likely as white people to have previous criminal records and they were arrested at the same rate following searches. Taken together, the evidence strongly suggested that – far from disappearing – disproportionality would actually get worse if officers were allowed only to search people in connection with crime reports. The only obvious way of achieving a reduction in the ethnic differential between black and white people in the search statistics, therefore, might be to weight the police response to victims of crime according to their description of the suspect. Yet it is hard to imagine how such an approach could be acceptably presented in the context of local community safety strategies, regardless of any implications for their successful implementation.

On the other hand, the research identified significant issues with regard to searches on Asians which had been overlooked in a debate framed by traditional assumptions about (dis)proportionality. As Figure 6.2a also shows, Asians were not searched disproportionately when compared with their presence in the population at large or even in relation to their presence in the school age population (6.2b). However, they were searched more than would be expected from descriptions of suspects in crime reports (6.2c). Moreover, this disparity was much starker in the few areas with relatively large Asian populations. At the same time, the arrest rates from searches for Asians at the beginning of the study were much lower than for white or black people; and those searched were much younger than the average for all groups. Proportionately many fewer of the Asians had criminal records; they were more likely to be searched in groups; those groups tend on average to be larger; and a higher proportion of searches on Asians were for drugs.

In other words, the Asians – and in particular the poorer, younger groups within this supposed community – were at special risk from the use of the power as a mechanism of social control. Their age structure meant that the cohort at the peak age for offending was now much larger than in the past, so increasingly large numbers of these young people had begun to experience the confrontational way in which the power was often applied. In so far as it was starting to criminalise them for possession of cannabis, the study argued that searches might yet prove the equivalent of the 'Sus' laws which did so much damage to police relations with the parallel generation of black youth twenty years ago (Demuth 1978).

For black people the implications of the research were different. They challenged the orthodox view that the 'over-representation' of black people in the figures relative to their presence in the population at large could serve as a proxy measure for police discrimination. But this did not imply that there was no particular cause for concern in relation to black people. Rather, black people were disproportionately suffering from the abuse of the power to harass people 'known' to the police. It also meant that the overbearing and aggressive manner of officers (whether or not they were using the power legitimately) was having a disproportionate impact on black people – including black people who were innocent of any crime. The bottom line, however, was that the extent to which the power is used would make little difference to 'disproportionality' as traditionally conceived. Whether the power was used more or whether it is cut back to the minimum, the black-white ratio within it was unlikely significantly to change.

Implications

Taken together, these findings posed a need for new thinking both about the effectiveness of the power and about whether it was being used fairly. Searches in general were not being used effectively to tackle crime. Although they had fallen dramatically, the fall had not occurred as the result of any explicit intervention – still less one which was coherently designed to target the power better or to address the problems associated with it. Yet, from the point of view of community safety, there was more risk associated with this sudden fall than might have been expected and some types of search (albeit a minority) might yet prove indispensable for the prevention of crime unless equally effective and more acceptable alternatives could be found.

At the same time, the disproportionate impact of the power on black people and the potential for damage to police relations with future generations of young Asians added particular urgency to the need to tackle generic problems with the way the search power was used. However, it was essential to recognise that these were problems which affected the community as a whole and to tackle them as such. Any attempt at remedial action which conceived of the problems as if they only affected the ethnic minority communities, would be treating symptoms rather than causes. The danger was that these problems were simply being scaled down until the Macpherson effect dissipated while crime would remain at the level to which it had risen during the time when the fall in searches was at its sharpest. Meanwhile, trends in recorded racial incidents also give cause for concern. They too call into question conventional interpretations based on simple headline statistics and suggest that these data also need to be seen in a wider context.

Racist incidents

Statistical sources

The issue of racial violence and harassment had long been a problem for minority communities in certain areas, but the issue reached the national policy agenda in the late 1970s and early 1980s. In 1985 the Association of Chief Police Officers responded to sustained criticism of the police response by adopting an all-embracing definition of a 'racial incident'. This attempted to overcome the frequent tensions between 'victims' and officers' perceptions of racial motivation by requiring forces henceforth to record all incidents reported to them in which it appears to the reporting or investigating officer that the complaint involves an element of racial motivation, or which includes an allegation of racial motivation made by any person. That is, the definition deliberately embraced non-criminal forms of harassment and it did not require racism to be the primary motivating factor. Hard evidence was not required, only a perception or 'an allegation' and officers were not to have the final decision about whether the incident should be recorded as racially motivated.

These figures, too, were soon requested by HMIC – albeit forces were only asked for a raw number. There was no suggestion that it might also be relevant to break the figures down by offence type or by the ethnicity of the victims and perpetrators. Publication of force totals was *ad hoc* at first, but the figures were among the few sources of relevant statistics available in 1991, so they appeared in the s95 publications from the outset. Meanwhile, the Home Office British

Crime Survey (BCS) had introduced an ethnic oversample in 1988; and in the same year it asked a question about racial harassment (Mayhew *et al.* 1989). Victims were asked if they believed what had happened to them was racially motivated. However, the question was only asked of black and Asian respondents and, while the survey covered threats as well as crimes, it did not cover the low level nuisance behaviour which was typical of much harassment.

A study carried out by the Home Office in 1997 showed that few police forces collected detailed figures on the racial incidents they recorded (Maynard and Read 1997). Where these were available, though, they broadly confirmed the consistent pattern of victims' experiences described by the British Crime Survey and earlier studies (FitzGerald and Ellis 1989). Unsurprisingly, the largest single category of racist incident (38 per cent) was 'verbal abuse', which is the most common currency of antagonism – whether between individuals or groups. Along with damage to property, verbal abuse accounted for well over half of all incidents across the fourteen forces covered by the study, with miscellaneous 'assaults' making up a further 21 per cent. Only 2 per cent of racial incidents were classified as 'serious crimes'.

In the same year, the Crown Prosecution Service published the first report of its 'Racial Incidents Monitoring Scheme'. This included a breakdown of the type of charges put by the police to the Crown Prosecution Service (CPS) in the previous year which the CPS viewed as racially motivated. It too showed a preponderance of less serious offences, with 49 per cent classified as public order and a further 14 per cent as criminal damage. Just over a quarter (27 per cent) were assaults (CPS 1997).

Part one of the Macpherson Inquiry was concerned with the most serious of all racially motivated offences: murder. But in part two it specifically criticised the police for failing to realise: 'the impact of less serious, non-crime incidents upon the minority communities'(Macpherson 1999: 313). It recommended a simplified version of the ACPO definition and it insisted on changing the term 'racial' to 'racist'. The new definition adopted by the Home Secretary and by all police forces was: 'an incident which is perceived to be racist by the victim or any other person'.

Recent trends

Despite its limitations, the BCS had become increasingly important as a benchmark against which to measure trends in the police figures. For it not only reflected the underlying levels of harassment experienced by victims, it also asked them whether they had reported incidents to the police. The police figures steadily began to rise through the early 1990s (see Figure 6.3). Although the British Crime Survey showed no change in the underlying rate of racist victimisation, it did suggest that there was a significant shortfall in the numbers of incidents being recorded by the police relative to those reported to them (Aye-Maung and Mirrlees-Black 1994; FitzGerald and Hale 1996a; Percy 1998). Since there was no evidence of any significant increase in levels of reporting

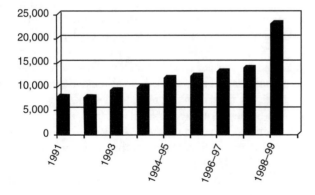

Figure 6.3 Recorded racial incidents in England and Wales, 1991–1999
Source: Home Office s95 reports

either, the gradual rise in the police figures up to 1996 mainly represented a closing of this recording gap.

As with searches, the Macpherson Inquiry appeared already to have had a significant impact on the racial incident figures before it even reported. Following year-on-year rises of less than 10 per cent since the first s95 report, the records for the financial year 1998 to 1999 showed a 66 per cent increase (see Figure 6.3).

Developments in London

Meanwhile, the MPS had been proactive on the issue of racial incidents as well as with regard to stop and search. The Race and Violent Crimes Task Force, set up at New Scotland Yard in August 1998, rapidly began to establish a high profile in the media and elsewhere. Under the charismatic leadership of Deputy Assistant Commissioner John Grieve, it publicly took a robust – even aggressive – approach to tackling racism. It mounted poster campaigns, opened the MPS to its critics by setting up a lay advisers group to assist it and took road shows out to public meetings across London. Within the force, the unit also spawned a wide range of initiatives to raise standards and to improve performance and co-ordination, including increasing the intelligence available for dealing with what it increasingly referred to as 'hate crime'.

The term 'hate crime' subsumed both racial and homophobic incidents. In recent years, both of these had increasingly fallen within the remit of 'Vulnerable Persons Units' which had developed somewhat *ad hoc* primarily to deal with domestic violence. Seizing the opportunities for restructuring in the move to borough-based policing, the Race and Violence Crimes Task Force had a specialist unit set up in each area. The core business of the units was their responsibility for racial and homophobic incidents as well as domestic violence (although there were some local additions to this), but the term 'vulnerable persons' was dropped. Despite the fact that their remit was limited to specified groups of victims, the new units were named 'Community Safety Units'.

While the total number of recorded incidents in England and Wales rose nationally by 66 per cent in 1998–1999 (i.e., the year of the Macpherson Inquiry), they increased by 188 per cent in London. This meant that the MPS now accounted for nearly half of all recorded racial incidents; and if London is removed from the total, the percentage increase in 1998–1999 would have been 50 per cent instead of 66 per cent. Figures available from the MPS at the time of writing showed a further, even larger increase for 1999–2000. The number of racial incidents recorded in London rose a further 211 per cent in the year following publication of the Macpherson report.

However, the more typical forms of victim experience appear consistently to have accounted for a much smaller proportion of incidents in London than those recorded elsewhere. The 1997 Home Office study, for example (op. cit.), showed that only 12 per cent of incidents were classified by the MPS as verbal abuse compared with an average of 38 per cent for all the forces in its sample. The CPS monitoring report showed a similar pattern. In 1998–1999, 50 per cent of charges were for public order offences in non-London forces compared to 28 per cent for assault; but the MPS figure for both was 37 per cent. This relative absence of incidents of low level harassment recorded by the MPS was identified as a problem by the police inspectorate in a report on community and race relations conducted in 1999. It fully acknowledged the pioneering work of the Race and Violent Crimes Task Force, but it specifically noted that 'the MPS was failing to capture those incidents referred to by some as low level harass-

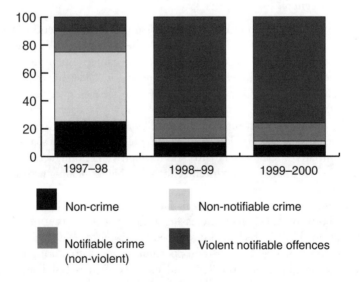

Figure 6.4 Trends in types of racial incidents recorded by the MPS, 1997–2000

Source: MPS Performance Information Bureau (PIB)

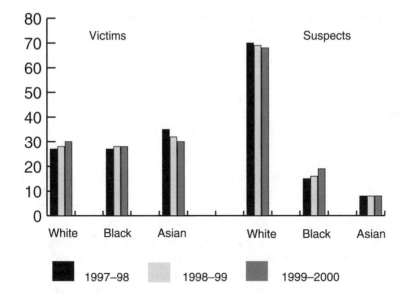

Figure 6.5 Victims and suspects of racist incidents by ethnic group, MPS 1997–2000
Source: MPS Performance Information Bureau (PIB)

ment, but which in fact do so much damage to the quality of life of victims' (Home Office 2000: 48).

The London figures during and after the Macpherson Inquiry show huge increases but they show little evidence to suggest that the concerns of Macpherson and the inspectorate with regard to 'low level harassment' are being addressed. The recorded increases were primarily in relation to crime rather than non-crime, and there was a further change in the balance of types of crime within this. Notifiable offences came to account for a much higher proportion of the crime incidents, and a progressively higher proportion of these were violent offences (see Figure 6.4).

Meanwhile, the MPS figures also present a more complex picture of the ethnicity of victims and of suspects than has been apparent from the terms in which the debate around racial incidents has usually been conducted. The debate has tended to assume that the victims of racism were primarily – if not exclusively – members of visible ethnic minorities and that the perpetrators were white. Yet both official definitions embrace all incidents irrespective of the ethnicity of the victim or the perpetrator, and the London figures had always shown a higher number of white victims than might have been supposed.

Following the publication of the Macpherson report, the proportion of victims of racist incidents recorded as white actually increased in the MPS. In 1999–2000, the proportion of white victims of racist incidents in London nearly equalled that of Asians, with a slightly smaller proportion of victims recorded as black. Meanwhile, although whites were still the main perpetrators (see Figure

6.5), a higher proportion of suspects were recorded as black than in previous years.

Implications

The statistics published by the Home Office tell us little about the real scale or nature of the problem of racist harassment and even less about how effectively the problem is being tackled. However, the BCS and the CPS reports provide some check, and the detailed information held by the MPS is capable of shedding further light on the situation in London.

With regard to the scale of the problem, the sudden increase in the crude s95 figures in 1998–1999 could have been due to any or all of three developments: (a) an increase in reporting; (b) an increase in the reported incidents which were actually recorded by the police; and/or (c) an increase in the underlying problem. Unfortunately, the BCS did not over-sample ethnic minorities in 1998, so there is no authoritative means of telling the extent to which each of these factors was implicated. Some tentative inferences can, however, be drawn.

It seems likely that reporting will have increased during a sustained period of sympathetic media coverage. High-profile statements of commitment by senior police officers may have encouraged more victims to report in the expectation that they would be taken seriously. Also, the Macpherson Inquiry had emphasised the extent to which racism could be implicit as well as explicit and this may have encouraged more victims who were reporting crimes additionally to identify any racist element to these. If so, this would also help to explain the increase in the MPS figures; for one would expect the serious crimes which were such an important component of this increase to have been reported in any event.

Additionally, though, the increase in the figures may include a backlash element. The 1999 study of searches (FitzGerald 1999a) produced incidental material which suggested that publicity surrounding the Macpherson Inquiry was indeed creating resentment among some white people. They believed that ethnic minorities were receiving privileged treatment; and several officers I interviewed spontaneously reported being taunted by white youths claiming that the police were picking on them because they no longer dared to search black people. One officer described a similar backlash among white victims of crime as follows:

> You know, people come up to you and they say 'I've just had this bloke smash the windows of my car in. What are you going to do about it?' And you say 'I'll take a report and that's the best I can do.' And they're turning round now and they're saying 'I suppose, if I was a black person you'd have detectives down here looking at my car', etc.

Anecdotally, it had always been claimed that some white victims of crime where the perpetrators were black have insisted *de facto* that these incidents were racially motivated. It seems entirely possible that such reporting may have increased in the context of the inquiry; and this would help to explain the increase in the proportion of white victims and of black suspects in the MPS figures.

Recording also seems likely to have increased as a result of the inquiry which is likely to have catalysed the pace at which the police had already begun to close the recording gap identified by the BCS. Alongside this, though, a back-lash element may also have been at work. Thus the officer quoted above had his own views on white victims' perceptions that black victims would receive special attention. He had added, 'They're probably right'.

The HMIC report had also noted:

> The view was widespread [among police officers] that the rationale behind the definition of racist incidents and the prescriptive approach to their recording was to provide a preferential service to minority ethnic communities thereby prejudicing the policing needs of the rest of society.
>
> (HMIC 2000: 44)

This suggests that some officers may themselves have actively connived in the white backlash by recording the type of perverse reporting referred to above. Both reporting and recording in this instance would, of course, fall strictly within the letter of the definition – even though they ran directly counter to its spirit.

The white backlash to the Macpherson Inquiry, however, will not only be reflected in the increase in the incidents reported to and recorded by the police. It seems almost inevitable that it also produced a rise in the *underlying level* of racial violence and harassment. The findings of existing studies of the actual and potential perpetrators of racial violence and harassment suggest that many come from marginalised groups within the white population. As justification for their activities, they draw heavily on perceptions of preferential treatment for minorities such as those cited above (Sibbitt 1997; Hewitt 1992 and 1996).

While the increase in the underlying level of racial violence and harassment may have occurred for reasons beyond the control of the police, it adds urgency to the need to show that the problem is being tackled effectively once it has occurred. However, the evidence of improvement here is, at best, limited. The most obvious measure of effectiveness comes from the CPS reports and from MPS data regarding judicial disposals, although these relate only to the minority of cases which are considered for prosecution. They show some improvement, but it is by no means commensurate with the scale of increase in the numbers of incidents recorded or their greater seriousness.

In 1998–1999 – the year which saw a 66 per cent overall increase in recorded incidents and a 188 per cent increase in London – there was also an increase in the number of actual charges involving racial motivation put to the CPS by the police. However, for England and Wales as a whole, the rise was only 10 per cent; and if the figures for London are removed it was only 4 per cent. Meanwhile in London, 12 per cent of recorded incidents resulted in judicial disposals (that is a charge or caution) in 1998–1999. This was exactly the same proportion as in the previous year; and in the following year there was an increase of just 1 per cent. Yet nearly two-thirds of all incidents were by now classified as violent notifiable offences compared to only 15 per cent in 1997–1998 (see Figure 6.4 above).

The Macpherson Inquiry and the government's response to its report significantly raised awareness of the problems of racial violence and harassment, along with expectations that the problem would be tackled with more vigour than in the past. Evidence of its impact to date, though, is mixed. The increase in the numbers recorded is encouraging in some degree, but is not matched by evidence of improved effectiveness – certainly in terms of dealing with the most common forms of the problem. These 'low level' incidents have a pervasive impact on the quality of life of victims and potential victims and this is compounded by heightened levels of fear associated with the problem (FitzGerald and Hale 1996b). For the present it seems possible that racist incidents in general may have increased. At the same time the heightened focus of the last two years on the relatively rare instances of extreme racial violence will have done nothing to allay the constant sense of threat felt by people whose level of fear of crime is already much higher than average (FitzGerald and Hale 1996b).

Discussion and conclusion

The Macpherson report was important as a symbol of the government's commitment to race equality in general. It also helped define that commitment in relation to the criminal justice system with regard to ethnic minorities both as suspects and as victims of crime. Yet there is little evidence that the expectations it raised on the part of ethnic minorities have been fulfilled; and at the same time tensions may arise between the priorities established by the report and the local priorities which have to be met under the Crime and Disorder Act (1998). The report's central finding of 'institutional racism' does little to resolve these tensions. For, once its cathartic effect has dissipated, it lacks analytical content. It has no legal force and, above all, it offers no practical basis for action. The problem as identified simply is the problem as described. The optimistic view is that this tautology will be enough to galvanise organisations to discern the causes of the problem for themselves and tackle them effectively. More pessimistically, though, the label of institutional racism may have three effects.

First, people who really are the cause of the problem may co-opt the idea that its nature is institutional rather than individual in order to deny any personal responsibility. Second, other individuals may feel personally accused because, collectively, they are the organisation, and the verdict that they are guilty of 'unconscious' racism is almost impossible to challenge. This may generate a sense of impotence at best and resentment at worst. Third, now the label is official, it is difficult to imagine it officially being lifted. But it is equally difficult to imagine how members of ethnic minorities can have confidence in a criminal justice system which is permanently marked in this way.

Inasmuch as the Macpherson report has any or all of these unforeseen consequences, it may further compound the potential tensions between the government's objectives on different fronts. To avoid this, additional thinking is needed which takes full account of the complex and fluid character of individuals' sense of community attachment. In particular, it needs to recognise that people do not define themselves exclusively in a single dimension – whether of ethnicity, gender, age or any of the other intersecting strands described by Yinger (1986). This means that individuals may be differentiated from each other on one dimension, but they have far more in common on other dimensions than may appear to divide them.

Achieving the government's objective of increasing the confidence of ethnic minorities in the criminal justice system does not require additional statistics so much as a more rigorous interrogation of those which are already available. In particular, it needs to take full account of the limitations of statistics. These include not only the crudeness of the ethnic categories used, which fail, for example, to capture especially vulnerable groups such as refugees and asylum seekers (many of whom will be subsumed within the omnibus 'white' category). Critical attention also needs to be paid to the ways in which administrative changes in recording practices may give a misleading impression of trends. Analyses of these data, in turn, need to take account of the fullest possible range of other relevant factors before assumptions are made about the reasons for apparent ethnic differences shown by the headline figures. Above all, though, the figures need to be interpreted in the light of understandings from qualitative research – especially when they are used to inform developments in policy and practice.

At the same time, systematic consideration needs to be given to the impact of criminal justice policy at its widest on different groups. Challenges to the abolition of the right to elect Crown Court trial have drawn attention to the potential implications for black defendants (Bridges 2000). However, less publicity has been given to other developments whose disproportionately adverse effect on ethnic minority suspects and offenders do not appear to have been taken into consideration at all. For example, the right of prospective employers to check on job applicants through the new Criminal Records Agency seems likely further to disadvantage young black men in the labour market.

Coupled with this, though, it is essential to make the link between aspects of criminal justice policy and practice whose disproportionate impact on certain groups highlights wider areas of concern. For example, the majority of the 3,000 miscarriages of justice predicted by Bridges (2000) as a result of the abolition of the right to trial by jury will be white. Moreover, the victims (of whatever ethnic origin) may be affected differentially depending on where they live – or even which court they appear before within that area. Thus the Home Office Criminal Statistics suggests that there are considerable variations by area in the rate at which magistrates themselves refer triable-either-way cases to the Crown Court; and a recent Home Office study highlighted the persistence of unevenness in sentencing practice in different areas (Flood-Page and Mackie 1998). Indeed, an important finding of Hood's study of sentencing of ethnic minorities in the Crown Court related to the differences in outcomes for defendants in general between different Crown Court centres within the West Midlands. It was only in some that he found further differences in the sentencing of the main ethnic group (Hood 1992).

As long as the criminal justice system remains capable of producing different outcomes for similarly placed individuals irrespective of ethnicity, it cannot be expected to treat any given group with consistent fairness. It is doubtful, therefore, that the government can achieve its particular aims with regard to ethnic minorities independently of its broader objective of 'improving the confidence of the community as a whole in the criminal justice system'. Ironically, if other sections of the community believe that the government is trying to address the unfair treatment received by minorities while neglecting their own grievances, this may further undermine their own confidence in the system, as well as having damaging consequences for minorities themselves.

This last point is highly relevant to the issues raised here about local community safety strategies. Especially in urban areas (where the larger part of the ethnic minority populations tend to live) these strategies address a notional community which is defined largely by administrative and political boundaries. In effect these local 'communities' comprise numbers of different communities of interest who simply happen to share (but may also contest) the same space, and this may pose particular difficulties in developing and implementing local community safety strategies. Yet, in fact, many different sections of local populations share the same concerns, but they may be unaware of what they have in common and they lack any framework in which they might work together on problems which affect them all. A study undertaken for the Home Office a number of years ago provided practical examples of how this could be achieved in a range of different local contexts. In particular, it showed what makes the difference between projects which effectively address common interests by transcending perceptions of ethnic difference and those which fail where the problems facing them become racialised (Jeffers *et al.* 1996).

Many of the concerns shared by local people regardless of ethnicity relate to issues of crime and disorder. Looked at in this way, the requirements of the Crime and Disorder Act (1998) could actually present opportunities for breaking down suspicion and antagonism based on perceived ethnic difference. Exploiting these opportunities would not be easy; nor would it eliminate the dilemmas and challenges identified by this chapter. It might, however, serve to minimise some of the tensions which have arisen from the perception that meeting the needs of ethnic minorities is inimical to meeting the needs of the majority population. As such, it might help offset the damage this perception may do to any prospect of achieving the ideal implied by the notion of 'the community as whole'.

References

Aye Maung, N. and Mirrlees-Black, C. (1994) *Racially Motivated Crime: a British Crime Survey Analysis*, London: Home Office.

Bridges, L. (2000) 'Limiting the Right to Jury Trial – Half Truths and False Assumptions', *Statewatch*, 10(1): 17–19.

Brown, D. (1997) *PACE Ten Years On: A Review of the Research*, London: Home Office.

Crown Prosecution Service (1997) *CPS Racist Incident Monitoring Scheme: Report on Year Ending 31 March 1997*, London: Crown Prosecution Service.

Demuth, C. (1978) *Sus, a Report on the Vagrancy Act 1824*, London: Runnymede Trust.

Euteneuer, R. (1999) *Education in London: Key Facts*, London: London Research Centre.

FitzGerald, M. (1999a) *Searches in London: Interim Evaluation of Year One of Programme of Action*, London: Metropolitan Police. Online. Available: http://www.met.police.uk/mps/htm

—— (1999b) *Searches in London: Final Report*, London: Metropolitan Police. Online. Available: http//www.met.police.uk/mps/htm

—— (2000) *London Borough Profiles: Social and Crime Characteristics. London*, London: London School of Economics and South Bank University. Online. Available: http//www.policingforlondon.org (September 2000).

FitzGerald, M. and Ellis, T. (1989) 'Racial Harassment: The Evidence', in C. Kemp (ed.) *Current Issues in Criminological Research*, Bristol: Bristol and Bath Centre for Criminal Justice.

FitzGerald, M. and Hale C. (1996a) *Ethnic Minorities: Victimisation and Racial Harassment: Findings From the 1988 and 1992 British Crime Surveys*, London: Home Office.

—— (1996b) 'Ethnic Minorities and Fear of Crime', unpublished paper presented to ESRC workshop on Fear of Crime. Manchester, 18 April.

—— (forthcoming) 'Stops, Searches and the Limitations of Ethnic Data', *Howard Journal*.

FitzGerald, M. and Sibbitt, R. (1997) *Ethnic Monitoring in Police Forces: A Beginning*, London: Home Office.

Flatley, J. (1999) *Social Care in London: Trends in Social Services' Activity 1993–97*, London: London Research Centre.

Flood-Page, C. and Mackie, A. (1998) *Sentencing Practice: An Examination of Decisions in Magistrates Courts and the Crown Court in the mid-1990's*, London: Home Office.

Her Majesty's Inspectorate of Constabulary (2000) *Policing in London: 'Winning Consent' – a Review of Murder Investigation and Community and Race Relations Issues in the Metropolitan Police Service*, London: Home Office.

Hewitt, R. (1992) *Sagaland: Youth Culture, Racism and Education: A Report on Research Carried out in Thamesmead*, London: University of London and London Borough of Greenwich.

—— (1996) *Routes of Racism: The Social Basis of Racist Action*, Staffordshire: Trentham Books.

Home Office (1999a) *Criminal Justice System: Strategic Plan 1999–2002 and Business Plan 1999–2000*, London: Home Office, Lord Chancellor's Department and Attorney General's Office.

—— (1999b) *Statistics on Race and the Criminal Justice System: A Home Office Publication Under section 95 of the Criminal Justice Act 1991*, London: Home Office.

—— (2000) *Statistics on Race and the Criminal Justice System*, London: Research, Development and Statistics Directorate, Home Office.

Hood, R. (1992) *Race and Sentencing*, Oxford: Oxford University Press.

Jeffers, S., Hoggett, P. and Harrison, L. (1996) 'Race, Ethnicity and Community in three Localities', *New Community*, 22(1): 111–26.

Macpherson, W. (1999) *The Stephen Lawrence Inquiry*, London: The Stationery Office.

Mayhew, P. Dowds, L. and Elliott, D. (1989) *The 1988 British Crime Survey*, London: Home Office.

Maynard, W. and Reed, T. (1997) *Policing Racially Motivated Incidents*, London: Home Office.

Metropolitan Police Performance Information Bureau: all statistics cited provided *ad hoc* to the author on request.

NACRO (1997) *The Tottenham Experiment*, London: National Association for the Care and Resettlement of Offenders.

Penzer, J. (1999) *Reported Crime and PACE Stop and Search Activity: An Investigation of the Possible Relationship*, London: London School of Economics. Online. Available: http://www.lse.ac.uk/Depts/statistics/ (26 October 1999).

Percy (1998) *Ethnicity and Victimisation: Findings From the 1996 British Crime Survey*, London: Home Office.

Runciman, R. (2000) *Drugs and the Law: Report of the Independent Inquiry into the Misuse of Drugs Act 1971*, London: The Police Foundation.

Sibbitt, R. (1997) *The Perpetrators of Racist Harassment and Racist Violence*, London: Home Office.

Yinger, M. (1986) 'Intersecting Strands in the Theorisation of Race and Ethnic Relations', in J. Rex and D. Mason (eds) *Theories of Race and Ethnic Relations*, Cambridge: Cambridge University Press.

Young, J. (1994) *Policing the Streets: Stops and Search in North London*, London: Centre for Criminology, Middlesex University.

7 The new correctionalism
Young people, Youth Justice and New Labour

John Pitts

Youth justice and community safety

An efficient and effective youth justice system was, and remains, a central plank of New Labour's community safety strategy. Hence, Section 37 of its Crime and Disorder Act (1998) states that: 'It shall be the principal aim of the Youth Justice system to prevent offending by children and young persons' (Home Office 1998a: 2). The Youth Justice Task Force, established by British Prime Minister Tony Blair immediately after the 1997 General Election, recommended that this goal could best be achieved via the swift administration of justice; confronting young offenders with the consequences of their offending; punishment proportionate to the seriousness and persistence of their offending; the reparation of victims; the enforcement of parental responsibility; and the provision of relevant help in areas deemed to be associated with offending, such as drug abuse and literacy.

This vision of an effective and efficient youth justice system stood in marked contrast with the account proffered by the Audit Commission in its report, *Misspent Youth*, published the year before which stated that:

> The current system for dealing with youth crime is inefficient and expensive, while little is being done to deal effectively with juvenile nuisance. The present arrangements are failing the young people – who are not being guided away from offending towards constructive activities. They are also failing victims – those who suffer from young people's inconsiderate behaviour, and from vandalism and loss of property from thefts and burglaries. And they lead to waste in a variety of forms, including lost time, as public servants process the same young offenders through the courts time and again, lost rents, as people refuse to live in high crime areas; lost business, as people steer clear of troubled areas; and waste of young people's potential.
>
> (Audit Commission 1996: 96)

Written by a Treasury economist and a social policy specialist, *Misspent Youth* posed both a critique of the inefficiency and ineffectiveness of the existing system and, through its specification of goals, administrative procedures, criminological theories and 'evidence-based' rehabilitative practices a blue-print for a new one. The report's emphasis upon the more effective integration of system elements, adherence to a limited range of shared objectives, the establishment of clear performance 'targets' and cost effectiveness, to be achieved via the adoption of evidence-based 'rehabilitative' techniques, had a strong resonance for New Labour and its Youth Justice Task Force, imbued as they were with the belief that prudent, popular and accountable 'good governance' was 'the only possible programme for contemporary governments' (Mair 2000). The Crime and Disorder Act (1998) was the legislative instrument by which these objectives were to be achieved.

The administrative structure of the new youth justice

The 1998 Act required chief executives of local authorities to bring into being Youth Offending Teams (YOTs) staffed by personnel seconded from the police, the probation service, education, social services, the health service and, in certain instances, the youth service or other relevant voluntary sector agencies if this were deemed appropriate. YOTs were required to produce a Youth Offending Plan specifying how the team would organise and discharge its functions, and how it would liaise with other statutory and voluntary bodies.

To oversee the development of the YOTs, the Act established the Youth Justice Board of England and Wales (YJB). The YJB has assumed management responsibility for what is now termed the Secure Estate. The Secure Estate comprises local authority Secure Units, the Secure Training Centres for 12 to 14 year olds (introduced by the Conservative government in 1993), the two specialist Youth Treatment Centres operated by the Department of Health and Young Offender Institutions and Young Offender wings, for youngsters aged 15 to 18, which are operated by the Prison Service. The role of the YJB is to specify and monitor standards of efficiency and effectiveness and provide advice, guidance and training for local authorities and institutions. The YJB also holds substantial budgets for which YOTs and institutions can bid in order to develop innovative working methods, such as mentoring schemes, bail support projects or outreach work with youngsters 'at risk', and specialist staff training. Beyond its developmental role, however, the YJB has reserve powers to take control of YOTs and institutions if they are not being run in accordance with the requirements of the 1998 Act or the standards promulgated by the YJB.

The government hopes that, in this way, similarly high standards of professional practice and provision will be achieved throughout England and Wales. These changes represent a significant move towards a national system of juvenile justice in England and Wales. They also represent an unprecedented centralisation of control over the system. However, if successful, they promise to inject a greater degree of equity between regions into a system which, as much previous research has noted, is characterised by significant variations in provision, quality of service and sentencing outcomes (ILYJS 1995; Audit Commission 1996).

The youth justice provisions of the Crime and Disorder Act (1998)

At the core of the deliberations of both *Misspent Youth* and the Youth Justice Task Force was an assumption that effective youth crime prevention could be achieved by drawing children, young people and their parents into the purview of the youth justice system at an early stage in the child's 'criminal career'. This marked a radical departure from the dominant orthodoxy of the 1980s and early 1990s, characterised by Elliott Currie (1985) as 'progressive minimalism', which held that whenever and wherever possible young offenders should be diverted away from the justice system in order to minimise stigma and re-integrate them into mainstream services and institutions. New Labour and its professional advisers rejected progressive minimalism out of hand. As Mark Perfect, joint author of *Misspent Youth* and subsequently secretary to the YJB, observed:

> The present system replicates the inconsistent parenting which most young offenders have received, making it necessary to replace it with a fast, efficient system with a progressive, comprehensible sentencing tariff, which offers the consistency and predictability which replicate 'good parenting'.
>
> (Perfect 1998)

The antipathy to 'progressive minimalism' found expression in the government's support for a robust interventionism. However, whereas Labour Party interventionism in the field of youth crime had traditionally focused upon the amelioration of the social and psychological needs and problems of young offenders, a 'tougher' New Labour government focused upon the deeds of young offenders, and their impact upon victims, rather than their needs. The youth justice provisions of the Crime and Disorder Act (1998) had four key elements: pre-emptive interventions, pre-court preventive interventions, non-custodial preventive disposals, and incarceration (see Figure 7.1).

Pre-emptive interventions

A remarkable feature of the 1998 Act is that it allows pre-emptive formal intervention with children and young people below the age of criminal responsibility (10 years), including those who have committed no offence but are deemed likely to do so, or who are deemed by the police and the local authority to constitute a nuisance in their neighbourhoods. These measures will, necessarily, draw more younger children and their parents, via Parenting Orders, into the purview of the justice system. These pre-emptive interventions are civil

Pre-emptive Interventions:
The Local Child Curfew
Child Safety Order
Parenting Order
Anti-Social Behaviour Order

Pre-Court Preventive Interventions:
Reprimand (once only)
Final Warning (once only)

Non-Custodial Preventive Disposals:
Fine
Referral Order (Youth Justice and Criminal Evidence Act 1999)
Action Plan Order
Reparation Order
Supervision Order
Probation Order
Community Service Order
Combination Order

Incarceration:
Detention and Training Order (Semi-Indeterminate)

Figure 7.1 The Crime and Disorder Act (1998)

measures but, in the cases of the Anti-Social Behaviour Order and the Parenting Order, breaches may be dealt with by criminal sanctions.

Pre-court 'preventive' interventions

The Act places strict limitations upon police discretion by replacing the more flexible police caution with the Reprimand and the Final Warning. These measures are to be backed-up by programmes of restorative justice, cognitive/behavioural change and parental education. The abandonment of police discretion to administer a series of repeat cautions if circumstances are seen to merit it, means that youngsters who are unresponsive to the new measures are likely to enter the Youth Court at a younger age and an earlier stage in their offending careers.

Non-custodial preventive disposals

The 1998 Act effectively abandoned the Conditional Discharge, a disposal previously imposed in 28 per cent of cases. Conditional Discharges required young offenders to desist from future offending as a condition of discharge. The Youth Justice and Criminal Evidence Act (1999) introduced a Referral Order to fill the gap left by the Conditional Discharge. When implemented, a young person subject to a Referral Order, and having been sentenced for his or her offence in the Youth Court, will be referred to a Youth Offender Panel. The constitution of these panels has yet to be finalised but it is likely that they will mirror the Scottish Children's Hearings in which there is both a professional and a lay presence. These panels will then decide on the type of programme the youngster should pursue. It is likely that the emphasis will be on victim-offender reparation and other 'restorative' interventions (Haines 2000). Whatever the merits of the Referral Order, the Danish experience suggests that it is likely to generate a higher volume of re-appearances in court, as a result of breaches of the Order, than the Conditional Discharge it replaces (Mehlbye *et al.* 1998). Whereas a breach of the Conditional Discharge required the young person to re-offend, to be detected, apprehended, charged, prosecuted and found guilty, a breach of the Referral Order requires only that the youngster fail to attend a session of the programme.

A failure to successfully complete a Referral Order will probably result in the imposition of an Action Plan Order, a Reparation Order or a Supervision Order by the Youth Court. The Act specifies that youngsters would not normally receive more than two community penalties so the imposition of such orders for a young person who has already completed or breached a Referral Order would, in effect, constitute a 'last chance'.

The assumption that the bulk of young offenders will, as a result of participation in the 'evidence-based' programmes of victim-offender mediation, mentoring and cognitive-behavioural change which underpin these orders, be made to desist from offending is, as I argue below, rooted in a particularly optimistic reading of that evidence (Pawson and Tilley 1997; Matthews and Pitts 1998).

Incarceration

In consequence, children and young people who breach an Action Plan, Reparation or Supervision Order, or re-offend following their completion, are likely to receive the new, partially indeterminate, Detention and Training Order (DTO) or have a 'residence requirement' inserted in their Supervision Order. This threatens to increase significantly the numbers of children and young people in custody. Indeed, in September 2000 the numbers of youngsters sentenced to custody was up 11.5 per cent on the preceding year. The 'fast-tracking' of persistent young offenders, who are now more likely to make a separate court appearance for each offence, or offending episode, exacerbates this tendency. This process will gain further momentum in 2001 with the introduction of the 'three strikes' sentencing strategy for young burglars, introduced in Michael Howard's Crime Sentences Act (1994). At this point, it is likely that the numbers of 12 to 14 year olds sentenced to Detention and Training Orders will increase substantially, quickly filling the 200 available places in the new Secure Training Centres and placing even greater pressure upon Prison Department young offender provision. And here lies one of the paradoxes of New Labour's new youth justice strategy.

The secure estate we're in

In its final report in 1998, the Youth Justice Task Force concluded that:

> The different types of facilities for young people that constitute the secure estate are in need of major reform. Current arrangements are both inconsistent and unsatisfactory. Young offender institutions are too large. Bullying and abuse of one young offender by another occurs too often while the education offered is often poor.
>
> (Youth Justice Task Force 1998: 3)

Inasmuch as the YJB may strive to develop a rational, effective and humane youth justice system and raise standards of provision and practice within the secure estate, its efforts are being systematically undermined by the logic of a system which, by default rather than design, is drawing in larger numbers of less problematic children at a younger age, and pushing them through the system more quickly. This systemic tendency is compounded by unequivocal signals sent to the Youth Courts by the Prime Minister, the Home Secretary and senior Home Office ministers that they should take a tough line on youth crime.

This tension between the political and professional spheres is nowhere more evident than in the case of Secure Training Centres (STCs). These were proposed by the Conservative administration in 1993, and were resisted by the then Shadow Home Secretary Tony Blair, who argued, correctly, that the evidence pointed to the folly of bringing together the most difficult and disturbed children in the country under one roof (Hoghughi 1983). However, STCs were subsequently embraced by Shadow Home Secretary Jack Straw in an attempt to beef-up New Labour's 'law and order' profile in the run-up to the 1997 General Election. Medway STC opened in the spring of 1998. The YJB required that staff were vetted in accordance with the recommendations of the Warner report, *Choosing with Care* (1996). Accountability was ensured by the recruitment of a resident Home Office monitor to ensure 'contract compliance', and regular inspections by the Social Services Inspectorate. The rights of inmates were to be vouchsafed by creating easy access to a variety of 'watchdog' organisations: Childline, The Samaritans, and the Voice of the Child in Care, this latter organisation also providing 'independent visitors'.

Thus, Medway STC represented the 'cutting-edge' in 'institutional transparency'. Yet in the Centre's first seven months of operation, more than 100 assaults on staff were recorded along with £100,000 worth of damage. Over this same period, thirty-five of the original 100 staff resigned. In June 1998, the London newspaper, the *Evening Standard*, reported that:

> More than 30 police wearing riot equipment had to use dogs to quell the disturbance at the Medway Secure Training Centre. Three staff were injured and windows smashed as 15 children, many wielding snooker cues

and balls, ran riot last night. It was an hour and a half before the incident was brought under control.

(*Evening Standard*, 26 June 1998: 1)

This was, more or less, a re-run of the scenes which had accompanied the launch of the similarly hyped DHSS Youth Treatment Centre in Brentwood, Essex, in the mid-1970s. Like Medway, Brentwood had also attempted to bring some of the most difficult and disturbed children in the country together under one roof.

The Social Services Inspectorate submitted a damning report on Medway STC in January 1999, recommending that it be shut down and that the other four STCs under construction, at an estimated cost of £30 million, should be put on hold. Government minister Paul Boateng, recently transferred from the Department of Health, where he launched the Quality Protects initiative to safeguard children in residential care, refused to be drawn on the issue of closure, referring to the Medway trainees as 'little monsters'.

Political imperatives displace professional considerations and ethical concerns while the problems identified by the Youth Justice Task Force, far from being ameliorated, become more acute. Similar tensions afflict the Youth Offending Teams.

What is a YOT and what is it not?

As noted, the 1998 Act required chief executives of local authorities to bring into being Youth Offending Teams (YOTs). The constitution of these teams echoes of the Multi-Agency Diversion Panels, comprising representatives from the police, social services, education, the youth service and the voluntary sector, which developed more or less spontaneously in the 1980s. *Misspent Youth* (Audit Commission 1996) had commended the exemplary Northamptonshire Diversion Scheme as a suggestive model for 'service delivery' within the new system. However, Multi-Agency Diversion Panels were developed in the heyday of 'progressive minimalism' and, as their name suggests, were designed to divert youngsters out of the justice system. Whereas in 1980, 71,000 boys and girls aged 14 to 16 were sentenced by the Juvenile Courts in England and Wales, by 1987 this figure had dropped to 37,300, a reduction of over 52 per cent. The most effective Diversion Panels strove to develop a non-stigmatising shadow tariff constituted from informal, but robust, contractually-based interventions in the spheres of education, family relationships, use of leisure, vocational training and drug abuse. This strategy had a remarkable impact upon police practice. Between 1980 and 1987 the cautioning rate for girls aged 14 to 16 rose from 58 to 82 per cent. For boys the figures were 34 and 58 per cent respectively. This rate was inflated in part by the development of 'Caution Plus', the practice of issuing repeat cautions if the young person agreed to comply with requirements specified by Diversion Panels (Pitts 1988).

For the first time, since the creation of a separate system of juvenile justice in the UK in 1908, the YOTs assemble in one place, on a statutory and fully funded basis, the 'minimum sufficient network' (Skynner 1974) of agencies, professionals and expertise necessary to make a 'holistic' response to the multiply disadvantaged young people who find themselves at the hard end of the youth justice system. Moreover, by dint of its multi-agency, multi-disciplinary structure, the YOT may also serve as a catalyst for positive change in the local authorities, the police, probation and voluntary sector services from which YOT personnel are seconded.

However, responding effectively to the troubled youngsters who find their way to the YOTs may take a long time and require the development of sensitive referral protocols with a range of agencies, plus regular follow-up contact. In a study of 270 young people involved with an inner London YOT (Jones 2001), 180 people (45 per cent) had been placed on the Local Authority Child Protection Register at least once. Most had spent some time in local authority care and the majority had a parent with recurrent mental health problems.

But the sheer volume of cases generated as a result of the propensity of the new system to draw in new populations and speed their progress through it (the Association for Youth Justice estimates an increase of 150 per cent per year, based on pre-1998 levels of throughput) means that in many YOTs professional staff, irrespective of their area of expertise, are simply concerned with the supervision of Court Orders.

These Orders are increasingly underpinned by offence-focused programmes devised, and in some cases quite literally scripted, by the Home Office Offending Behaviour Programme Unit or the Community Justice National Training Organisation (Pitts 2000a and b). These programmes aim, quite explicitly, to eliminate the exercise of judgement or discretion on the part of the professionals administering them in order to avoid compromising 'programme integrity'. This means that efforts to develop reflexive, holistic, responses to youngsters in trouble, in which specialists come together to devise programmes which will not only challenge young people's behaviour, but also address the underlying problems associated with their offending, is jeopardised, and in some cases abandoned. Moreover, preliminary results from the forthcoming YJB evaluation of 'pilot' YOTs suggest that professionals may be spending less time in face-to-face contact with young offenders than in 1996, when *Misspent Youth* bemoaned the paucity of professional contact with young offenders.

On 25 September 2000, Jack Straw announced new measures, involving the use of electronic tagging and voice verification systems, to keep Britain's '2,500 most persistent tearaways' under twenty-four hour surveillance (*Guardian*, 25 Sept. 2000: 6). He had earlier announced a cash injection to create several thousand more probation officers. While at a political level this is an obvious attempt to 'steal a march' on New Labour's right-wing critics, it may also indicate that the government is concerned that correctionalism has not fulfilled its early promise, and is now seeking more direct, certain and cost-effective measures with which to control young offenders.

The politics of the new youth justice

As noted at the beginning of this chapter, there is a clear tension between the professional and political dimensions of New Labour's youth justice strategy. At a political level, New Labour's strategy on youth crime mirrors the 'toughening' of youth justice which has been evident in the US, as well as mainland Europe, in recent years.

New Labour's strategy was designed to seize the mantle of 'law and order' by synthesising the authoritarian populism of its most powerful opponents and most vociferous critics while show-casing a new sort of politics in which economy efficiency and effectiveness were the watchwords. For Tony Blair, this was a strategy which also held the promise of bridging some of the political divisions in his own Party by promising to be both 'tough' enough 'on crime' for the 'modernisers' and 'tough' enough on the 'causes of crime' for Old Labour's remaining 'social engineers'. This marked a shift from what Johnstone (2000) has described as the elitist policy-making, which characterised the development of the minimalist youth justice policies of the 1980s, to forms of policy-making 'based on a growing bureaucracy of administrators and experts as well as a media driven relationship to individual voters' (Simon 2000).

The Crime and Disorder Act (1998) marked a repudiation of both 1960s 'welfarism' (Pitts 1988) and 1980s 'progressive minimalism' (Currie 1985) on the grounds that both approaches represented soft options which failed to confront the moral dimension of youth crime and disregarded the 'rights' of victims. However, this strategy diverged from developments in the US, in its unwillingness to adopt explicitly 'cruel' measures such as the 'boot camps', 'house of pain' regimes and 'chain gangs' which have re-emerged in several US youth justice systems in recent times (Simon 2001). 'Toughness' for New Labour may mean the extension of custodial confinement and the community supervision of a broader range of young offenders and troublesome children, but its stated purpose is to provide a forum in which 'evidence-based' programmes can be administered in a setting bounded by administrative protections against violations of children's rights. This is not to suggest, of course, that, 'on the ground', institutions, regimes and professional practices in the English youth justice system may not sometimes be negligent, brutal or inimical to the best interests of young offenders in a variety of ways (Crimmens and Pitts 2000).

Dejuvenilisation

The onus on children's rights in the new youth justice is, however, in tension with the attempt to erode the distinctiveness of the juvenile jurisdiction and to ascribe greater levels of culpability to juveniles. As Jonathan Simon (2001) has argued, the erosion of the juvenile jurisdiction in the US has been powered by the belief amongst 'opinion-formers' and policy-makers, hostile to both 'welfarism' in youth justice and the welfare state in general, that the rehabilitative responses developed in the 1960s and 1970s had failed and that only the re-assertion of patently retributive responses would restore moral hegemony and reduce crime. In the UK, pressures towards 'dejuvenilisation' were intensified in the wake of the killing in 1993 of 2-year-old James Bulger by two 10-year-old boys, Jon Venables and Robert Thompson. Since then, there has been a steady movement away from strategies of informalism and normalisation and the abandonment of attempts to divert less serious young offenders from prosecution and custody. As I have already noted, this has been accompanied by the steady growth of custodial disposals for 15 to 18 year olds, and the introduction of new types of secure and custodial penalties and institutions for youngsters aged between 12 and 14.

Popular anxieties triggered by the Bulger case gave rise to a debate in the media, the police and, eventually, Parliament, concerning the existence of a 'new breed' of under-age criminals whom the law 'could not touch' (Hagell and Newburn 1994; Pitts 2000b). One of the political fruits of this debate was the Home Secretary Jack Straw's decision, shortly after the 1997 election, to abandon the principle of *doli incapax*, a defining feature of the juvenile jurisdiction in the UK from its inception. The problem with *doli incapax*, Straw maintained, was that it pre-supposed that children aged between 10 and 13 were incapable of differentiating between right and wrong. In fact, the principle of *doli incapax* means no such thing. Rather, it holds that in its dealings with children below the age of 14 who have broken the law, the courts must proceed from the assumption that, by dint of their immaturity, and even though they may have known that they were doing wrong, the child does not have criminal intent and does not fully understand the consequences of their actions for themselves or their victim(s). As a result, the onus is upon the prosecution to demonstrate criminal intent. In the case of 14 to 17 year olds, by contrast, the onus is on the defence to demonstrate the absence of criminal intent. This was a symbolic intervention; an unequivocal indication that considerations of responsibility, culpability and retribution were henceforth to be a legitimate concern of the youth justice system and its agents. The other principle overturned by the Home Secretary, that in order to minimise the stigma of involvement in the youth justice system, the identity of defendants should not be revealed to the press or the public, was supplanted by discretionary powers for Youth Courts to 'name and shame' young offenders if they felt it to be warranted. Moreover, the Crime and Disorder Act (1998) allowed curfews, enforced by electronic tagging, to be extended to children and young people of 10 years and over, even though this measure would not be supervised by a member of the new YOTs. However, the lowering to 12, or to 10 if the Home Secretary deems it politic, of the age at which youngsters can be sentenced to custodial confinement in a Secure Training Centre constitutes the radical edge of the government's dejuvenilising thrust.

The re-assertion of the responsibilities of young offenders which dejuvenilisation represents, and the suspicion that welfarism, and by extension the welfare state *per se*, might in fact foster youthful misbehaviour finds expression in New Labour's conflation of the problem of youth crime with the problem of 'the family'.

Failing families

In the 1980s the 'family', and in particular the criminogenic, lower-class, 'welfare-dependent' family, became a key focus for neo-liberal politicians and a newly emergent neo-liberal intelligentsia. Their lament, in essence, was that the rules of civilised social life were no longer observed, that absolute moral values and their associated norms and practices had been trashed and abandoned by irresponsible 'intellectuals' on the one hand, and lower-class malcontents on the other hand. Moreover, a culture, which had once placed a premium on duty and responsibility, had now been supplanted by a culture of complaint, dependency and entitlement. Thus, they rejected the traditional ethos of the welfare state, which emphasised the rights of poor families, focusing instead upon the economic burden placed by welfare recipients upon the hardworking majority. In its dealings with families, they maintained, the welfare state has been counterproductive because it:

> failed to reinforce the work ethic; the goal of self sufficiency, self support and self-initiative; the importance of intact families; the fiscal responsibility of the parents to the child; and the notion of reciprocity, the idea that recipients have a social obligation to perform in return for receiving assistance.
>
> (Karger and Stoesz 1990: 65, cited in Glennester and Midgley 1991)

In the US, Charles Murray (1994) had argued that the US government should scrap its Aid to Families with Dependent Children programme (AFDC), Medicaid, Food Stamps and Unemployment Insurance, in order to 'drive young women back into marriage'. Imported to do a similar job in the UK by the influential right-wing political journalist Andrew Neil and the *Sunday Times* newspaper, Murray argued that:

> the civilising process cannot occur in communities where the two parent family is not the norm, and this will turn out to be as true in England as America. The real problem with the 'alternative' of unmarried parenthood is that it offers no ethical alternative for socialising little boys. For males, the ethical code of the two-parent family is the only game in town.
>
> (Murray 1994: 26)

Journalist Melanie Phillips (1994) was one of the first erstwhile left-leaning celebrities to embrace what Murray described as the New Victorianism in the UK, and in an article for the *Observer* newspaper she gleefully monitored its colonisation of metropolitan opinion in the 1990s:

> Peter Lilley and Sue Slipman, doughty defender of single parents, are suddenly singing in close harmony. In a speech last week, the Social Security Secretary blamed low pay and unemployment for turning young men into unmarriageable prospects. Miss Slipman talks about how the

collapse of the male role through lack of work is manufacturing the kind of yob no self-respecting woman would choose as a spouse. Suddenly a government widely assumed to be hostile to single mothers seems to agree that the real problem is men. ... The question being asked is how can we civilise young men when family structures, employment and moral authority are so weakened?

(Phillips 1994: 27)

In a somewhat similar vein, but coming this time from the 'post-Marxist left', Beatrix Campbell (1995) argued that unemployment and the 'collapse of the male role' had forced men back into spaces which, by day, have traditionally been occupied by women. However, she states that far from:

Co-operating in the creation of a democratic domesticity ... what they admired and serviced was the criminalised brotherhood; what they harassed and hurt was community politics. It was an entirely and explicitly gendered formation.

(Campbell 1995: 249)

Thus, for Campbell, there is 'an underclass' but it is a gendered underclass made up exclusively of men. What united these critiques was their conflation of moral and fiscal concerns which found expression in a desire for the state to control the bad behaviour of young men and their feckless fathers while, Slipman and Campbell excepted, withdrawing support from their welfare-dependent mothers.

These attempts to locate the origins of crime in the lower-class family ranged from the blatantly rhetorical (Phillips 1994), through the pseudo-scientific (Dennis 1997; Murray 1994), to accounts which inferred an aetiology from empirically established correlates. *Crime and the Family* (1993) by Utting et al., drew upon data generated by West and Farrington's (1973) Cambridge study of 'delinquent development' to argue that 'the tangled roots of delinquency lie, to a considerable extent, inside the family'. This timely publication paralleled, and gave considerable impetus to, New Labour's growing interest in the lower-class family and in crime. Thus, by 1995, New Labour's emergent 'family policy' was virtually synonymous with its 'criminal justice policy'. Indeed, the advent of the Parenting Order in the 1998 Act must be seen against the backdrop of New Labour's high-profile commitment to the rejuvenation of the family as an 'effective caring and controlling social unit', and the pre-eminence it ascribed to what Jack Straw described as family forms characterised by 'two participating parents'. As Tony Blair declared in his speech to the 1995 Labour Party conference: 'a young country that wants to be a strong country cannot be morally neutral about the family.'

Clearly, families play an important role in determining whether, or to what extent, children and young people become involved in a broad range of socially deviant and illegal behaviours. However, the causal primacy ascribed to the 'criminogenic' lower-class family in New Labour's youth justice strategy suffers from what Elliott Currie (1985) has termed the 'fallacy of autonomy'. This is because it denies or ignores the relationship between socio-economic stress, neighbourhood poverty and the biographies of young offenders (Braithwaite 1979 and 1981; Field 1990; Hope 1994; Wikstrom and Loeber 1997; Sampson *et al.* 1997; Pitts and Hope 1998; Hagedorn 1998; Young 1999), the peculiar, mutually-reinforcing, negative contingencies set in train by socially deviant acts perpetrated by lower-class children and young people (Hagan 1993; Sampson and Laub 1993), and the role of state agencies in the construction and amplification of their 'deviant careers' (Muncie 1999; Goldson 1999 and 2000).

The appeal of this perspective for New Labour is fairly clear. In a time when politicians are unwilling to countenance robust, 'demand side', social and economic intervention to counter social problems, and are eager to demonstrate that they are 'tough on the crime', an analysis which identifies poor child-rearing practices and weak parental control as the fundamental problem, and a strategy which targets families and their capacity to inculcate self-control in unruly and disruptive children which, moreover, resonates with the moral sensibilities of New Labour's new constituencies in 'Middle England', is a political godsend.

Professional perfidy

New Labour's onslaught upon the lower-class family was paralleled by an assault upon the public professionals responsible for keeping the lower-class family in order. This critique owed much to the neo-liberal account of the role of the welfare state in fostering a 'culture of dependency' and New Labour's neo-Thatcherite suspicion of local government and the political orientation of members of the 'social professions'. In post-Thatcherite Britain, anti-professional ire was characteristically directed against teachers and social workers, although the police are not always exempt, as Campbell's account of their collusive involvement in the 1991 youth riots in England testifies (Campbell 1995).

Teachers were castigated as defenders of entrenched, outmoded and almost invariably 'permissive', professional doctrines to which they apparently clung in the face of 'widely accepted contrary scientific evidence', and 'informed opinion'. Social workers, for their part, were admonished for blundering into normal families on the basis of 'child protection' hearsay while failing to protect and control the children of the poor, even as they colluded with the fecklessness and criminality of their parents. While the problem of youth crime was presented as, first and foremost, a product of the moral failure of families, this failure was, it appeared, nurtured and amplified by the stupidity, cupidity, collusion, incompetence or sheer bloody-mindedness of the professionals who were supposed to contain and educate them. These themes are articulated succinctly in *The Blair Revolution* by Peter Mandelson and Roger Liddle (1996). The authors write:

Schools require a new, much tougher, set of disciplinary sanctions to deal with unruly and uncooperative pupils – such as compulsory homework on school premises, weekend and Saturday night detention, and the banning of favourite leisure pursuits such as football matches.

This greater emphasis on discipline should be matched in the local community. The police, schools and local authority services must work together closely to crack down on vandalism and other antisocial behaviour. Excessive tolerance of low-level sub-criminal behaviour by unruly young people undermines general respect for the rule of law, ruins the environment and makes a misery of the lives of many innocent people – and provides a breeding ground for more serious crime.

(Mandelson and Liddle 1996: 17)

New Labour's solution to the unpredictability of state professionals has been threefold. It has privatised state services, inserting detailed conditions for contract compliance and penalty clauses for deviation. In the new Secure Treatment Centres, for example, the Home Office monitors, mentioned above, are on hand twenty-four hours a day to ensure that staff are managing proscribed behaviours among the children in the stipulated manner. It has supported the de-professionalisation of the professional task by allowing recruitment of far more easily managed, unqualified workers to undertake face-to-face work with offenders in both youth justice and the Probation Service. It has also taken to video monitoring correctional programme 'delivery', most notably in Prison Department establishments and the Probation Service. These videotapes are then sent to monitors in the Home Office who determine whether the level of compliance with the scripted interventions means that programme providers may be accredited to run these programmes. At present there is discussion in the Home Office concerning whether lectures and seminars on the new university-based Community Justice degrees, which now train Probation Officers, should be similarly monitored and accredited. In these ways, the government aims to ensure that its policies go 'all the way down' and are not subverted by the exercise of professional judgement or discretion.

The metamorphosis of rehabilitation

The idea that youth justice systems might rehabilitate children and young people fell from favour in the 1970s in the face of research which appeared to show that official intervention with young offenders tended to worsen the problems they were designed to solve (Martinson 1974; Preston 1980; Pitts 1992). However, the 'progressive minimalism' to which these findings gave impetus fell from favour in the early 1990s in the face of a protracted economic recession, rising crime rates and the murder of James Bulger, which pulled youth crime back to the centre of the political stage.

As more young people were drawn into the system, the 'nothing works' orthodoxy of the 1970s and 1980s gave way to a new rhetoric of 'what works'

(Pitts 1992). This 'rehabilitation of rehabilitation' was palpably political in intent. As Christopher Nutall, described by the *Independent* newspaper as the 'hard-headed' director of research and statistics at the Home Office, told a meeting of chief probation officers: ' "Nothing Works' should be killed; not just because it's not right but because it has had a terrible effect. Let's not talk about it any more. Let's talk about what does work. (*Independent*, 27 Oct. 1992).

The 'what works' movement emanating from the Home Office set about exhuming aetiological theories and rehabilitative techniques, some of which had lain abandoned since the 1950s (Pitts 1992). Whereas the rehabilitative techniques of the 1960s had aimed to ameliorate emotional and social deprivation, these newly disinterred rehabilitations aimed to restructure the modes of thought, the values, the attitudes and the behaviour of young offenders, the control strategies of their parents, and the classroom regimes presided over by their teachers. While presenting themselves as new forms of rehabilitation, these techniques were straightforwardly 'correctional' in both intent and content.

The promise of correction

The 'what works' correctionalist phenomenon was important to New Labour's project in two main ways. First, after two decades in which criminological theory had appeared to be incapable of making any coherent contribution to criminal justice policy, the policy implications of the new correctionalism were self-evident and straightforward (Vanstone 2000). This was of particular importance to New Labour which, through the YJB, was endeavouring to control its policies 'all the way down' to the point of implementation.

It is an axiom of the new correctionalism that, if 'properly applied', evidence-based techniques will arrest the development of 'offending careers', thereby averting subsequent custodial sentences and maximising the economy, efficiency and effectiveness of the youth justice system. Much has therefore been made of the fact that these correctional measures – cognitive skills training (also known as reasoning and rehabilitation), restorative justice and mentoring – are 'those which research points to as the most thorough and best designed programmes showing the most "promising" results' (Farrington 1996). Indeed, this phrase has become a kind of official mantra amongst Home Office ministers, within the YJB, amongst senior personnel in the welfare, justice and community safety industries and the denizens of some university senior common rooms. However, their apparent confidence in these measures appears to be rooted in a partial reading of the 'evidence' and an over-estimation of their 'promise'.

When the word 'promising' is used to describe such correctional ventures, it has a very specific meaning; one bestowed upon it by the National Institute of Justice (NIJ), a division of the US Department of Justice, in elaborating national criteria for evaluating 'correctional programs'. By promising, the NIJ means:

programmes for which the level of certainty from available evidence is too low to support generalisable conclusions, but for which there is some empirical basis for predicting that further research could support such conclusions.

(Sherman *et al.* 1998: 10)

However, should further research support such conclusions, the NIJ cautions, these findings would only be valid if applied in 'similar settings in other places and times'. This raises important questions concerning whether, and to what extent, the youth justice system of England and Wales might represent such an analogous social context.

Cognitive skills training

Among the promising programmes cited by the NIJ are cognitive skills training programmes. Those currently operating in the UK have their origins in the Reasoning and Rehabilitation programmes developed by cognitive psychologist Robert Ross and his associates, based on research done in Canadian jails. In the 1990s, the apparent success of these programmes led to their widespread adoption by prison and probation services in England and Wales and latterly by YOTs. The programmes 'attempt to teach delinquents the cognitive (thinking skills) in which they are deficient', in the expectation that this would lead to a decrease in their offending (Farrington 1996: 22).

The research evidence

The most frequently cited example of the effectiveness of cognitive skills training is the correctional programme designed by Robert Ross and undertaken in a Canadian jail in the mid-1990s. This programme was evaluated by Ross' colleagues Porporino and Robinson (1995). The programme was, as Pawson and Tilley (1997) observe, 'probably the most ambitious and comprehensive rehabilitation programme ever attempted by this or any other prison service. By the end of March 1993, 2,500 offenders had been assessed as suitable cases for treatment and 1,400 had completed the programme.' Porporino and Robinson's evaluation reveals that prisoners who volunteered for the programme had a far lower reconviction rate, in the twelve months following release, than prisoners who did not volunteer for the programme – around 20 per cent for the volunteers against 50 per cent and greater for non-volunteers. However, in addition to the group who volunteered and completed the programme and those who did not volunteer for the programme, there was a third group who volunteered for the programme, were randomly allocated to a waiting list, and never actually undertook the programme. Whereas 19.7 per cent of programme 'completers' were reconvicted in the twelve months following release, 23 per cent of the control group were reconvicted. When other contingencies and inconsistencies are taken into account the measurable impact of the cognitive skills training programme evaporates (Pawson and Tilley 1997; Matthews and Pitts 1998).

Meta-analyses of evaluations of cognitive behavioural programmes suggest that, for the programmes to be effective, certain key elements must be present. In the case of high-risk offenders, programmes should occupy between 40 and 70 per cent of the offenders time (Gendreau 1996) and should last for at least twenty-three weeks (Lipsey and Wilson 1998). In addition to matching the duration and intensity of programmes to the 'risk', 'criminogenic needs' and 'learning styles' of offenders, programme providers must attempt to match the programme to the offender's personality characteristics. 'High anxiety' offenders, for example, do not respond well to confrontation, 'egocentric' offenders show a poor appreciation of the victim's perspective, while offenders with both 'below average' and 'above average' intellectual ability tend to be, respectively, perplexed or under-stimulated by cognitive skills programmes (Fabiano *et al.* 1991). Meta-analyses also show that programmes are successful only if providers relate to juveniles in 'interpersonally sensitive' and 'constructive' ways and are trained and supervised appropriately. Moreover, in the case of more serious young offenders, 'relapse prevention programmes' need to be employed in the community to monitor and anticipate problematic situations and train offenders to rehearse alternative behaviours (Vanstone 2000). Alongside this, programme staff need to be active in linking young people into other services which meet their needs. However, even when all these criteria are achieved the average recidivism rate remains relatively high at around 50 per cent (Andrews *et al.* 1990). Similarly inconclusive results are reported by Maurice Vanstone (2000), although he reports positive, if not statistically significant, rehabilitative outcomes in some UK programmes for motivated adult offenders.

The community penalties administered by the YOTs are unlikely to offer either the levels of intensity or the consistency of application necessary to effect change with the persistent or serious young offenders upon whom they will be imposed. Meanwhile, if these interventions mix low- and high-risk offenders in, for example, a drugs awareness or literacy element of the programme, they may trigger an 'interaction effect' (Clear and Hardeyman 1990) in which offending amongst low-risk groups, prematurely drawn into the system by the new measures introduced by the 1998 Act, may escalate.

Theoretical problems

Beyond the frailty of the evidence about the impact of cognitive skills training are other concerns about the flimsy theoretical rationale upon which cognitive skills training is built. At its core is an assumption that offenders can be taught new cognitive skills which will enable them to anticipate the consequences of their behaviour for themselves and others, and so make 'appropriate' moral choices. It is assumed that if they can think 'straight' they will go 'straight'. In so reasoning, the purveyors of cognitive skills training, like the eighteenth-century Classicists, conflate rational/logical thinking with moral/law-abiding thinking and, in so doing, commit a categorical error since they fail to distinguish between the cognitive 'machinery' which enables logical thought and the ethical choices made possible by a capacity for logical thought. The assumption that people engage in crime because they lack a capacity for logical thought is, at least, tendentious since in reality people often resort to crime, violence or deception because, in the circumstances in which they find themselves, it 'works' for them (Sutherland 1934). Thus their involvement in crime, while morally reprehensible, is nonetheless rational.

Restorative justice

The fundamental precepts of restorative justice hold that when an offence is committed, both the immediate victims and the communities to which they belong have been harmed and that the relationship which has been fractured by that offence is in need of restoration. In this perspective, the primary victims are those most directly affected by the offence, but others, such as family members of victims and offenders, witnesses and other members of the affected community, are regarded as having been victimised by the offence. The restorative justice process encourages victims to participate in defining the obligations of offenders, who are then offered opportunities to understand the harm they have caused to victims and the community and to devise a way of making restitution. In this process, obligations to victims take priority over sanctions or obligations to the state. In its original form, restorative justice emerged as a local, colloquial and informal alternative to formal systems of retributive justice administered by state agencies (Christie 1977; Braithwaite and Daly 1994). Latterly in most Western youth justice systems, as in the UK Crime and Disorder Act (1998), restorative elements have been incorporated into an avowedly retributive youth justice system.

The research evidence

The Northamptonshire Youth Diversion Scheme (the Northants Scheme) in the UK, appears to have had a remarkable degree of success in terms of both victim/offender satisfaction and reconviction. Victims and offenders reach agreement about appropriate remedies in over 60 per cent of cases, and both groups report high levels of satisfaction in terms of the restorative process and its outcomes. These findings echo those of Elejabarrieta *et al.* (1993) who found that, of the 40.2 per cent of cases dealt with in this way in the Catalonian youth justice system in 1993, 68.5 per cent resulted in agreement between victim and offender about an appropriate remedy. Of these cases, 78.2 per cent were rated successful by both victims and offenders although, as was also the case in Northants, there was a tendency for victim satisfaction to fade with time. In the bulk of these cases the remedy involved 'dialogue' between the victim and the offender. It proved hardest to reach agreement in cases with initial 'not guilty' pleas and those involving peer violence. It proved easiest to reach agreement in cases of 12 and 13 year olds involved in 'criminal damage'. It is important to note that when success rates for restorative justice programmes are cited, they usually refer to victim-offender satisfaction rather than offender reconviction.

Nonetheless, the Northants Scheme boasts of a 23 per cent reconviction rate over a two-year follow-up period for the youngsters passing through its programmes. However, although this is a cause for celebration, it is important to note that the Northants Scheme is voluntary, operating outside and as an alternative to formal involvement in the youth justice system. Moreover, because the scheme has only initial administrative contact with the most serious and persistent offenders and is open to any child or young person who is apprehended for an offence, many of whom are low risk and unlikely to reoffend, it is difficult to identify whether, or to what extent, the scheme, or natural 'evaporation', accounts for its low reconviction rate.

The Northants Scheme offers a comprehensive range of rehabilitative, educational, vocational and 'use of leisure' programmes alongside the restorative elements; but hereby hangs a key methodological problem. Because restorative justice is just one component of a more complex and extensive programme of intervention, it is difficult, if not impossible, to isolate its effects.

In their meta-analysis of ten US 'restitutive' intervention programmes, Lipsey and Wilson (1998) found little effect on the recidivism rates of 'non-institutionalised' but persistent juvenile offenders. Van Hooris (1985) found that restorative justice routinely failed to change the attitudes of 'low-maturity persistent offenders'. A study undertaken by Gendreau (1996), found even less promising results in terms of recidivism, but divined an 'interaction effect' which resulted in an escalation of offending rates amongst low-risk offenders. This was largely because referral into the programme put them at heightened risk of non-compliance and, as a result, vulnerable to the penal sanctions which could then be imposed upon them. On the other hand, these programmes were deemed to be insufficiently intensive to meet the needs of higher-risk offenders.

Theoretical problems

At the level of theory, there is an important question about the mechanisms of change which are triggered by restorative interventions. We do not know whether, or to what extent, young offenders can generalise their identification with the particular victim they have harmed to an empathy with other potential victims. The Kirkholt study (Forrester et al. 1990) suggests that 'burglars' divide the world into legitimate and illegitimate targets, raising the possibility, suggested by reconviction studies, that even restorative justice programmes rated 'successful' by both victims and offenders may serve only to delegitimise a specific victim, rather than all potential victims, in the minds of young offenders.

Mentoring

New Labour has wholeheartedly embraced the idea of mentoring. A central aim of its Quality Protects, Leaving Residential Care and Connexions programmes, as well as its youth justice strategy, requires that each young person should have a mentor. At present, the YJB funds approximately fifty mentoring schemes in YOTs.

The term 'mentor' denotes a loyal, wise and trusted teacher, guide and friend. In recent years in the US, mentoring, in the guise of 'buddying', 'big brothering', 'positive peer influence programs' or 'companionship therapy', has been utilised extensively with young people experiencing problems of academic attainment, personal conduct and crime and violence. Mentoring was embraced by African-American activists in the 1980s as a means of transcending the barriers to social mobility occasioned by the profound socio-economic disadvantages experienced by about one-third of black Americans, and the 'institutionalised racism' encountered by them all. This approach to mentoring proceeds from the assumption that the mentor and the mentee share similar aspirations, values and goals. What distinguishes the mentee is his or her lack of access to opportunities for the realisation of these aspirations, values and goals. Thus, mentoring becomes a tool for emancipation, a means whereby the mentee is helped to navigate hostile social terrain.

However, as mentoring has spread, it has been adopted by a broad range of educational, employment, social welfare and youth justice organisations with different goals and different priorities. In the process the focus of mentoring has shifted from advice, guidance and advocacy to a concern to 'correct' those shortcomings in the mentee which prevent him or her from entering the social, economic or moral mainstream. While 'emancipatory' mentoring is borne of a critique of an inequitable social order which keeps lower-class young people down, and out, 'correctional mentoring' finds the origins of such 'social exclusion' within the mentee.

Government minister Margaret Hodge, for example, writing in *The Times*, notes that: 'Mentors can help to break the vicious circle. They are invaluable in helping boys who lack a father figure at home. It could be simply by making sure that they get up in time for school (*The Times*, 10 April 1998). In most mentoring schemes, 'role modelling' is identified as the key medium of change. The usual rationales for role modelling are redolent of the traditional approaches to the teaching of history which assert that the young need heroes with whom to identify and emulate. However, what a 'role model' actually is, and the mechanisms whereby its positive or negative attributes are transmitted to, and introjected by, the mentee is the subject of continuing controversy.

The research evidence

Unsurprisingly, perhaps, the evaluations of mentoring cited by the Youth Justice Board are remarkably upbeat, deriving as they do mainly from studies undertaken by members of the US-based National Mentoring Association. The

Association cites a number of studies which suggest positive outcomes for mentoring. A comparison of 500 children in the Big Brothers and Big Sisters of America scheme and a control group of non-participants, revealed that participants were 46 per cent less likely to be using illegal drugs, 27 per cent less likely to begin using alcohol, and 52 per cent less likely to truant. The programme also claimed to reduce violence by one-third. The Quantum Opportunities Program found that its mentees were more likely to graduate from high school, have fewer arrests, become involved in community service and, interestingly, have fewer children (Pitts 2000a). The benefits of mentoring cited most frequently in such evaluations are reduced offending, reduced school exclusion, improved school performance, the achievement of paid employment, enhanced self-esteem and confidence and improved relationships with peers and adults.

Methodological problems

However, these claims have tended to be most frequent in evaluations undertaken by the agencies which provide mentoring programmes and they must therefore be regarded with a degree of scepticism. Such evaluations may tend, for understandable reasons, to 'accentuate the positive' and overlook, or underplay, areas where no change occurs or where problems actually worsen. As with certain evaluations of cognitive skills training programmes, some mentoring schemes select their 'control groups' from young people who decline the offer to join the scheme. The danger here is that they may then be comparing a group of youngsters who are motivated to change with a control group which is not.

Other American research, on the effectiveness of mentoring with young offenders, is far less encouraging. An analysis of the ten 'best-evaluated' mentoring programmes, carried out for the US Department of Justice in the early 1990s (Brewer et al. 1995), suggests that 'non-contingent supportive mentoring relationships' (i.e., programmes which did not utilise a cognitive-skills training approach involving the systematic manipulation of rewards and sanctions – but see above for a critique of cognitive-skills training), failed to achieve their goals in terms of academic attainment, 'dropping out', behavioural change or employment. This analysis also points to 'interaction effects', citing evaluations which revealed significantly increased delinquency for young people with no previous offences but significantly decreased recidivism for youngsters with prior offences (Goodman 1972; Fo and O'Donnell 1974).

Hellen Colley (2000) points to a key problem at the heart of mentoring programmes developed in furtherance of particular government policies:

> It [the study] revealed significant gaps between the goals and assumptions of the scheme, and the desires and needs of the mentees. Many mentees and mentors felt unduly constrained by the tight focus. ... Some mentees developed resistance strategies to avoid scheme requirements, whilst others were dismissed from the scheme. Some mentors accepted the young person's agenda whilst others tried to impose the official view. Either way

subversion resulted. Consequently, some mentors became highly critical of the young people they were trying to help, reinforcing negative stereotypes of them as feckless and inadequate. A combination of these factors risked making things worse for some of the very people the scheme was supposed to help.

(Colley 2000: 11)

Inadmissible evidence

Although the Home Office and the Youth Justice Board make great play of the fact that the correctional techniques which underpin the community-based and custodial penalties in the youth justice provision of the 1998 Act are 'evidence-based', the evidence is, at least, equivocal. Clearly it is much harder to specify, institutionalise and regulate a restricted repertoire of professional practices, as the Home Office, the Youth Justice Board and the agencies and organisations associated with them aim to do, if the evidence upon which they are based is shown to be ambiguous. As a result, these powerful 'claim-making agencies' tend to cite only the evidence which indicates that the theories and practices they have championed 'work'. Yet, as Pawson and Tilley (1997) argue, whether or not an intervention 'works', in the sense that it promotes the desired behavioural change in a young offender, may have little to do with the correctional technique applied to them. Like Colley (2000), they challenge the assumption at the heart of the new correctionalism, that programmes somehow work 'on' individuals; arguing instead that programmes can only work 'through' individuals. They write:

Social programs involve a continual round of interactions and opportunities and decisions. Regardless of whether they are born of inspiration or ignorance, the subject's choice at each of these junctures will frame the extent and nature of change. What we are describing here is not just the moment when the subject signs up to enter a program but the entire learning process. The act of volunteering merely marks a moment in a whole evolving pattern of choice. Potential subjects will consider a program (or not), co-operate closely (or not), stay the course (or not), learn lessons (or not), apply the lessons (or not). Each one of these decisions will be internally complex and take its meaning according to the chooser's circumstances.

(Pawson and Tilley 1997: 38)

Conclusion

The judicial and administrative arrangements brought into being by the Crime and Disorder Act (1998) threaten to draw greater numbers of younger, less problematic, children and young people into the youth justice system, to subject them to modes of correctional intervention which have not been shown to be particularly effective and, in consequence, to propel many more of them into the custodial institutions from which, Sir David Ramsbotham the Chief Inspector of Prisons believes, anybody under 18 should be immediately removed (Home Office 1998b).

However, the effectiveness, or otherwise, of these correctional techniques or institutional regimes does not appear to be the main criterion by which New Labour's youth justice system will stand or fall. While it is of course true that these techniques have, at some times, in some places and with some people, 'worked', their incorporation into policy is, as I have argued above, largely determined by pre-scientific, ideological and managerial imperatives. And this is because the primary target of New Labour's youth justice strategy is not the criminal behaviour of a handful of young offenders, but the voting habits of a far larger and much older constituency. New Labour has placed youth crime at the core of its social and criminal justice policies, alongside, and inextricably linked with, its assault upon 'welfare mothers', 'failing families', laggard education authorities, self-serving public professionals and 'neighbours from hell'. In the process, the claims of justice for juveniles have been subordinated to the political allure of correctionalism. As a result, it seems unlikely that the new youth justice will contribute significantly to community safety.

References

Andrews, D., Zinger, R., Hoge, J., Bonta, P., Gendreau, P. and Cullen, F. (1990) 'Does Correctional Treatment Work? Clinically Relevant and Psychologically Informed Meta-Analysis', *Criminology*, 28: 369–404.

Audit Commission (1996) *Misspent Youth: Young People and Crime*, London: The Audit Commission.

Braithwaite, J. (1979) *Inequality, Crime and Social Policy*, London: Routledge and Kegan Paul.

—— (1981) 'The Myth of Social Class and Criminality Reconsidered', *American Sociological Review*, 46: 36–57.

—— (1989) *Reintegrative Shaming*, Cambridge: Cambridge University Press.

—— and Daly, K. (1994) 'Masculinities, Violence, and Communitarian Control', in T. Stanko and T. Newburn (eds) *Just Boys Doing Business*, London: Routledge.

Brewer, D., Hawkins, J., Catalano, B. and Neckerman, H. (1995) 'Preventing Serious, Violent and Chronic Juvenile Offending: A Review of Evaluations of Selected Strategies in Childhood, Adolescence and the Community', in J. Howell, B. Krisburg, J. Hawkins and J. Wilson, *Serious, Violent and Chronic Juvenile Offenders*, London: Sage Publications.

Campbell, B. (1995) *Goliath, Britain's Dangerous Places*, London: Methuen.

Christie, N. (1977) 'Conflicts as Property', *British Journal of Criminology*, 17: 1–15.

Clear, H. and Hardeyman, C. (1990) 'The New Intensive Supervision Movement', *Crime and Delinquency*, 36: 42–60.

Colley, H. (2000) *What Do We Think We're Doing? How Mentors' Beliefs About Disaffection Influence the Process of Mentoring Disaffected Young People*, Paper presented to BERA Post-16 Special Interest Group, Milton Keynes.

Crimmens, D. and Pitts, J. (2000) *Positive Residential Practice, Learning the Lessons of the 1990s*, Lyme Regis: Russell House Publishing.

Currie, E. (1985) *Confronting Crime*, New York: Pantheon Books.

Dennis, N. (1997) *Zero Tolerance: Policing in a Free Society*, London: Institute for Economic Affairs.

Department of Health and Social Security (1969) *Children and Young Persons Act*, London: HMSO.

Elejabarrieta, F. *et al.* (1993) *Els Programes de Mediacio: Que Pensen i Com Els Viuen Les Parts Implicades*, Barcelona: Universitata Autonoma de Barcelona.

Fabiano, E., Porporino, F. and Robinson, D. (1991) 'Canada's Cognitive Skills Program Corrects Faulty Thinking', *Corrections Today*, 53 (August): 102–8.

Farrington, D. (1996) *Understanding and Preventing Youth Crime*, York: Joseph Rowntree Foundation.

Field, S. (1990) *Trends in Crime and Their Interpretation*, Home Office Research Study No. 119, London: HMSO.

Fo, W. and O'Donnell, C. (1974) 'The Buddy System: Relationship and Contingency Conditioning in a Community Intervention Program for Youth with Non-Professionals as Behaviour Change Agents', *Journal of Consulting and Clinical Psychology*, 42: 163–96.

Forrester, D., Frenz, S., O'Connell, M. and Pease, K. (1990) *The Kirkholt Burglary Prevention Project: Phase II*, London: Home Office.

Gendreau, P. (1996) 'The Principles of Effective Intervention with Offenders', in A. Harland (ed.) *Choosing Correctional Options That Work*, Thousand Oaks: Sage Publications.

Glennester, H. and Midgley, J. (1991) *The Radical Right and the Welfare State: An International Assessment*, London: Harvester Wheatsheaf.

Goldson, B. (1999) 'Youth (In)justice: Contemporary Developments in Policy and Practice', in B. Goldson (ed.) *Youth Justice: Contemporary Policy and Practice*, London: Ashgate.

—— (2000) (ed.) *The New Youth Justice*, Lyme Regis: Russell House Publishing.

Goodman, T. (1972) *Companionship Therapy: Studies in Structured Intimacy*, New York: Jossey Bass.

Graham, J. and Bowling, B. (1995) *Young People and Crime*, London: Home Office.

Hagan, J. (1993) 'The Social Embeddedness of Crime and Unemployment', *Criminology*, 31: 455–91.

Hagedorn, J. (1998) *People and Folks: Gangs, Crime and the Underclass in a Rustbelt City*, Chicago: Lakeview Press.

Hagell, J. and Newburn, T. (1994) *Persistent Young Offenders*, London: Policy Studies Institute.

Haines, K. (2000) 'Referral Orders and Youth Offender Panels: Restorative Approaches and the New Youth Justice', in B. Goldson (ed.) *The New Youth Justice*, Lyme Regis: Russell House Publishing.

Hoghughi, M. (1983) *The Delinquent*, London: Burnett Books.

Home Office (1982) *Criminal Justice Act*, London: Home Office.

—— (1997a) *Crime (Sentences) Act*, London: Home Office.

—— (1997b) *No More Excuses*, London: Home Office.

—— (1998a) *Crime and Disorder Act*, London: Home Office.

—— (1998b) *The Chief Inspector of Prisons Report on Werrington Young Offenders Institution*, London: Home Office.

Hope, T. (1994) *Communities Crime and Inequality in England and Wales*, Paper presented to the Cropwood Round Table Conference Preventing Crime and Disorder, Cambridge, 14–15 September.

ILYJS (1995) *Statement of Principles and Practice*, London: National Association for the Care and Resettlement of Offenders.

Johnstone, G. (2000) 'Penal Policy Making: Elitist, Populist or Participatory', *Punishment and Society*, 2(2): 161–80.

Jones, K. (2001) 'An Analysis of the Deviant Careers of Young People Placed Upon the Child Protection Register of One London Borough', unpublished M.Phil. thesis, University of Luton.

Karger, H. J. (1991) 'The Radical Right and Welfare Reform in the United States', in H. Glennester and J. Midgley (eds) *The Radical Right and the Welfare State: An International Assessment*, London: Harvester Wheatsheaf.

Lea, J. and Young, J. (1988) *What is to Be Done About Law and Order?*, Harmondsworth: Penguin.

Lipsey, M. and Wilson, D. (1998) 'Effective Intervention for Serious Juvenile Offenders: A Synthesis of Research', in R. Loeber and D. Farrington (eds) *Serious and Violent Juvenile Offenders: Risk Factors and Successful Interventions*, Thousand Oaks: Sage Publications.

Loveday, B. and Marlow, A. (2000) *Policing After MacPherson*, Lyme Regis: Russell House Publishing.

Mair, P. (2000) 'Partyless Democracy: Solving the Paradox of New Labour', *New Left Review*, March/April: 21–36.

Mandelson, P. and Liddle, R. (1996) *The Blair Revolution*, London: Faber.

Marquand, D. (1999) 'Progressive or Populist? The Blair Paradox', in D. Marquand (ed.) *The Progressive Dilemma: From Lloyd George to Blair*, 2nd edition, London: Verso, 225–46.

Martinson, R. (1974) 'What Works? – Questions About Prison Reform', *The Public Interest*, Spring: 22–54.

Matthews, R. and Pitts, J. (1998) 'Rehabilitation, Recidivism and Realism: Evaluating Violence Reduction Programs in Prison', *The Prison Journal*, 78(4): 390–405.

Mehlbye, J., Sommer, B. and Walgrave, L. (1998) *Confronting Youth in Europe: Juvenile Crime and Juvenile Justice*, Denmark: AKF.

Mika, H. and Zehr, H. (1997) *Fundamental Concepts of Restorative Justice*, Harrisonburg, VA: Mennonite Central Committee USA.

Muncie, J. (1999) *Youth and Crime*, London: Sage Publications.

Murray, C. (1994) *Underclass: The Crisis Deepens*, London: Institute of Economic Affairs.

NACRO Young Offenders Committee (1997) *3Rs: Responsibility, Restoration and Reintegration*, London: NACRO.

Newburn, T. (1995) *Crime and Criminal Justice Policy*, London: Longman.

Pawson, R. and Tilley, N. (1997) *Realistic Evaluation*, London: Sage Publications.

Perfect, M. (1998) unpublished speech on the 1998 Criminal Justice Act delivered to the Crime and Disorder Conference, Anglia Polytechnic University, New Hall, Cambridge, September.

Phillips, M. (1994) 'Is the Male Redundant Now?', *Observer*, 26 May: 27.

Pitts, J. (1988) *The Politics of Juvenile Crime*, London: Sage Publications.

—— (1992) 'The End of an Era', *Howard Journal*, 31(2): 133–49.

—— (1997) 'Youth Crime, Social Change and Crime Control in Britain and France in the 1980s and 1990s', in H. Jones (ed.) *Towards a Classless Society*, London: Routledge.

—— (2000a) *Youth Justice*, Research Matters, Community Care/Reed Business Information, April–October: 56–60.

—— (2000b) 'The New Youth Justice and the Politics of Electoral Anxiety', in B. Goldson (ed.) *The New Youth Justice*, Lyme Regis: Russell House Publishing.

—— and Hope, T. (1998) 'The Local Politics of Inclusion: The State and Community Safety', *Social Policy and Administration*, 31(5): 37–58.

Porporino, F. and Robinson, D. (1995) 'An Evaluation of the Reasoning and Rehabilitation Program with Canadian Federal Offenders', in R. Ross and R. Ross (eds) *Thinking Straight*, Ottawa: Air Training Publications.

Preston, R. H. (1980) 'Social Theology and Penal Theory and Practice: The Collapse of the Rehabilitative Ideal and the Search for an Alternative', in A. E. Bottoms and R. H. Preston (eds) *The Coming Penal Crisis*, Edinburgh: Scottish Academic Press.

Sampson, R. J. and Laub, J. (1993) *Crime in the Making: Pathways and Turning Points*, Cambridge, Mass.: Harvard University Press.

——, Raudenbush, S. W. and Earls, F. (1997) 'Neighbourhoods and Violent Crime: A Multi-Level Study of Collective Efficacy', *Science* 277 (15 August): (page nos. not known).

Sherman, L., Gottfredson, D., MacKenzie, J., Reuter, P. and Bushway, S. (1998) *Preventing Crime: What Works, What Doesn't, What's Promising*, Washington, DC: US Department of Justice.

Simon, J. (2000) 'From the Big House to the Warehouse: Rethinking Prisons and State Government in the 20th century', *Punishment and Society*, 2(2): 213–34.

—— (2001) 'Entitlement to Cruelty: Neo-liberalism and the Punitive Mentality in the United States', in K. Stenson and R. Sullivan (eds) *Crime, Risk and Justice*, Devon: Willan.

Skynner, R. (1974) 'The Minimum Sufficient Network', *Social Work Today*, 14 July.

Sutherland, E. (1934) *Principles of Criminology*, Chicago: J. B. Lippincott and Co.

Thorpe, D., Smith, D., Green, C. and Paley, J. (1980) *Out of Care*, London: Allen & Unwin.

Utting, W., Bright, J. and Hendrickson, B. (1993) *Crime and the Family, Improving Child Rearing and Preventing Delinquency*, Family Policy Studies Centre, Paper no.16, London: Family Policy Studies Centre.

Van Hooris, P. (1985) 'Restitution Outcome and Probationer's Assessments of Restitution: The Effects of Moral Development', *Criminal Justice and Behaviour*, 12: 259–87.

Vanstone, M. (2000) 'Cognitive-Behavioural Work with Offenders in the UK: A History of Influential Endeavour', *The Howard Journal*, 39(2): 171–83.

Warner Report (1996) *Choosing with Care*, London: Department of Health.

West, D. and Farrington, D. (1973) *Who Becomes Delinquent?*, London: Heinemann.

Wikstrom, T. and Loeber, R.(1997) 'Individual Risk Factors, Neighbourhood SES and Juvenile Offending', in M. Tonry (ed.) *The Handbook of Crime and Punishment*, New York: Oxford University Press.

Wilson, J. Q. and Kelling, G. (1982) 'Broken Windows: The Police and Neighbourhood Safety', *Atlantic Monthly* (March): 29–38.

Young, J. (1999) *The Exclusive Society*, London: Sage Publications.

Youth Justice Task Force (1998) *The Final Report of the Youth Justice Task Force*, London: Youth Justice Board of England and Wales.

8   Crime victimisation and inequality in risk society

Tim Hope

Introduction

We live in both a *risk society* (Beck 1992) and an *exclusive society* (Young 1999). At the same time as we orient ourselves around the risks and dangers which we see surrounding us in our everyday lives, so also do our social and political arrangements lend themselves to the magnification of inequalities in access to those goods which reassure, protect or expose ourselves to risk. As our perception of the 'bads' increases, so do we seek to garner the 'goods' which would keep them at bay, trading on our capital reserves and capacities across the various spheres of economy, community and culture. The 'ontological insecurity' which the condition of late modernity inspires in us (Giddens 1990; Young 1999) fuses with the apprehension of mundane insecurities, pressurising us to invest in the means of *risk avoidance* (Hope and Sparks 2000). As we feel increasingly that the public sphere alone can no longer guarantee sufficiently the *public goods* of everyday safety (see Garland 1996), so we are thrown upon our own individual and collective resources and strategies to acquire the *private goods* which would remedy our perceived security deficit. And our incapacity to protect ourselves from risk leads to frustration with government – still seen as the primary provider of safety in modern society – and with ourselves, as a reflection of our own powerlessness in the face of the risks and harms that surround us.

Yet, access to capital in one sphere – for instance, through income and wealth – remains an important commodity for acquiring capital in another sphere – for example, in 'community safety' – promising to buy ourselves out of risk and into security. That the dynamic of consuming private security itself may be inherently and literally unsatisfying (Loader 1997) is not in itself a guarantee that we will not continue to consume at an ever increasingly voracious rate. And if security is a relative or 'positional' good – one that acquires value for its possessor to the extent that others do not possess it to the same degree (Hirsch 1977) – then to the degree that those with capital successfully pursue their private strategies of risk avoidance, those without will become increasingly excluded from access to the goods of private security (Hope 1999; 2000). Existing social inequalities will thus be reproduced in the newer spheres of risk and risk avoidance.

If such a process is at work in contemporary society we might expect to see its consequences in the observed structure of outcomes – both of risk and of risk avoidance. Even if we have little access to the decision-making processes of individuals, and little chance of observing their pursuit of strategies of risk avoidance in their everyday lives, we may still be able to infer their operation from the observed structural patterns of risk. In this vein, this chapter essays an 'actuarial' analysis of the distribution of the risk to private citizens of household property crime victimisation in England and Wales, as measured by the British Crime Survey.

Crime risk in risk society

Actuarialism and criminology

Actuarialism in criminology has an ambivalent role. On the one hand,

> The actuarial stance is calculative of risk, it is wary and probabilistic, it is not concerned with causes but with probabilities; not with justice but with harm minimisation. It does not seek a world free of crime but one where the best practices of damage limitation have been put in place; not a utopia but a series of gated havens in a hostile world.
>
> (Young 1999: 66)

If actuarialism is 'a major motif of social control in late modern society' (*ibid.*), a criminology whose methodology is actuarial may also collude with the newer manifestations of domination and injustice inherent in the risk society, elevating principles of societal risk management above those of individual justice and liberty (Feeley and Simon 1993). Actuarial analysis thus becomes a tool not only for key-players in the emerging markets of private insurance and security but also more generally for many governance projects in social control (Simon 1987) – an 'administrative criminology' for the risk society (Young 1999). Actuarial criminology may then become as complicit in social control as did once a 'modern' (positivist) criminology in correctional penology (Hope and Sparks 2000; Taylor *et al*. 1973).

Yet, on the other hand, in risk society, actuarialism itself has also become a primary medium through which individuals, organisations and institutions make sense of their world, communicate with one another and pursue strategies of self-interest (Beck 1992). If society is becoming organised around considerations of risk management and risk avoidance – not only in governmental projects for the social control of dangerous classes (Feeley and Simon 1993), but also profoundly in everyday lives and private practices (O'Malley 1992) – then actuarial analysis must also constitute a major way of interpreting strategies of risk management, including relations of inequality which may underlie them; with the possibility that it could be critical of, as well as complicit in, strategies of social control.

In respect of household property crime – including, burglary, theft and criminal damage – 'risk factors' such as where you live and how much you own, or owe, have already become key factors informing insurers about your present and future risk and what kind of contract they are willing to enter into with you to deal with your apprehension of that risk. In risk society, people become increasingly reflexive of the risks facing them (even if they cannot calculate their risks precisely) and, especially, how their own risks are viewed by powerful institutions which have the capacity to affect their individual, private security. For instance, those who cannot get household insurance, or face high premiums, rapidly acquire an everyday knowledge of how the crime risk of their community is viewed by the master institutions of contemporary society. Similarly, research has shown for some time that residents of 'problem estates' are often acutely aware of the stigma attached to their community and will often hotly resist the reinforcement of that stigma by external bodies, particularly their social welfare landlords (Hope 1997). As research into the phenomenon of neighbourhood watch suggests, the publication of local crime figures by the police may not only stimulate increased security consciousness but also the worry and anxiety which is supposed to be allayed (Hope 1995).

In light of the declining efficacy of the state to provide universal security from crime, *reflexivity towards crime risk* becomes a more significant strategy of everyday life. People may seek actively to provide themselves with private security, and to 'react to crime' in their everyday lives, albeit with imperfect knowledge of the risks confronting them or the means which might be available for their protection (Skogan and Maxfield 1981). What is of interest, though, are the *collective consequences* of these individual actions, not only for the level but also for the *distribution* of private security.

The critique of 'actuarial justice' is concerned primarily to protect the erosion of civil liberty which occurs when people are dealt with solely on the basis of group characteristics. For example, where decisions to grant parole to prisoners are based on the statistical probability of reconviction for the applicant's reference group (defined by age, gender, etc.) rather than on more personal or moral criteria (Feeley and Simon 1993). Yet in its focus on individual liberty, this critique may render itself less able to address genuinely *collective issues* of social justice, such as class, race or gender bias in criminal justice processes and outcomes, which are only likely to be revealed by aggregate statistical analysis. So, in the interests of distributive justice, we would need to know whether the emergent distribution of crime risk heightens 'unjustifiable inequalities' in access to the rights and goods of private safety and how the reflexive implementation of private security in response to risk is distributed socially. And for this we need 'actuarial' criteria on which to base our moral and political discourse about the new insecurities of the risk society.

Over the past twenty years, household crime victimisation surveys have become a major *technology* for measuring crime risk and informing practice; and their deployment has contributed both to the definition and management of crime risk. The scale and resources necessary to conduct these have meant that they are a tool usually only available to large-scale organisations, primarily governments. Their use in crime management seems set to grow. For instance, at the time of writing, the Home Office for England and Wales has announced plans to double the sample size of the British Crime Survey and to make its coverage more consistent with police areas, presumably with the intention of setting it alongside the current 'official statistics' of crimes recorded by the police as another part of the state's national accounting of crime risk. To be sure, dominant modes of surveying may have major biases of response and coverage which distort estimations of risk – most notably in the case of violence against women (Stanko 2000) – but such distortions may be less to do with the technology *per se* than with the practices and uses built into particular survey *techniques* commonly used (see Mooney 1998). The burgeoning technology of risk control *per se* is not necessarily dystopian – in this case, more actuarial knowledge of crime risk is not an inevitable precursor of greater dominance. What is more at stake in the politics of risk society is the *reflexivity* with which the actuarial analysis of risk is handled (Beck 1992). In particular, whether risk is treated as if it were an *accidental misfortune* emanating from the seemingly 'natural' or given environment of its potential victims (see Felson 1998) or as a *manufactured risk* (Giddens 1990), embedded in the social structure, inherent in the social positions in which people are located and in the distributions of opportunities and threats to which they are differentially exposed (Ewald 2000). Consequently, before we conduct an actuarial analysis of victimisation risks, it is necessary to be reflexive about the framework used to make sense of such analysis.

Risk positions and crime victimisation

As risks become regular or routine – or, alternatively, as risk-generating routines proliferate – so risks become embedded into the structure of everyday life (see Giddens 1984) and thus, consequentially, people come to acquire *social risk positions* in relation to them. Yet these positions are not *necessarily* identical to, or consequential upon, 'traditional' social or class positions (Beck 1992). In the social conditions of late modernity, neither risks nor social positions are fixed or ascribed by traditions of community, culture or the inheritance of capital. Risks fall widely amongst those who take part in modernity's routines and activities. Indeed, one of the most influential explanations for the growth of property crime in contemporary society is that of the growth and change in the structure of *opportunities for crime* produced by changes in everyday *routine activities* – especially the growth of desirable and stealable goods – such as televisions, hi-fis and CD players, computers and motor vehicles – and the increase of activities away from the home and domestic environment (Felson 1998). That such growth could be identified under macro-social conditions of apparently increasing wealth, economic opportunity and equality (Cohen and Felson, 1979) presented an argument against traditional, class-based explanations of vulnerability to crime risk. Moreover, while in industrial society, the distribution of crime risk primarily reflected the ecological patterns of urban growth and industrial production, produced chiefly as a consequence of social and spatial proximity to populations vulnerable to offending, in late modern society, crime risk patterns no longer so closely follow these imperatives, reflecting more divergent patterns of distribution of communication and consumption rather than of production (see Bottoms and Wiles 1997; Felson 1998).

Arguably, in the conditions of early modernity (industrial society) crime risk flowed as a consequence of incumbency in positions *ascribed by the social order*: since the lower classes were more prone to offending (as most prevailing explanations predicted), lower-class people would generally be more vulnerable to the risks of crime, in all its forms, since they were socially, culturally and spatially *proximate to and familiar with 'offenders'*. The higher classes would be relatively free of crime risk since they were distant and socially segregated from the lower (crime prone) classes and the places in which the latter were concentrated ecologically. In contrast, in late modern, risk society, incumbency in a particular socio-economic position does not in and of itself guarantee safety or generate risk. Opportunities for stealing and for being stolen from are abundant in most walks of life; the 'new ghettos' are not necessarily segregated spatially from the affluent suburbs (Logan and Molotch 1987); and society is open and mobile to the extent that, in theory, 'offenders' are able to gain access to a potentially large number of victims of all classes with fewer formal or practical impediments to their mobility (Felson 1998).

In risk society, vulnerability to risk becomes *individualised* because people are now presented with a proliferating range of options and choices which they are in principle free to adopt in their everyday lives, freed from the proscribed folkways of class, status or cultural identity (Beck 1992). Criminologists have (rather unreflexively) conceptualised this individualisation of potential choice and its consequences for crime risk in terms of a 'lifestyle' theory of victimisation. Here, it is not class or status *per se* which bestow risk or security; it is individuals' lifestyles which *differentially expose or protect* people from risk. Thus, for instance, whether and when a person leaves their home unattended, where they go to and for how long, whom they associate with and where, what they own and consume, and in what quantities, and so on, all become *variables* affecting individuals' differential exposure to risk and the opportunities they afford for self-protection or the protection available from other people. In such explanations, other forms of difference and opportunity in addition to class – for example, in gender, sexual preference and age – become more prominent, all components of differential 'lifestyles' which may vary as much within income groups as between them.

Nevertheless, as Beck (1992) notes, this does not necessarily imply that every kind of risk is classless in its incidence, especially those risks, like crime victimisation, which are not necessarily 'global' in nature, as are global warming or pollution. The seeming 'classless-ness' of risk apparent in some writings on modernity, such as Giddens (1998) and Beck (1992) himself, is perhaps a consequence of a focus on the latter and a down-playing of the importance of the former kind of risk. For more 'mundane' risks, like crime victimisation, it is not so much that risk society abolishes income- and status-based inequalities through individualisation but that these embedded, structural and cultural inequalities will re-emerge, despite the new arenas of life and opportunities for self-expression which modernity has opened-up. Beck writes that:

> The history of risk distribution shows that, like wealth, risks adhere to the class pattern, only inversely: wealth accumulates at the top, risks at the bottom. To that extent, risks seem to *strengthen*, not to abolish, the class society. Poverty attracts an unfortunate abundance of risks. By contrast, the wealthy (in income, power or education) can *purchase* safety and freedom from risk.
>
> (Beck 1992: 35, original emphases)

What differentiates the allocation of risks and safety between rich and poor in risk society is precisely the individualisation which sunders traditional class-based risks:

> The ability to chose and maintain one's own social relations is not an ability everyone has by nature. It is, as sociologists of class know, a *learned* ability which depends on *special social and family backgrounds*. The reflexive conduct of life, the planning of one's own biography and social relations, gives rise to a new inequality, the *inequality of dealing with insecurity and reflexivity*.
>
> (Beck 1992: 98 original emphases)

As Pierre Bourdieu (1998) has shown in his various works, while the possession of economic capital is a great enabler, the power of economic capital to shape its possessors' lifestyles and opportunities finds its expression and reinforcement chiefly through its capacity to accumulate other forms of capital – social, cultural, symbolic – which operate to achieve advantages for their possessors in varying ways in diverse social spaces. In this respect, then, inequality in income and status no longer ascribes a fixed quota of risk so much as it facilitates or impedes *the deployment of necessary and effective capital and capacities for avoiding risk and/or acquiring safety*. Though these acquisitions are achieved through individualised strategies of everyday life, reflecting diversity and differentiation of lifestyle and routine activity, their *collective consequences and outcomes* may nevertheless reveal the aggregate inequalities of income and status that affect the distribution of individual capacities and choices. The next part of this chapter seeks to test this proposition in relation to the risk of property crime victimisation.

Crime risk and the distribution of rich and poor

In conceptual terms, much of the difficulty in sorting out the risk factors of crime victimisation as they are presented in the general population arises because the victimising act itself is the result of a convergence of two separate processes:

> A fundamental aspect of predatory crime is that it occurs in a social context where there exists a convergence of victims and offenders in time and space.
>
> (Miethe and Meier 1994: 44)

This convergence has been expressed also in terms of the conditions necessary for a criminal event to happen – what has become known as the *routine activity* approach, comprising the convergence of 'suitable' victims (or targets) and 'motivated' offenders in conditions (i.e., low 'guardianship') where it is unlikely that a third party capable of exercising control over the situation will intervene (Cohen and Felson 1979). Two basic distributions affecting the likelihood of property crime victimisation risk can be distilled from this literature (for which see Felson 1998; Miethe and Meier 1994):

1   *Opportunities for crime*, as presented by potential victims to putative offenders.
2   *Exposure to risk*, as attributes of victims in relation to supplies of offenders.

The phenomenal growth of household property crime victimisation, especially burglary, during the second half of the twentieth century suggests the proliferation of a 'modernisation risk' within post-industrial societies (Cohen and Felson 1979). Broadly, this risk would seem to consist of a number of characteristics of people's homes and lifestyles (see Winchester and Jackson 1982) which may have proliferated:

- *environment*: expressed in physical forms which combine *privacy* – for example, the degree to which the property is not under the surveillance of others – with *accessibility* – for example, the ease with which it is possible to gain physical access to all parts of the residential property (Hope 1999);
- *occupancy* – the extent to which domestic property is unoccupied and unguarded due to the routine activities of people's lives in work and leisure away from the home environment (Cohen and Felson 1979);
- *value*: the extent to which domestic property is 'valuable' as a commodity which can be exchanged illicitly for other commodities (e.g., cash, drugs) – the most valuable commodities in this regard (including cash itself) usually have a high exchange value relative to their portability (Felson 1998);
- *security*: the extent to which domestic property is guarded by physical, electronic or human means which deny or increase the risk of unauthorised access and appropriation (Winchester and Jackson 1982).

Nevertheless, there are different social positions which the 'rich' and 'poor' are able to take up in relation to these risks (I use these terms for ease of presentation, though advisedly).

Opportunities for crime

There are a number of ways in which opportunity theories of crime would suggest that the 'rich' may be *more* vulnerable to household property crime victimisation than are the 'poor'.

1   The rich have more valuable and attractive *property to steal* – and may be relatively more casual in safeguarding it if they have full household insurance and relatively low premiums and excesses – i.e., the phenomenon of moral hazard (Litton 1982).
2   As more household members are likely to be in full-time employment, they are more likely to *leave their homes unattended* during weekdays and holidays.
3   Their dwellings may be *easier to enter unobserved* – for example, larger, detached houses in their own grounds may afford more opportunities for unobserved and undisturbed access to property (Hope 1984; 1999; 2000; Winchester and Jackson 1982; Maguire 1982).

Nevertheless, the rich may be *less* vulnerable than the poor because:

1   They are more likely to purchase or adopt a greater range of *household security measures*, especially more expensive home surveillance systems (Hope 2000).
2   They may take *greater security precautions* in their everyday lives because they may be more 'risk-averse' (Field and Hope 1990) – for example, by believing they have much to lose from crime victimisation, including the peace and tranquillity of their communities (Loader *et al.* 2000).

The 'poor' may also be *more* vulnerable to household property crime than the rich, because they are less able to afford, or have available, *security measures and protection* (Hope 2000). But they may be *less* vulnerable to victimisation because, being poor or unemployed, they may be more likely to spend time in the home environment, thus exercising more *guardianship* over their household property (Cantor and Land 1985).

Exposure to risk

In the context of household property crime, exposure to risk primarily means exposure to active property crime offenders. Here, the likelihood is that the poor will be *more* exposed to risk than the rich because they are more likely to *live in areas where active property offenders are also likely to live* (Wikstrom 1998).

People who live near poor people are also likely to be active in property crime against the poor because:

1   Having a greater likelihood of being poor themselves, they have (variously) more or greater *motivations to commit crime* (especially if they are also young and male).

2   Young males in poor areas may also be subject to *less supervision and social control* in the community, and spend more time in public in the company of their peers, all of which are conducive to the development of active criminality (see Wikstrom 1998).

3   They may also be more *frequent property criminals* because they have a need for a greater return from crime – for example, to supplement income, or support a drug habit (cf. Sullivan 1989) – or because their (poor) victims yield a lower per offence return of valuable items.

4   They are *less likely to travel* to other areas to commit crime because (a) they lack transport or (b) are averse to committing crime in unfamiliar areas, where they might stand out (Bottoms and Wiles 1997).

As a corollary, the rich may be *less* exposed to risk than the poor because they are more likely to avoid crime by living in the *kinds of area* which are *orderly* (i.e., they do not contain active resident offenders or keep such potential persons under some kind of social control), *distant* (i.e., not close to places containing offenders) and/or *buffered* from criminal areas (i.e., there are other areas or obstacles lying between them and source of criminals – see Hope 1999).

Nonetheless, some of the rich may be more at risk than other rich, or even than other poor, if they live in closer proximity to the poor (see above) by living in 'mixed class' neighbourhoods or 'gentrified enclaves' in otherwise deprived urban areas (see Hope 2000; Hirschfield and Bowers 1997).

In sum, various considerations of both opportunities for crime and exposure to risk result in differing predictions about the risks of household property crime for the 'rich' and the 'poor' respectively. These contradictory predictions may be enough to satisfy those who regard only universal consistency as 'proof' of any axiom (e.g., Wilson and Herrnstein 1985). Because the rich are, in this case, sometimes more at risk than the poor, then victimisation it is suggested must be classless. Nevertheless, as will be suggested below, while the above predictions are apparent *only with other things being equal* (as they are in multivariate, statistical analysis) the likely reality is usually that other things are *not equal*. And one of the key inequalities is that rich and poor have, in sum, unequal propensities towards the various opportunity and risk factors of property crime victimisation.

Models of risk

A certain kind of approach to causation tends to see these as separate questions. In this kind of reasoning, the existence of opportunities and exposure processes are thought to indicate particular explanations of crime. For example, that offending is a matter of rational choice on the part of the offender such that the task of explanation is to demonstrate that these are general processes, irrespective of their observed correlation with other distributions, such as income and wealth which, likewise, are taken to be indicators of competing explanations of crime, offender motivation, or the absence of social control. In some versions of this approach, the causal contenders are required to 'slug it out' to see which one wins outright. In other versions, the task is to apportion the explanatory spoils – so much to this one, so much to that – so as to develop and test 'integrated' theories. Methodologically, these causal strategies require clear specification of expected effects, the development of measurement indicators which are unambiguous (i.e., which either measure opportunity/exposure processes or those of motivation and control), reliable sampling strategies, and the use of appropriate multivariate techniques of statistical analysis (see Miethe and Meier 1994, for an elaboration of this research strategy).

Although in the past we had only officially-recorded crime data, now we routinely possess one other source of data containing potential risk factors

Table 8.1 Household and area risk factors for household property crime

Household risk factors
The worse off?
council tenant (+)
young head of household (+)
children in household (+)
lone-parent household (+)
Asian sub-continent origin (+)
low level of household security (+)

The better off?
non-manual occupation (+)
house-dweller (+)
number of cars (+)
detached house (+)
income (+)

Area risk factors
Deprivation?
single parents (+)
children aged 5–15 (+)
private rented housing (+)
inner city (+)
'rich' ACORN groups (+)

Affluence?
cars per household (–)
deprivation index (–):
• overcrowded households
• large families
• housing association rental
• male unemployment
'poor' ACORN groups (+)

Source: 1992 British Crime Survey (BCS), 1991 UK Census (Osborn and Tseloni 1998; Ellingworth *et al.* 1997); 1996/1998 BCS, 1991 UK Census (Budd 1999).
Note: Household property crime includes: burglary, theft from dwelling and criminal damage to property associated with the dwelling, its contents or grounds. A plus sign (+) = a positive risk factor (crime risk is increased); a minus sign (–) = a negative risk factor (crime risk is reduced).

(predominantly socio-demographic) – the 'cross-sectional' household victimisation survey. However, since these are surveys of reported victimisation events, information on the likely activities of offenders is bound-up with information on the characteristics and activities of victims. As a result, ambiguities remain within the risk models developed, leading to inconsistent predictions of the crime victimisation risk as it affects, respectively, the rich and the poor (for examples, see Pantazis and Gordon 1999).

This can be illustrated, in Table 8.1, with reference to the risk factors identified in three recent efforts to model risks of household property crimes using British Crime Survey (BCS) data (Budd 1999; Osborn and Tseloni 1998; Ellingworth *et al.* 1997). Despite utilising differing sweeps of the BCS, modelling assumptions, selections of explanatory variables, levels of measurement of variables, and the inclusion of information on prior victimisation, the three models come up with consistent findings regarding the socio-demographic predictors of risk. Nevertheless, there is also inconsistency within each model as to the predictors associated with rich and poor. Each of these models include risk factors associated not only with *households* but also (contextual) factors associated with the *residential area* in which the household is located; yet for both levels there are contradictory patterns – both rich and poor areas and households seem at risk.

Nevertheless, looking just at the *ecological distribution* of rich and poor (again estimated from the BCS) we find a much simpler and straightforward relationship with household property crime risk, as illustrated in Figure 8.1. Here, victimisation risk seems unambiguously correlated with the distribution of rich and poor areas. How, then, can we account for this paradox – an ambiguity of risk at the individual level but a consistency of risk at the community level? Notwithstanding the relative propensities of rich and poor respectively to be

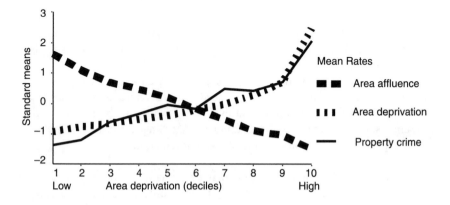

Figure 8.1 Inequality and property crime
Source: 1992 British Crime Survey/1991 Census

associated with particular opportunities and risks, part of the answer at least lies in addressing two questions:

1   What is the *appropriate level* at which risk factors for household property crime operate – are they a product of communities or individuals, and which risk factors operate at which level?
2   How are rich and poor *distributed within and between communities* so that, even if they had different propensities towards risk, the pattern of their respective ecological distributions would result in the observed area pattern of outcomes?

One strategy for research would be to allocate risk factors *a priori* to each level – for example so that factors conjectured to be indexing the supply of offenders would be allocated to the community level, while those indexing opportunities would be allocated to the individual level (Miethe and Meier 1994). Yet while there may be some merit in this approach, again, it relies upon unambiguous specification, not only in the measurement of indicators but also in their allocation to the appropriate level. In practice, few data sets are able to afford this, even if it were conceptually possible to do so with respect to every risk factor. Yet even if the rich and poor had consistently different types of risk propensity, we would still be left with how to handle the possibility that the varying outcomes observed were due to the different distributions of rich and poor within and between communities. In other words, we need to consider how community and household risk *interacts* to produce victimisation outcomes (Miethe and Meier 1994) and how such interaction is *conditioned* by the respective distributions of rich and poor between and within communities.

If we consider area level risk factors to have in common the possibility that differences in victimisation represent differences in exposure to risk (in the shape of active property offenders), then residents of poor areas will have *more exposure to risk* than those in rich areas, because poor areas may contain or attract more frequent and active property offenders than rich areas (Felson 1998: Chapter 2).

Consequently, how the different propensities of rich and poor to household property crime victimisation are produced will therefore depend upon the *balance* of opportunities to crime and exposures to risk attaching to individual households, *relative to the social context in which they are located*. For example, we might expect to observe some of the following interactions:

1   That the *poor in poor areas* have a higher risk than, say, the *poor in rich areas* because, over and above the balance of opportunity and risk associated with poverty, they are more exposed to risk by virtue of their area of residence.
2   The *rich in poor areas* also have higher risks than the *rich in rich areas* because they are more exposed to offenders and have more goods to steal.

3   The *rich in rich areas* may have a higher risk than the *poor in rich areas* because they present more opportunities.

Nevertheless, whether we can observe these interactions will also depend upon how the individual rich and poor are distributed between rich and poor areas. In this respect, the overall pattern of outcomes of property crime victimisation risk – whether in respect of individuals or communities – will depend upon the *class mix* distribution of potential risk propensities attaching to the rich and the poor as they are distributed, 'ecologically', across the range of communities (see Braithwaite 1979, for an investigation of the class mix hypothesis with regard mainly to offending propensities). Even though the 'modernisation risks' of property crime victimisation may be similar for rich and poor, the specific positions which they may be able to take with regard to these risks may vary according both to their personal and social circumstances. The next section provides an empirical investigation of these possibilities.

The distribution of risk

Data in the subsequent analysis is taken from the 1992 British Crime Survey. Information on households comes from the survey, while information on area characteristics is taken from the 1991 Census and refers to the postcode sector in which the household was located (i.e., areas of around 2,000 households defined by the first half of the standard six-figure unit British postcode, plus the next digit, for example AB1 2). The analysis is concerned with variation in the number of household property crimes (defined above) experienced by responding households over the twelve month BCS recall period. The specific types of risk factors used in this analysis are those identified as having a statistically significant effect on the risk of household property crime in the multivariate model estimated by Ellingworth *et al.* (1997) (see also Table 8.1, above), to which the reader is referred for more details about data, measurement and model specification. In this analysis, the aim was to construct four different indices of affluence and deprivation applying to each respondent. These were:

- an *area deprivation* index
- an *area affluence* index
- a *household deprivation* index
- a *household affluence* index.

These are listed in Table 8.2. None of these indices constitutes a perfect measure of affluence or deprivation, and some relevant BCS data are left out. For instance, household income in the 1992 BCS has a high non-response rate and may be unreliable – *pace* Pantazis and Gordon (1999) who conclude on the basis of this variable that the rich experience more crime than the poor. Nevertheless, the variables used aim to capture primary aspects of economic opportunity (e.g., educational level) and consumption (e.g., car access and housing tenure) which have come to be seen increasingly as important surrogate measures for income and quality of life (JRF 1995). Additionally, these variables have already been used in multivariate models of risk (see Table 8.1). Finally, given the binary nature of the indicators – and the observation that the frequency distribution of victimisation is not normally distributed (Osborn and Tseloni 1998), relatively simple descriptive and distribution-free statistical techniques were used to investigate the possibility of interaction effects of the kind noted above.

Table 8.3 shows the correlation between the various indices and property crime victimisation. As a check on the validity of our indices, there is a strong,

Table 8.2 Indices of individual and area deprivation and affluence

---

*Area deprivation index**
proportions of households with:
- overcrowding (> one person per room)
- three or more children
- housing association accommodation
proportion of adult males:
- unemployed

*Area affluence index**
average number of cars per household
proportion of detached dwellings

*Household deprivation index***
rental tenure (household)
not in employment (respondent)
children under 5 years old (household)
lone-parent household (household)
under 30 years old (respondent)
no use of car (household)
completed full-time education under 17 years old (respondent)

*Household affluence index***
owner-occupier (household)
aged 30–59 (respondent)
in full-time work (respondent)
two or more cars (household)
completed education at 20 years old or later (respondent)
detached dwelling (household)

Source: 1991 Census (area deprivation and affluence indices); 1992 British Crime Survey (household deprivation and affluence indices)
Notes:
In the 'Area deprivation index' and the 'Area affluence index', variables were identified for the area level indices using principal components analysis – the variables in the two scales showing collinearity (Ellingworth *et al.* 1997: 213)
*Variables standardised, additive scale
**Variables binary coded, additive scale

negative correlation between the respective indices of deprivation and affluence at both the area $(-.815)$ and individual $(-.770)$ levels, so we can be confident that the indices are measuring the different dimensions of rich and poor. Table 8.3 also shows that residents in poor areas face a higher risk, and those in rich areas a lower risk; and also that poor households have a higher risk and rich households have a lower risk of victimisation. Nevertheless, these correlations, though statistically significant, are relatively weak. What are also relatively weak are the correlations between area and household deprivation and affluence. Though a definite tendency, by no means all the rich live in rich areas $(.319)$ nor do all the poor in poor areas $(.248)$, at least as defined in this analysis. These weak inter-correlations provide some grounds for investigating whether there are stronger patterns of victimisation risk evident from the interaction between household deprivation (or affluence) and area deprivation (or affluence).

Such patterns are indeed evident from the findings presented in Table 8.4 which shows the correlation between household deprivation (or affluence) and property crime victimisation *within* different levels of area deprivation (arranged in quintiles from the 20 per cent least deprived areas to the most deprived quintile of areas). Clearly, property crime risk increases appreciably according to the level of deprivation of the community (see Figure 8.1). Nevertheless, as anticipated, there is also evidence of the *conditioning of individual risk* according to the level of area deprivation. Thus, in the least deprived (most affluent) areas the *rich have higher risk rates than the poor*. Indeed, contrary to the overall pattern (Table 8.3), in the least deprived areas (first quintile), the more deprived the household on our measure, the *less at risk* they seem to be. The pattern of higher risk rates for the 'rich' relative to the 'poor' seems to hold generally in the 40 per cent least deprived areas in the national sample. However, the pattern of risk seems to reverse when one begins to approach the 'other Britain' – the half of the country with the more deprived or less advantaged communities. Here, it is the poor who are more likely to be at risk than the rich.

Table 8.3 Property crime victimisation, deprivation and affluence

Rank-order correlation coefficients (Spearman's Rho)				
	Household victimisation incidents (n.)	*Area deprivation*	*Area affluence*	*Household deprivation*
Area deprivation	.133			
Area affluence	−.154	−.815		
Household deprivation	.051	.248	−.284	
Household affluence	−.029	−.269	.319	−.770

Source: 1992 British Crime Survey, 1991 UK Census
Notes: All coefficients significant at p<.01. Weighted data. Base no. 11,730.

Table 8.4 Correlation between property crime victimisation, (a) household
deprivation (b) household affluence, within levels of areas deprivation

Rank-order correlation (Spearman's Rho)

Area deprivation	Property crime incidence rate per 100 households	Correlation household deprivation and property crime	Correlation household affluence and property crime
1st quintile (lowest 20 %)	17	−.043*	.064*
2nd quintile	26	−.022	.043*
3rd quintile	31	.055*	−.028
4th quintile	38	.063*	−.038
5th quintile (highest 20 %)	49	.034	.021

Source: 1992 British Crime Survey, 1991 UK Census
Notes: Weighted data. Base no. 11,739
* Correlation statistically significant at p<.05

Table 8.5 summarises patterns of risk according to the individual risk factors
used in our overall indices. In the least deprived parts of the country (first and
second quintiles), those most at risk are younger households, and those with
young children and/or two or more cars. Those least at risk are persons not in
work, including the elderly, and those who do not own a car. In the most
deprived parts of the country (fourth and fifth quintiles), those most at risk
include renters, families with young children, lone-parent households and both
young adults and the middle-aged. In both rich and poor Britain, then, there
would seem to be a clear divide in household property crime risk between the
younger population and the older, less mobile, and retired populations.
Arguably, much the same sort of risk processes apply: for instance, younger
households are more likely to leave their homes unoccupied and to have fewer
adults around the home environment to supervise activity (Felson 1998).
Additionally, the relatively more affluent households may also be more vulnerable because of their possession of more desirable goods – in richer Britain these
may be the two-car-plus households; in poorer Britain they are likely to be the
middle-aged. Yet at the extremes of income, households may be able to buy (or
not buy) themselves out of risk. Thus, in affluent Britain, owners of detached
houses may be able to afford sufficient security in order to offset their attractiveness to burglars at the level of risk present in their communities (see Hope
1999; 2000); something perhaps unachievable for detached house dwellers in
poorer neighbourhoods, as their relatively greater risk in the fourth quintile
suggests. Similarly, in poorer Britain, renters may be more vulnerable to victimisation than owners, not only because they are living in the same
neighbourhoods (e.g., social housing estates) as offenders but also because they
are unable to take many security precautions (Hope 2000).

Finally, how does the class mix of an area affect its crime rate? Looking at the
distribution of property crime rates between neighbourhoods, we can estimate
that around one-fifth of the victims of household property crime live in the 10

Table 8.5 Risk factors for household property crime victimisation by level of area deprivation

Level of deprivation of area (quintiles, from lowest to highest)

Risk factor	Q1	Q2	Q3	Q4	Q5
renter	0	0	+	+	+
not in work	–	0	0	0	0
young children	+	0	+	+	+
lone parent	0	0	+	0	+
young adult	+	0	+	+	0
no car	–	0	0	0	0
low education	0	0	0	0	0
middle-aged	+	+	0	0	+
two-plus cars	+	+	0	0	0
detached house	0	–	–	+	0

Source: 1992 British Crime Survey, 1991 UK Census
Notes: + signifies a positive risk; – signifies a negative risk; 0 signifies no significant risk. All differences in means significant at p < .055 (Mann-Whitney U-Test)

per cent of the residential areas with the highest crime rates, and suffer *over one-third* of the total of household property crime (which itself constitutes just under one half of all victimisation recorded in the BCS). Over half of all property crime – and over one-third of all property crime victims – are likely to be found in just one-fifth of the communities of England and Wales. Conversely, the 50 per cent of communities of England and Wales with the lowest crime rates suffer merely *15 per cent* of household property crime victimisation, spread between a quarter of victims (Hope 1996; 1997). Inequality in both individual and area distributions go together – victims who are multiply (or repeatedly) victimised in a given period are more likely to live in high crime rate areas than are other, less frequently victimised victims (Osborn and Tseloni 1998; Trickett *et al.* 1992).

Figure 8.2 suggests, broadly, that this inequality in the distribution of community crime risks is correlated with the ratio of the poor to the rich within the community. It suggests not only that as the crime rate of the community increases, so does the ratio between poor and rich within the community *but also* that the concentration of the crime rate coincides with the increasing rate of concentration of the poor. Thus, the 20 per cent of communities with the highest crime rates not only have appreciably higher crime rates than other communities but also have much greater numbers of the 'poor' relative to the 'rich'.

Although the data presented here are relatively crude measures of risk and social position they derive nevertheless from a representative national survey and provide some guidance about crime victimisation risk, albeit roughly calibrated. In general, they provide some evidence on the likely social risk positions of the 'rich' and the 'poor' with respect to property crime victimisation. Although the

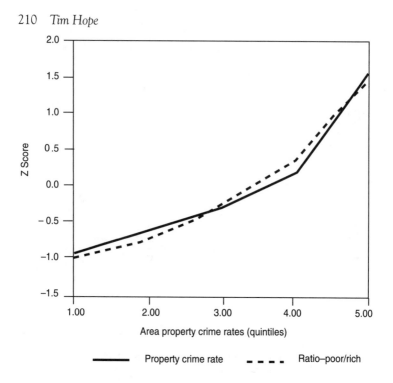

Figure 8.2 Property crime rates and poverty concentration

'modernisation risks' of residential crime – that is, the risk attaching to environ-ment, occupancy, value and security – may be generally applicable to most instances of victimisation and are therefore, in a broad sense, 'classless', the specific social risk positions which rich and poor adopt in respect of these risks vary considerably. Moreover, there does not seem to be any intrinsic risk attaching to individual class position; rather, the risk of victimisation associated with being rich or poor depends upon the social (community) context in which individuals are located. And a primary feature of that social context is its class mix: specifically, the concentration of the 'poor' relative to the 'rich'. The concluding section of this chapter considers some of the political ramifications.

The politics of risk avoidance

Risk strategies of rich and poor

While the state may claim to have the power to prevent crime by being autho-rised to take action directly against 'offenders', private citizens are able to do no more than try to pursue individualised strategies of risk avoidance. Clearly, contemporary governments hope that individualised strategies will also reduce crime in the aggregate – an expectation that has come to be more fervently wished for by politicians as they come to terms with the declining capacity of the 'sovereign state' to deliver overarching (public good) security at a level expected by its citizens (Garland 1996). Yet, this *responsibilisation strategy* on the part of the state *vis-à-vis* its citizens does not necessarily contain within it a conception of the public good. Citizens are not being asked to carry out altruistic acts of intervention, such as to mount guard on other people's homes, to engage in self-denial, or to give up the desire for or possession of CD players or portable televisions. Rather, they are being expected to attain security both for themselves *and* in the aggregate, largely through the pursuit of their own individual self-interest in the avoidance of risk. This is not unlike developments in other areas of social welfare provision and may be part of an emerging 'new orthodoxy' of welfare (Jordan 1998). Yet a core belief in rational self-interest is no guarantee that the resulting outcomes in terms of the distribution of risk and safety will be equitable nor, as important, deducible simply from the summation of individual rational strategies. Rather, it will involve:

> An understanding of the interactions between the (often unintended) collective consequences of individual actions; the emergence of new kinds of risks, and new methods of managing them; changing technologies in the creation of exclusive 'clubs' for sharing risks and collective benefits; and the role of nation states as providers of public goods in a global economic environment.
>
> (Jordan 1998: 113)

Class differences in income and wealth may result in different risk positions occupied respectively by rich and poor via the resources and strategies which affect individuals' ability to avoid risk. Yet the *collective consequences of individuals' strategies may produce inequalities in access to safety and the avoidance of risk.* We can illustrate some of the resulting problems with reference to the data presented in this chapter.

Simply put, the likely most effective strategy of property crime risk avoidance on the part of the poor is for them *to remove themselves from high-risk areas and live amongst richer neighbours.* Reference to Table 8.4 suggests that if they can get into the richest neighbourhoods their risk will greatly reduce, possibly to the extent that they become less at risk than the rich. Unfortunately for them, the most rational individual strategy for the rich to avoid property crime is *to avoid the poor.* Risk seems to increase the greater the ratio of poor to rich in a community (see Figure 8.2), and the rich in poor areas face a higher risk than that of the rich in rich areas. Other things being equal (which they rarely are), neither poor nor rich have intrinsic crime victimisation propensities which they carry around with them (Table 8.4). So, in principle, the individual rich do not have anything to fear from the individual poor by allowing them to live alongside them (see Table 8.5). But they do seem to have something to fear by way of increased risk if they allow *too many* poor to be their neighbours (Figure 8.2), presumably because this would increase the chances of living in closer proximity to active offenders. Whatever the niceties of the situation, the strategies of risk avoidance for rich and poor end up as radically opposed because, rationally, each would see the other as part of their solution to their individual problems of risk avoidance.

The risk pools of rich and poor

Over and above individual class propensities – which this analysis shows not to be invariant across social situations – property crime risk varies according to the community of residence – specifically, the nature of the people amongst whom one lives. On this basis, other things being equal, the most rational strategy for the rich would seem to be to *insulate* themselves from the poor. Neither the individual rich nor the individual poor can control or impose limits on their neighbours and only the very rich can insulate (fortify) themselves and their property to the degree that it does not matter in terms of their perceived security how many poor surround them. In lieu, insulation from risk can be achieved most cost-effectively through *a collective strategy of pooling risk* (Jordan 1998) – by 'voting with one's feet' to ensure that one is living amongst 'low-risk' people. By pooling risk with others a security 'club' is created with the advantage that the low risks enjoyed by your neighbours are also enjoyed by you, and vice versa. In this respect, the 'club' offers collective goods to members – including sharing in the benefits of other people's individualised strategies of risk avoidance – which are not available to those who are excluded (Hope 2000; see also Jordan 1996).

Entry into the private security 'club' of the better-off neighbourhood is, of course, determined by property prices – the capacity which provides individuals with capital to buy into more affluent neighbourhoods also allows the purchaser to buy into the collective security goods of the suburb (Hope 1999). Yet the collective security goods available to residents may be undermined unless their *exclusive nature* can be maintained. Our analysis suggests that this is because private security resembles what Hirsch (1977) called a *positional good* – something which has value to its possessor *only* because others cannot possess it to the same degree and whose supply cannot be increased greatly by changes in the basic factors of production. The positional advantage offered by the 'exclusive' suburb itself diminishes through congestion unless external demand for its goods can be resisted (Hirsch 1977). Positional goods, which residents might once have enjoyed exclusively, loose their value if everyone has equal access to them. If the cost of private security can be reduced by avoiding risk in the first place – particularly by avoiding proximity to a 'supply' of offenders – then the private security value of the suburb will depend upon the extent to which it can maintain its exclusivity by preventing others, including would-be offenders, from encroaching upon it (Hope 1999). Having done so, it can then provide members with the collective benefits of individuals' security actions. That is, keeping the collective *externality benefits* generated by individual private security actions within the club (Hope 2000). It is thus in the interests of the rich within their (low-) risk pool to resist encroachment by the less rich; ironically for the poor, the positional advantage of the exclusive suburban risk pool diminishes the more that the poor successfully overcome the barriers to sharing the positional security advantages of the rich. As Table 8.4 and Figure 8.2 show, the fewer the rich who live among them, the more their risk increases.

Thus, the defence of the better-off community against 'encroachment' becomes an important weapon in the preservation of neighbourhood values and amenities, including security. Much community action in suburbs is 'preservationist' (Savage *et al*. 1992), not least with regard to anti-crime efforts (Skogan 1988), and better-off communities do have some advantages in generating resources to defend themselves. The 'weak', overlapping ties which characterise social relationships in better-off suburbs (see Baumgartner 1988; Loader *et al*. 2000) provide linkages between sources of power and influence within a community (Granovetter 1973). These also provide opportunities for network 'closure', creating a collective reciprocity of social obligation from which *social capital* can be generated (Coleman 1990). In turn, social capital can be mobilised to create collective goods like community organisations and residents associations. These groups can then cash-in the (symbolic and cultural) capital which the neighbourhood holds with extra-communal sources of power, such as public police and local government, to mobilise resources to preserve neighbourhood amenities, including security (Skogan 1988). Without external intervention, the market in private security becomes a struggle for positional advantage amongst competing risk pools – a struggle to avoid the congesting and crowding of positional security advantages. As Mike Davis observes of the 'home-owner' politics of the communities of Los Angeles:

> The market provision of 'security' generates its own paranoid demand. Security becomes a positional good defined by income access to private 'protective services' and membership in some hardened residential enclave or restricted suburb. As a prestige symbol ... 'security' has less to do with personal safety than with the degree of personal insulation, in residential, work, consumption and travel environments, from 'unsavoury' groups and individuals, even crowds in general.
>
> (Davis 1990: 224)

In contrast to the rich, increasing poverty in the social mix of the community seems to be associated with a greater victimisation of the poor (Figure 8.2). Further, *a concentration of poverty in the community results in a greater concentration of victimisation amongst the poorer sectors of such communities* (Table 8.4). And to the extent that the poor are excluded, whether consciously or not, from the security pools of the rich, they face the danger of becoming trapped in the risk pools of poor neighbourhoods and neighbours. In late modernity a key characteristic of the communities of concentrated poverty is the *concentration of social dislocation* (Waquant 1995; Lash and Urry 1994; Wilson 1987). The experience of destabilised neighbourhoods caught in a spiral of economic and social deterioration is increasingly one where adverse circumstances ratchet together to produce compounded social dislocations for both residents individually and communities collectively – for instance, the compounding of offending with other dislocations including youth poverty and drug abuse (Stewart and Stewart 1993, cited in Smith and Stewart 1997). Such compounding of dislocation within the community not only intensifies the harm suffered by residents but also has knock-on effects on the 'institutions' of the community, which themselves might comprise some of the social defences against such harm (Hope 1995; 1997).

Severe economic decline and resource inequality may be producing a vicious spiral in which not only does crime and disorder impinge on the effectiveness of local institutions – for example, schools, youth services and voluntary organisations – but also cripples their ability to provide the kind of framework of order which might ameliorate or offset the dislocations and heightened risks of disadvantage. In sum, the risk pools of concentrated poverty:

> may be due to a failure to prevent the process of criminal embeddedness of local youth [see Hagan 1994] – fuelled by low economic opportunity – which escalates their offending activities, with certain vulnerable groups of residents coming to be repeatedly victimised as a consequence, particularly as social controls progressively diminish and the neighbourhood tips into increasing disorderliness. Each element in the process may interact dynamically with the others to account for the sharp growth of crime in particular communities caught in the spiral of deterioration.
>
> (Hope 1996: 178)

Conclusion: the politics of risk avoidance

As has been said often enough before, the rich live in communities of choice, the poor in communities of fate. The capacity or incapacity to avoid risk underpins the social risk positions taken up by rich and poor and leads to distributive injustice – simply put, the rich have unequal access to security from crime relative to the poor. Although once the meanings of a social good are clarified it becomes possible to work out how and on what criterion the good *ought* to be distributed justly, there is equally nothing intrinsic to the meaning of the good which guarantees how, and by what means, it *can* be distributed feasibly in practice. In the case of private security, as with the delivery of many other social goods, that becomes a political task (Walzer 1983).

The political problem for governments in the face of high crime rates has been seen as that of ensuring, by one means or another, a *level* of provision of security goods sufficient to meet at least some minimum level of need (demand) for the collective good. For these reasons, Garland (1996) identifies two strategies which have been pursued by governments: one consists of greater investment in the punitive, deterrent and incarcerative services provided by the state; the other, the *responsibilisation strategy*, summarises efforts to generate more 'private' (including citizen) investment in the production of collective security. An optimistic prognosis is the hope that by raising the overall (national) aggregate level of provision of private security goods of any kind, the collective need for security will be met. For example, British governments over the past couple of decades have pursued campaigns and programmes of exhortation, demonstration and (modest) investment in crime prevention with the principal aim of raising security levels for and amongst private citizens. And governments remain attached to the 'performance indicator' of achieving reductions in national reported crime rates (Barr and Pease 1990). In a potent political sense, the reduction of the national crime rate is what governments of nation-states see as their mandate from the electorate as a whole (Home Office 1999).

Nevertheless, it appears that the threat to the collective good of private security, *when it is disaggregated as individual risk*, is inequitably distributed amongst members of the population. Not everyone seems actuarially 'at risk' of property crime victimisation to the same degree. This apparent inequality in need poses problems for the project of maintaining the collective provision of private security, particularly through growth in the total amount of privately-provided security. It is not that inequality in the distribution of a social harm itself poses a problem for social justice, but that the available goods to remedy the harm are not distributed on the basis of need but on some other criteria (say income and wealth) which comes to dominate their provision, irrespective of the way in which the meaning of the good implies that it ought to be distributed (Walzer 1983). Thus, we may be far more egalitarian about the distribution of the collective good of private safety than we are about the distribution of private wealth. So it becomes unjust if we allow the distribution of wealth to dominate the distribution of safety – the inequality which we tolerate in one sphere becomes intolerable when it comes to determine the distribution of another, separate and more equitably regarded, sphere. It is not so much that the 'commodification' of access to private security is unjust in an intrinsic sense – that fetishistic, private consumption corrupts the nature of the collective good – but rather that the injustice lies in the *consequences* of commodification – that is, the facility which commodification allows (i.e., money purchase) for those with greater capital to distort the basis on which the good might otherwise be distributed (see also Waldron 1995).

Tackling inequality in the distribution of private safety, then, lies not in the direction of redistributing insecurity (see Barr and Pease 1990), since it is not feasible to assume that members of a society predicated on the pursuit of individual self-interest would accept or let such a redistribution of harm take place, but in safeguarding the autonomy of the just criteria for distributing private security. To paraphrase Walzer (1983: 20): 'private security should not be denied to people who do not possess some other good – for example, wealth – merely because they do not possess wealth and without regard to the way we think private security ought to be distributed'. The problem in implementing this principle, however, is that the distribution of private *insecurity* is intimately connected to the distribution of private *security*. That is, the strategies which are adopted by private actors to provide security for themselves usually at best do not benefit others less protected than themselves and, at worst, reinforce the latter's insecurity.

The collective consequences of crime risk avoidance in risk society is the creation of risk pools dictated according to one's social position, either by choice or fate. The collapse of the state's universal insurance policy against crime victimisation risk (Garland 1996) may have induced a dynamic which encourages the *clubbing of private security* (Hope 2000). As Jordan (1996) argues with respect to social security in general, the logic of collective action – albeit the unintended consequence of individualised strategies of risk pooling and risk avoidance – may act to reinforce *social exclusion* – the transformation of individual disadvantage into an ascribed social position. In a great many respects, in risk society the threat of crime victimisation is not just a consequence of social exclusion but also a contributory cause. The challenge facing government remains whether and how to intervene – not just to reduce risk but also how to distribute fairly the means for dealing with risk.

References

Barr, R. and Pease, K. (1990) 'Crime Placement, Displacement and Deflection', in M. Tonry and N. Morris (eds) *Crime and Justice*, volume 12, Chicago: University of Chicago Press.

Baumgartner, M. P. (1988) *The Moral Order of a Suburb*, New York: Oxford University Press.

Beck, U. (1992) *Risk Society*, London: Sage.

Bourdieu, P. (1998) *Practical Reason*, Cambridge: Polity Press.

Bottoms, A. E. and Wiles, P. (1997) 'Environmental Criminology', in M. Maguire, R. Morgan and R. Reiner (1997) *The Oxford Handbook of Criminology*, 2nd edition, Oxford: Clarendon Press.

Braithwaite, J. (1979) *Inequality, Crime and Public Policy*, London: Routledge and Kegan Paul.

Budd, T. (1999) *Burglary of Domestic Dwellings: Findings from the British Crime Survey*, Home Office Statistical Bulletin, no. 4, London: Home Office.

Cantor, D. and Land, K. C. (1985) 'Unemployment and Crime Rates in the Post-World War II United States: A Theoretical and Empirical Analysis', *American Sociological Review*, 50: 317–23.

Cohen, L. E. and Felson, M. (1979) 'Social Change and Crime Rate Trends: A Routine Activities Approach', *American Sociological Review*, 44: 588–608.

Coleman, J. S. (1990) *Foundations of Social Theory*, Cambridge, MA: Belknap Press.

Davis, M. (1990) *City of Quartz*, London: Verso.

Ellingworth, D., Hope, T., Osborn, D. R., Trickett, A. and Pease, K. (1997) 'Prior Victimisation and Crime Risk', *Journal of Crime Prevention and Risk Management*, 2: 201–14.

Ewald, U. (2000) 'Criminal Victimization and Social Adaptation in Modernity: Fear of Crime and Risk Perception in the New Germany', in T. Hope and R. Sparks (eds) *Crime, Risk and Insecurity*, London: Routledge.

Feeley, M. and Simon, J. (1993) 'The New Penology: Notes on the Emerging Strategy of Corrections and its Implications', *Criminology*, 30: 449–74.

Felson, M. (1998) *Crime and Everyday Life*, 2nd edition, Thousand Oaks, CA: Pine Forge Press.

Field, S. and Hope, T. (1990) 'Economics, the Consumer and Under-Provision in Crime Prevention', in R. Morgan (ed.) *Policing, Organised Crime and Crime Prevention*, British Criminology Conference 1989, volume 4, Bristol: Bristol Centre for Criminal Justice.

Garland, D. (1996) 'The Limits of the Sovereign State: Strategies of Crime Control in Contemporary Society', *British Journal of Criminology*, 36: 445–71.

Giddens, A.(1984) *The Constitution of Society*, Cambridge: Polity Press.

—— (1990) *The Consequences of Modernity*, Cambridge: Polity Press.

—— (1998) *The Third Way*, Cambridge: Polity Press.

Granovetter, M. S. (1973) 'The Strength of Weak Ties', *American Journal of Sociology*, 78: 1360–80.

Hirsch, F. (1977) *Social Limits to Growth*, London: Routledge.

Hirschfield, A. and Bowers, K. J. (1997) 'The Development of a Social, Demographic and Land Use Profiler for Areas of High Crime', *British Journal of Criminology*, 37: 103–20.

Home Office (1999) *The Government's Crime Reduction Strategy*, London: Home Office Communication Directorate.

Hope, T. (1984) 'Building Design and Burglary', in R. Clarke and T. Hope (eds) *Coping with Burglary: Research Perspectives in Policy*, Boston, MA: Kluwer Nijhoff.

—— (1995) 'Community Crime Prevention', in M. Tonry and D. P. Farrington (eds) *Building a Safer Society: Strategic Approaches to Crime Prevention*, Crime and Justice, volume 19, Chicago: University of Chicago Press.

—— (1996) 'Communities, Crime and Inequality in England and Wales', in T. Bennett (ed.) *Preventing Crime and Disorder: Targeting Strategies and Responsibilities*, Cambridge: Institute of Criminology.

—— (1997) 'Inequality and the Future of Community Crime Prevention', in S. P. Lab (ed.) *Crime Prevention at a Crossroads*, American Academy of Criminal Justice Sciences Monograph Series, Cincinnati, Ohio: Anderson Publishing.

—— (1999) 'Privatopia on Trial? Property Guardianship in the Suburbs', in K. Painter and N. Tilley (eds) *Surveillance of Public Space*, Crime Prevention Studies, volume 10, Monsey, NY: Criminal Justice Press.

—— (2000) 'Inequality and the Clubbing of Private Security', in T. Hope and R. Sparks (eds) *Crime, Risk and Insecurity*, London: Routledge.

—— and R. Sparks (2000) (eds) *Crime, Risk and Insecurity*, London: Routledge.

Jordan, B. (1996) *A Theory of Poverty and Social Exclusion*, Cambridge: Polity Press.

—— (1998) *The New Politics of Welfare*, London: Sage.

JRF (1995) *Joseph Rowntree Foundation Inquiry into Income and Wealth*, volumes 1 and 2, York: Joseph Rowntree Foundation.

Lash, S. and Urry, J. (1994) *Economies of Signs and Space*, London: Sage.

Litton, R. A. (1982) 'Crime Prevention and Insurance', *Howard Journal*, 21: 6–22. Reprinted in P. O'Malley (1998) (ed.) *Crime and the Risk Society*, Aldershot: Ashgate/Dartmouth.

Loader, I. (1997) 'Thinking Normatively About Private Security', *Journal of Law and Society*, 24: 377–94.

——, Girling, E. and Sparks, R. (2000) 'After Success? Anxieties of Affluence in an English Village', in T. Hope and R. Sparks (eds) *Crime, Risk and Insecurity*, London: Routledge.

Logan, J. H. and Molotch, H. (1987) *Urban Fortunes: The Political Economy of Place*, Berkeley: University of California Press.

Maguire, M. (1982) *Burglary in a Dwelling*, London: Heinemann.

Miethe, T. D and Meier, R. F. (1994) *Crime and its Social Context*, Albany, NY: SUNY Press.

Mooney, J. (1998) *Gender, Violence and the Social Order*, London: Macmillan.

O'Malley, P. (1992) 'Risk, Power and Crime Prevention', *Economy and Society*, 21: 252–75. Reprinted in P. O'Malley (1998) (ed.) *Crime and the Risk Society*, Aldershot: Ashgate/Dartmouth.

Osborn, D. R. and Tseloni, A. (1998) 'The Distribution of Household Property Crimes', *Journal of Quantitative Criminology*, 14: 307–30.

Pantazis, C. and Gordon, D. (1999) 'Are Crime and Fear of Crime More Likely to be Experienced by the Poor?', in D. Dorling and S. Simpson (eds) *Statistics in Society*, London: Arnold.

Savage, M., Barlow, J., Dickens, P. and Fielding, T. (1992) *Property, Bureaucracy and Culture*, London: Routledge.

Simon, J. (1987) 'The Emergence of a Risk Society: Insurance, Law and the State', *Socialist Review*, 95: 93–108.

Skogan, W. G. (1988) 'Community Organisations and Crime', in M. Tonry and N. Morris (eds) *Crime and Justice: A Review of Research*, volume 10, Chicago: University of Chicago Press.

—— and Maxfield, M. G. (1981) *Coping with Crime*, Beverly Hills: Sage.

Smith, D. and Stewart, J. (1997) 'Probation and Social Exclusion', *Social Policy and Administration*, 31: 96–115.

Stanko, E. A. (2000) 'Victims R US: The Life History of "Fear of Crime" and the Politicization of Violence', in T. Hope and R. Sparks (eds) *Crime, Risk and Insecurity*, London: Routledge.

Sullivan, M. L. (1989) *Getting Paid: Youth Crime and Work in the Inner City*, Ithaca, NY: Cornell University Press.

Taylor, I., Walton, P. and Young, J. (1973) *The New Criminology: For a Social Theory of Deviance*, London: Routledge and Kegan Paul.

Trickett, A., Osborn, D., Seymour, J. and Pease, K. (1992) 'What is Different About High Crime Areas?', *British Journal of Criminology*, 32: 81–90.

Waldron, J. (1995) 'Money and Complex Equality', in D. Miller and M. Walzer (eds) *Pluralism, Justice and Equality*, New York: Oxford University Press.

Walzer, M. (1983) *Spheres of Justice: A Defence of Pluralism and Equality*, Oxford: Blackwell.

Waquant, L. J. D. (1995) 'The Ghetto, the State and the New Capitalist Economy', in P. Kasinitz (ed.) *Metropolis: Centre and Symbol of Our Times*, London: Macmillan.

Wikstrom, P. -O. H. (1998) 'Communities and Crime', in M. Tonry (ed.) *Handbook of Crime and Punishment*, New York: Oxford University Press.

Wilson, J. Q and Herrnstein, R. (1985) *Crime and Human Nature*, New York: Simon and Schuster.

Wilson, W. J. (1987) *The Truly Disadvantaged: The Inner City, the Underclass and Public Policy*, Chicago: University of Chicago Press.

Winchester, S. and Jackson, H. (1982) *Residential Burglary*, Home Office Research Study. London: HMSO.

Young, J. (1999) *The Exclusive Society*, London: Sage.

9   Distributive justice and crime

Paul Wiles and Ken Pease

Distributive justice concerns the dispensation of benefits and services to people, and the tax and other burdens which make that possible. It lies at the core of most political values. In the literature on distributive justice, the central notions include justifications of deviations from equality, means whereby such deviations may be understood, and how fair distribution may be achieved and recognised once achieved. Much sophisticated work has been carried out within this tradition. Notions of justice as impartiality, mutual advantage, primary social goods, 'offensive tastes' and fetishist handicaps (Sen 1980; Nussbaum and Sen 1993) feature in a diverse, complex and important literature. The levels of discord among leading scholars reflect both the complexity of the area and the passion which scholars bring to it. This chapter takes up a few of the ideas of leading thinkers, notably Rawls' (1971) difference principle and Walzer's (1983) elaboration of 'spheres of justice' thinking, to suggest some ways in which crime policy could be shaped with distributive concerns in mind.

The questing criminologist, having become somewhat familiar with (not to say confused by) the leading theories, will seek examples which speak directly to crime issues. These are not plentiful. S/he will find the distributive justice literature to be full of examples featuring goods like education, income and power. Crime tends not to feature explicitly, even as its inverse, safety. Roemer (1996: 64) comments that: 'If one idea must be singled out as the most prominent in contemporary theories of distributive justice, it is that personal responsibility justifiably restricts the degree of outcome equality'. However, in the literature, discussion of benefits and services are typically distanced from the actions (such as crime) of those amongst whom the distribution is to occur, although discussion of pre-existing attributes (such as ability) is plentiful. Thus, while personal responsibility is mentioned as a reason for fairly permitting departure from equality, it is difficult to make explicit links between this and crime policy.

Although there is little in the literature we have read which speaks directly to the distribution of crime, much can be adapted to that purpose. In this chapter, we will:

1   Describe some of the ideas which can be put to work by criminologists.

2   Discuss the linkage between distributive justice and its sub-types, retributive and restorative justice, and how this linkage has been invoked in crime policy.
3   Outline the current distribution of crime opportunities, and conclude that their extreme inequality, and linkage with other social indices, suggests distributive unfairness.
4   Set out some policy suggestions which would have the effect of remedying such unfairness.

Key ideas in distributive justice

Perhaps the best-known heuristic device in work on distributive justice is that used by John Rawls (1971). In this, the fair solution is the one which would be chosen from behind a veil of ignorance by rational people knowing nothing of their own situation and confronting an abstract set of goods. One of the principles which Rawls deemed would apply from behind the veil of ignorance – the difference principle – is that inequalities are justified only if they are designed to bring the greatest benefit to the least advantaged social grouping. Dworkin (1981a and b) also used the veil of ignorance device. His concern was rightly to identify the thing to be equalised (equalisandum) for an egalitarian theory of justice. He distinguished transferable resources, like wealth and power, from non-transferable resources, like talent. He argued that the just solution would involve equalisation of transferable resources as well as the kind of insurance arrangements against deficits in non-transferable resources, which would be taken out by someone knowing their preferences but not their non-transferable resources.

Many philosophers have been sceptical of a single distributively fair solution, and concentrate instead on the permeability of advantage conferred by the possession of goods of certain types. This perspective is known as 'complex equality' and Pascal (1658/1961) is cited as its first clear proponent. Its essence is stated by Walzer (1983) thus:

> The regime of complex equality is the opposite of tyranny. It establishes a set of relationships such that domination is impossible. In formal terms, complex equality means that no citizen's standing in one sphere or with regard to one social good can be undercut by his standing in some other sphere, with regard to some other good. Thus, citizen X may be chosen over citizen Y for political office, and then the two of them will be unequal in the sphere of politics. But they will not be unequal generally so long as X's office gives him no advantages over Y in any other sphere – superior medical care, access to better schools for his children, entrepreneurial opportunities and so on. So long as office is not a dominant good, is not generally convertible, office holders will stand, or at least can stand, in a relation of inequality to the men and women they govern.
>
> (Walzer 1983: 20)

The notion of parallel 'spheres of justice' has been elaborated and applied to specific policy choices by Elster (1989; 1992) and Young (1994). The same notion is of potential importance to a resolution of the opposition taken by Fraser (1997) to exist between justices of recognition and redistribution. In brief, complex equality permits the elaboration of a differentiated view of what should be equalised, and specifies relationships between status of different types. Recognition is achieved when the attribute recognised carries no penalty in other spheres, when for example gender carries no cost in violent victimisation and pension entitlements. Young's (1990) first attribute of ideal city life, 'social differentiation without exclusion', describes a state of independence of status in different spheres.

Fraser (1997: 13) makes a clear distinction between justices of redistribution and recognition. The first is socio-economic injustice, 'which is rooted in the political-economic structure of society'. Examples include exploitation; economic marginalisation and deprivation. This is contrasted with cultural or symbolic injustice. Here injustice is rooted in social patterns of representation, interpretation and communication. Examples include cultural domination, non-recognition and disrespect. The problem of the Marxian working class instances the first type of injustice. That of the gay community instances the second. Fraser points out that the first kind of injustice is remedied by denying the specificity of the disadvantaged group. The second kind of injustice is remedied by asserting its specificity:

> The upshot is that the politics of recognition and the politics of redistribution often appear to have mutually contradictory aims. Whereas the first tends to promote group differentiation, the second tends to undermine it. Thus, the two kinds of claim stand in tension with one another; they can interfere with, or even work against, each other.
>
> (Fraser 1997: 16)

The central distinction made by Fraser (and the elaborated view by Young [1990; 1999]) must either shape the whole of this chapter, or be reconciled with another approach. We believe that it is readily reconcilable with a 'spheres of justice' approach to redistribution. Complex equality is achieved according to Walzer when status is not transferable across spheres. The formulation of sphere is the key to reconciliation with Fraser. In a differentiated society, spheres proliferate. People occupy spheres by race, sexuality, profession and sporting club allegiance. Walzer's approach requires that status is not correlated across spheres. Thus sexuality must not be translatable into professional success. Attempts to do so are unfair (indeed, actionable under employment legislation). Thus a group suffering from injustices of recognition acts not by de-differentiation but by asserting and seeking to establish the *de facto* separation of spheres. This approach requires similar action taken in respect of all those in a disadvantaged set, not *ad hoc* action in respect of those who are in the intersecting set of two forms of disadvantage. For example, it may involve remediation of disadvantage incidental to disability, and remediation of disadvantage incidental to a minority sexual orientation, but not towards the disabled of minority sexual orientation. This becomes crucial (and familiar) when we think of, say, the dyslexic offender. Action may not be taken in respect of the dyslexic offender because it is unfair to dyslexic non-offenders and non-dyslexic offenders. In this way it resolves the 'goodies for baddies' dilemma in criminal justice, described later in this chapter.

Fraser's approach to achieving both distributive justice and justice of recognition, which she collectively terms 'transformation remedies', proceeds by destabilising group differentiation, for example in the case of sexuality by nuancing general notions of sexuality. This is translatable into Walzer's formulation by seeking to change perceptions of spheres of justice, perhaps to the point at which a human characteristic is no longer seen usefully to constitute a viable sphere of justice, and be relegated to an incidental attribute. Fraser's work certainly helps one think in terms of the repertoire of spheres of justice as culture and time limited, and that perceptions of justice will depend upon consistency in distinguishing between human attributes which are salient in judging fairness, and those which are incidental. In sum, Fraser's distinction is seen as helpful in advancing the 'spheres of justice' argument and as being entirely consistent with it. Thus, an informing theme throughout the chapter will be spheres of justice, rather than the central distinction between justices of distribution and recognition, advocated by Fraser.

Crime contingent distributive justice

Before considering the implications of 'spheres of justice' for crime, we must first establish the relationship between distributive justice and the evocations of justice familiar in the criminological literature. It will be concluded that retributive and restorative justice, together with victim support and compensation schemes, are sub-types of distributive justice whose uniting feature is that they are triggered by the crime event.

Criminology takes as its starting point the crime event. Much work has concerned itself with social differences in the probability of an act being classified as criminal, and retribution ensuing. Race has been the social categorisation featuring in much of this work (see, for example, Hood 1992; von Hirsch and Roberts 1997). Retributive justice involves a consideration of the expected probability and degree of sanction consequent on a criminal act and the scaling of penalties in proportion to harm inflicted. This is achieved (however imperfectly) by the specification of maximum allowable penalties and the maintenance of proportionality between crime seriousness and punishment below that maximum. By disadvantaging offenders, it attempts to offset gains achieved by the commission of crime. Restorative justice involves negotiation between the offender and victim to repair and rearrange matters, economically and/or psychologically, between them. Both retribution and restitution seek, however crudely, to restore an approximation of the *status quo ante* of the distribution of resources as between victim and offender. Victim support and criminal injuries compensation also represent attempts to promote distributive justice and this remains possible even when an offender's identity is not known.

Retribution, restoration, victim compensation/support and distribution as modes of justice are linked through their attempts to establish a balance of effort and advantage between citizens. Viewed thus, retribution, restoration and compensation are simply means of moving towards distributive justice in the wake of an offence. Distributive justice can be seen as the overarching notion, with retribution, restoration and compensation becoming relevant (in the service of promoting distributive justice) once a crime has been committed. The debates on race and sentencing note that the formulation of the criminal law itself can generate patterns of ethnicity among offenders, on the basis of differential criminalisation of lifestyles. This well illustrates the limits of distributive justice achievable through the operation of a criminal justice system.

Classifying retribution as a form of distributive justice seems contentious. It could be argued that it is precisely the appeal of these responses that they do not involve any redistribution of resources. But the sanctions of criminal justice do involve a redistribution of resources. A two-year prison sentence delays the development of a career and family life by two years, in comparison with immediate colleagues. An eye for an eye redistributes visual impairment. A fine redistributes disposable income. The problem appears to us to be a consequence of equating the search for distributive justice with policy choices which improve the lot of people. Criminal justice is perhaps unique in seeking distributive justice by deliberately disadvantaging people, but it is no less redistributive for that. One can as well equalise height by chopping off the legs of the tall as by good nutrition of the short.

In what follows, the distinction will be made between initial distributive justice and contingent distributive justice. The former concerns allocation across society. The second concerns re-allocations, which follow disruptions of distribution occasioned by an offence. It should be stressed that the distinction concerns the circumstances of application of fair distribution, not the point at which fairness is to be decided. Fairness should be determined in advance. Only its application is contingent. The principles of retributive justice are general. Their application is contingent on case facts.

Tough on crime, tough on the causes of crime

Because it seems implicit in much thinking about crime, we should explicitly reject the notion that addressing material inequality directly is a sensible way of reducing crime. In a spheres of justice approach, we should strive to make them independent. Some of the key relationships are counter-intuitive, and the research on the penal effectiveness of providing benefits to offenders does not inspire much hope. In Field's (1991) analysis, violence appears linked with affluence. Property crime is linked inversely with GDP/head, which is not a measure of distribution. Moreover, the association is direct rather than delayed, so must therefore be more a function of anticipated than current poverty. The link between violent victimisation and wealth goes against the notion that the poor are most victimised by violence (Skogan 1991). In the analysis of the British Crime Survey, it is the better-off households within the worst areas which are most prone to victimisation (Trickett *et al.* 1995). Improving the job prospects of offenders by training or subsidised employment is not one of the favoured approaches identified by the major review of what works in crime reduction – although there are isolated instances of success (Sherman *et al.* 1997). Crime and deprivation do co-vary at the areal level, but the relationship is imperfect. The simple presumption that economic inequality causes crime is seductive but far too simple. Remedying material inequality is not the royal road to crime reduction.

While remedying material inequality would not be the finding of an evidence-led approach to crime reduction, it is one which seems politically ingrained in parties of the Left. For this reason we will, for the moment, take the debate on these terms. What is the policy link between unfairness in material distribution and the appropriate response to crimes committed by those disadvantaged in the initial shake-out? This link is central to the New Labour mantra heading this section: 'Tough on crime, tough on the causes of crime'. Let us assume causes of crime are taken to include early material and social disadvantage (but, as noted above, the reality is complex). If this constitutes distributive unfairness to the pre-delinquent child, being tough on the causes of crime means reducing material and social disadvantage. If being tough on crime means being tough on the criminal (it can mean nothing else), one is tough on offenders even though distributive unfairness led to their offending. If one is tough on the (presumed) causes of crime, it becomes unnecessary to be tough on offenders. If people offend because of their exposure to the causes of crime, it is unfair to be tough on them. So being tough on crime and tough on the causes of crime at the same time is cruel or dishonest. The problem can perhaps be resolved by being tough on the causes of crime now and later becoming tough on offenders who wilfully offend despite the removal of the circumstances which may contribute to crime.

In practice, the interactive link between toughness towards criminals and toughness towards the causes of criminality, between distributive justice and its sub-types, retribution and restoration, is confused, and most of what is controversial about criminal justice stems from that confusion. The fact that the New Labour mantra has survived without frequent identification of its central tension is itself remarkable.

The nub of the confusion stems from the assumption that if we had delivered distributive justice to someone before he or she embarked upon a criminal career, we would not need to dispense retributive or restorative justice now. For example, many pre-sentence reports and most pleas in mitigation attribute offenders' misdeeds to their failure to have received a fair deal initially. If they had received a fairer share of love, abuse, education, training or the like, they would not be in the dock. When sentences are deemed unduly lenient, this is often because initial distributive injustice has been taken into account. When sentences are deemed unduly harsh, this is often because of a failure to take initial injustice into account. Because these are matters of judgement, the same sentence may be judged both too severe and too lenient. This is typically the case where women have killed abusive partners. Also, probation officers and social workers invite criticism from the press when they use the decisions of retributive justice as a springboard in the attempt to remedy actual or perceived distributive injustice. These hoped-for remedies dispense 'goodies for baddies' where holidays, driver education and the like are offered to the errant and denied to the righteous.

In a society where no one is deprived by initial distribution, retribution (at least towards adults) could be dispensed without any angst on the part of the punisher,[1] and 'goodies for baddies' would be perverse. In the real world, where systemic or individual distributive injustice is presumed to intrude, and the language of the court conspires in that presumption, all criminal justice personnel have to make judgement calls about how the degree of a sanction must be adjusted in individual cases. Arguments about juvenile justice and means of dealing with mentally disordered offenders are difficult because of differing presumptions about the proper scope of remediation of past distributive injustice.

This is not to say that offenders who have experienced initial distributive justice (in so far as society can dispense it) are easy to sentence. Initial injustice starts at conception. Are genes distributed in a just way? Are we the victim of injustice if we have genes making for risk-taking and shortness of temper? Is short stature, and consequent feelings of inferiority and tendency to violence, the product of parental smoking and poor nutrition? The Dworkin formulation described above, and as developed by Arneson (1989) and Cohen (1989), offers at least a way of thinking about these issues. The central shift is from welfare equalisation to resource equalisation. Since resources include native talents, compensation is necessary for inequalities in resources for which individuals are not responsible. This requires a sense of community or fraternity, and requires the talented not to be self-regarding.

In sum, the language, pronouncements and decisions surrounding caution, prosecution, sentence imposition, sentence administration and release – in fact, all decisions dealing with criminal offenders – become difficult in so far as issues of initial distributive justice are taken to interact with contingent justice. Apologetic retribution follows when punitive intervention is moderated by reason of presumed initial distributive injustice. Distribution blindness occurs when punitive intervention is greater by the neglect of such injustice. Apologetic retribution and distribution blindness are the Scylla and Charybdis of offence contingent justice.

In the foregoing, there was too easy a transition from discussions of contingent justice to concerns about what to do with offenders. Leslie Wilkins (1999), instancing his work in preventing aircraft accidents, repeatedly bemoaned the reduction of the problem of crime (paralleling the crash) to the problem of the offender (paralleling the pilot or ground crew). Historically, offence contingent justice has been centred on the offender. Sanctions are generally tempered or wholly by-passed on the basis of the offender's failure to receive distributive fairness in the past. Offender-oriented crime reduction methods are based upon belated attempts to afford distributive justice to perpetrators. This translates into those applications for crime prevention funding providing facilities for offenders. It is interesting that all long-term person-oriented crime prevention programmes are focused on offenders, or those at risk of becoming offenders, rather than victims or those for whom victimisation is a future hazard.[2] Even if effective, this assigns to crime victims a secondary role, whose future protection is dependent upon the response of perpetrators to efforts made on their behalf. The fact of a crime leads to two sets of responses, one through the detection and processing of putative offenders, the other to direct protection of the person and property of the victim. Distributive justice is perceived to be important for the offender and to be achieved to benefit the victim only through the achievement of change to the perpetrator.

Is it a fact of nature that the allocation of long-term person-oriented crime prevention has to be centred upon the perpetrator rather than the victim? It is not. The sad fact is that we know little of how victim careers work. We know a great deal about how offender careers work. Victimisation surveys such as the British Crime Survey (see, for example, Hales and Stratford 1997) are cross-sectional, and do not allow us to view the trajectory of crime victimisation across a lifetime. Just as notions of fairness in criminology have been overwhelmingly discussed in relation to the offender, so the inequities of crime distribution from the victim perspective have been neglected. Farrell *et al.* (2001) propose an accelerated longitudinal design using data from the US National Victimisation Survey, to yield some early answers.[3] The introduction of a longitudinal element into the British Crime Survey will in due course show something about how victim careers develop, but the modest extent of the longitudinal element means that it will be many years before a picture emerges to rival the proposed accelerated longitudinal design from the American data. The fact that we are having to play catch-up on a topic of such importance is astonishing.

Distributive justice and crime victimisation

Perhaps the first problem in recognising victimisation as an issue in distributive justice is linguistic. One talks about inequalities in health and education rather than illness and illiteracy/innumeracy. This is because it is the protective and remedial services against illness and illiteracy whose distribution is at issue. To be comparable, should one cast the victimisation debates in terms of safety rather than risk? The objection may be raised that we cannot come close to guaranteeing safety. However, the same is true in the health arena. Preventive and appropriate remedial treatment can reduce the risks of illness, but some illnesses are intractable, and in many cases, citizen lifestyle may offset the health benefits of preventive measures deployed.

A second problem, more apparent than real, concerns the wilfulness of actions taken to make citizens unsafe – actions taken by the criminally inclined and by those who carelessly dispense crime opportunities as part of their business. Should such actions be excluded from the range of convenience of distributive justice? Why is there no just distribution of directed malice?

Safety has been chosen as the currency of choice only to be rejected. This is because it focuses primarily on the potential victim. One can think more generally about the distribution of crime opportunities. This has the effect of simultaneously regulating victim safety and offender temptation. By choosing crime opportunities, one recognises that it may be as unfair to present someone with a host of criminal opportunities by which to be tempted, as to allow a person or situation to be chronically victimised by those who succumb to that temptation. In short, by choosing the supply of opportunities over safety one considers the welfare of both potential victim and potential offender at the same time.

Considering the distribution of crime opportunities in terms of the well-being of both offenders and victims creates new problems. They should be addressed, but doing so is beyond the scope of this chapter. Probably all human action has an ethical 'range of convenience'. When a society is grossly unfair, the removal of temptations is not defensible. 'Give us this day our daily bread' in the Lord's Prayer comes before 'lead us not into temptation'. Target hardening the baker's shop is not acceptable in a city of starving and penniless people. Target hardening stores selling electronic goods in affluent societies is acceptable. Where is the crossover point? This is not an argument for omitting temptations and delivery from evil from the list of variables to which distributive justice is relevant, rather a balancing of the harms inflicted upon the starving, those who lust after electronic gizmos, PC World and bakers. This is no different from organ transplantation, where insensitive harvesting of the organs from the dead causes their loved ones suffering which has to be set against the suffering involved in repeated dialysis or slow death.

A second apparent problem lies in the interpretation of diminishing crime opportunities as diminished freedom of action. In particular, CCTV is demonised as the sign of the surveillance society in headlong pursuit of crime reduction. In fact, more sophisticated crime reduction measures, such as biometric access control (e.g., your computer logs on in response to your fingerprint on the screen) and location-aware electronic goods (which cease to work when they are moved from where they 'ought' to be), do not reduce the non-criminal options available to a citizen. How one engineers a society which favours such options over cruder forms of opportunity reduction is a debate in itself. For the moment, it should be asserted that controlling the supply of opportunities will not necessarily reduce freedom of action generally.

Before addressing the fairness of current distributions of victimisation by crime, it may be appropriate to summarise the argument to this point. First, it has been suggested that retribution, compensation and restoration are sub-types of distributive justice applied crudely in the wake of an offence to restore the balance of effort and advantage between citizens. Second, some of the most difficult issues in criminal justice come with the interaction between retributive/restorative justice and presumptions about the causal role of distributive unfairness in causing offending. Third, while notions of fairness to offenders are well theorised, no similar development has taken place with respect to crime victims. This is reflected in the absence of research on victim careers, by contrast with the extensive research on criminal careers; and finally, thinking about the distributive fairness of crime opportunities (in preference to the fair distribution of safety or risk) incorporates both victims and offenders as people to whom justice must be done.

Is the distribution of crime fair?

Crime is distributed very unequally across even small areas, and across people within areas with similar aggregate levels of crime (Farrell *et al.* 1996; Hope 1996; Pease 1998). One of the major developments in criminology over the last two decades has been the recognition of these facts and their implications. This has occurred by a number of routes, including the recognition of crimes whose rate of repetition is huge. These include domestic violence, bullying and racial harassment. The smallest geographic unit to be found in the standard volumes on crime, the annual Criminal Statistics, will be seen to be the police force area. Adding up crimes and expressing them as a total for a command unit or police force area obscures how crime experience varies street by street, home by home and pub by pub. The oldest joke about statistics is that if you have got your head in the oven and your feet in the freezer, on average you will be comfortable. Combining quiet areas like Bramhall and difficult ones like Wythenshawe to produce an overall figure for Greater Manchester Police and expecting the resulting total to be meaningful makes no more sense for the corporate body of the police than the oven-freezer predicament does for the human body. Furthermore, the fact that the numbers are routinely expressed in this way shows an apparent indifference to the distribution of suffering which they entail.

Figure 9.1 shows the total number of crimes experienced in each sampling unit of the British Crime Survey. Readers will be aware that this survey reports an enquiry, which now takes place every year, of crime, both reported and unreported to the police, in England and Wales. The data in Figure 9.1 come from the 1988 Survey and refer to property crime, but the picture is much the same in different years and for crime against the person too. The survey employed some 600 sampling points, at each of which some thirty people were interviewed. The 600 areas were then divided into the 10 per cent of areas with the most crime, the 10 per cent with the next most crime, and so on, up to the 10 per cent with least crime. Figure 9.1 simply takes the total number of crimes captured in the 10 per cent (decile) of areas with most crime, the 10 per cent with next most, and so on, and makes evident the ratios between these areas (i.e., how many times more crime is suffered by the worst than the best areas).

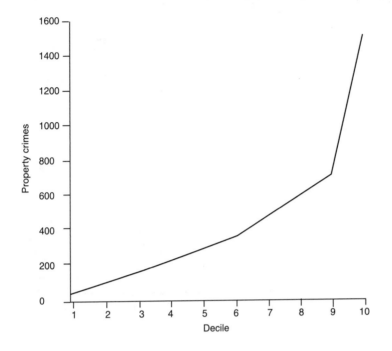

Figure 9.1 Property crime by area crime levels
Source: 1988 British Crime Survey

The shape of the curve shows that the 10 per cent of areas with most crime has more than double the amount of crime in the next most crime prone 10 per cent of areas. Looking at the worst 10 per cent of areas against the best 10 per cent, the worst 10 per cent suffer forty-three times as much crime as the least victimised 10 per cent. Another way of saying this is that some 40 per cent of all crime experienced happens in the 10 per cent most crime prone areas. Well over half occurs in the 20 per cent most crime prone areas. Calls logged from the public will also show a massive range of crime densities.

The 10 per cent of areas with most crime can get to be that way via one or both of two different routes. First, increasing proportions of people living in the area may become victims, so that perhaps 80 or 90 per cent of people in the worst areas suffer some crime. Alternatively, the same proportion of people could become victims of crime in the worst and best areas, but those victimised in the worst areas would suffer crime more often. The old and unfunny joke is that in England and Wales somebody is getting robbed every thirty minutes – and she's getting sick of it. Unfunny as it is, it shows that more people do not necessarily have to fall victim to crime for the crime rate to rise.

Figure 9.2 shows the proportion of people victimised in each area decile. Thus in decile 10 (the 10 per cent of areas with most crime) some 28 per cent of people are victims of crime over the year. The proportion increases steadily to

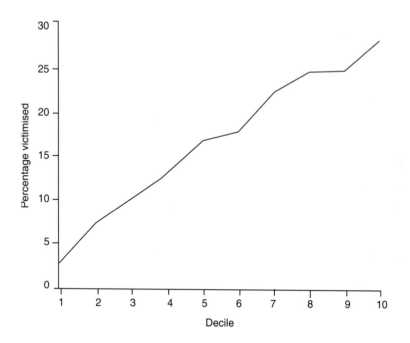

Figure 9.2 Property crime by area victim prevalence
Source: 1988 British Crime Survey

that figure from 3 per cent in the least crime-ridden areas. The point to stress, however, is that even if you live in one of 10 per cent most crime prone areas, you have a 72 per cent chance of not being a victim over a one-year period. However, Figure 9.3 shows the number of crimes which people who are victims each suffer. It will be seen that in the worst areas, each victim of property crime suffers an average of nearly five.

The same pattern is even more marked for crimes of violence, where 15 per cent of people in the worst areas suffer crimes against the person, but each of those who do suffer crime has to endure six crimes, on average. Most people in the worst areas do not suffer crime over the course of a year. Those who do, suffer it several times each. Since areas which suffer much property crime are by and large also those which suffer most personal crime, looking at all crime combined yields an even more marked difference between areas in levels of chronic victimisation.[4]

One should not rely on the precision of the numbers presented to measure crime concentration. There are conventions in the British Crime Survey concerning the maximum number of victimisation forms which a victim may complete, the maximum number of events recordable as a series against a chronic victim, and the like. Such conventions change the exact numbers arrived at. Neither should one stereotype all crime victims as the innocent and put upon. As yet unpublished research by the first author with Andrew Costello

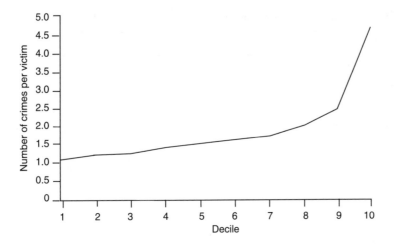

Figure 9.3 Property crime by area victim concentration
Source: 1988 British Crime Survey

suggests recent criminal involvement is a characteristic of some repeat victims.[5] Insurance fraud is another possibility to explain some repeat victimisation. However, there is no challenge to the fact that crime is heavily concentrated, both by area and within area by victim and household. If one wants to address the problem of crime, repeat victims in high crime areas would be where most effect is to be had, whatever the dynamics of the problem.

The reason for developing the point about concentration at such length is that questions about how crime opportunities are distributed is the single fact about crime that one would wish to know if notions of fairness of that distribution were regarded as a salient feature of crime. Yet such statistics are not to be found in Criminal Statistics, and have in the past had to be dragged out of British Crime Survey data after much effort. As criminologists, we have largely behaved as though indifferent to the concentration of crime opportunities.

Even now, criminologists have paid less attention than they should to risk differences across non-geographic dimensions. Over the last two decades, much attention has been given to the development of tools to aid precise spatial location of crime. This has not been accompanied by equivalent attention being given to the social mapping of crime. Even now, the allocation of resource to high crime areas by the Home Office takes the police Operational Command Unit (OCU) to be the appropriate unit defining a high crime area. Given what we know about variation within OCUs, social patterning of crime risks, and the role of prior victimisation in marking out those at high risk, this seems crass. Many people and places outside the designated 'high crime' OCUs will be at greater risk than many of those within it. Illustrations of the social patterning of victimisation opportunities will now be given.

Table 9.1 Risks of domestic burglary by household type

Household is:	Relative risk
head of household 16–24	2.71
one adult living with children	2.00
head of household is single	1.73
head of household is separated	1.63
respondent is Asian	1.77
head of household is unemployed	1.80
head of household is economically inactive	1.70
home is privately rented	1.73s
respondent resident for less than one year	1.75
home has no security measures	2.71
home in inner city	1.52
home in area with high levels of physical disorder	2.14

Source: calculated from Budd 1999

Table 9.1 is calculated from Budd (1999) and represents the risk of domestic burglary victimisation in relation to a national average of 1. It will be seen that certain social groups suffer much more than their 'fair' share of burglary, with young householders suffering some 2.7 times the national rate, the recently moved some 1.75, and so on.

What gets counted, counts

The primacy of geographic over other forms of classification reflected in Criminal Statistics defines the scope of what we can regard as distributively just.[6] We cannot dispense justice when we do not know the variables in terms of which distribution is unfair, however fairness is defined. We cannot know whether health care is distributed fairly in terms of gender, ethnicity or whatever without having breakdowns of health care by these variables. We are ill-equipped to begin to dispense justice because of the paucity of analyses along non-geographic lines. Counting new things may be the most important change one could advocate. Allocating events according to the variables across which the equalisandum must be equalised may be the most fundamental necessary condition for achieving fairness.

Even when thinking geographically, the unit of analysis defines the degree of concentration. Hence even when counting old things (places and people victimised) we must do so in ways which reflect crime experience, rather than aggregated by administrative boundaries. As hinted earlier, the smaller the unit of analysis the higher the degree of concentration. Figure 9.4 shows Lorenz curves for crime data disaggregated at force and OCU level. The most crime prone 2.5 per cent of forces accounts for some 8 per cent of crime, whereas the

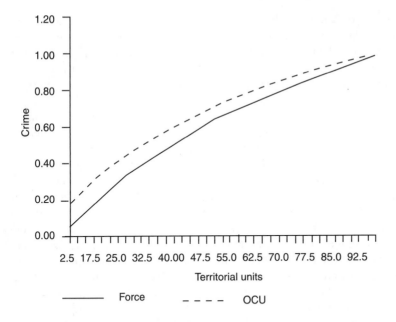

Figure 9.4 Inequality at force and OCU level

most crime-prone 2.5 per cent of OCUs account for some 17 per cent of crime. The difference between the curves remains along their length. The smaller the unit, the higher the degree of concentration.

Displacement

In the late 1980s, the geographer Robert Barr and one of the writers of this chapter (Pease) became interested in the terms in which the debate about crime displacement was being conducted. The debate centred upon whether displacement happened, the extent to which it did so, and the limits on crime prevention efficacy which that entailed. Absent from the literature was any suggestion that some distributions of crime were to be preferred to others. Barr and Pease (1990) expressed the view that:

> 'Displacement' is discussed as a limit on the efficacy of crime prevention. In the gloom that attends such discussion, it is too readily forgotten that for a crime to be displaced, it must first be unplaced; in other words, that a crime at a particular place and time must have been prevented. The word 'deflected' gives a better sense of the achievement at the heart of the process. ... [W]e should ask ourselves what kinds of crimes, perpetrated against whom, would we most like to prevent? Such a question does not admit of a sensible, unqualified answer.
>
> (Barr and Pease 1990: 280–1)

The notion of benign displacement was introduced by Barr and Pease (1990). Benign displacement is said to exist when the distribution of crime after deflection is judged to be fairer than its distribution beforehand. Malign displacement is its opposite. There is a judgement to be made about the fair distribution of unavoidable crime, a point which the lack of differentiation of the concept of displacement obscures.

Barr and Pease's argument has been extended by Barnes (1995). The importance of the argument lies simply in the recognition that the previous literature had been written as though 'a crime is a crime is a crime', with no apparent recognition that the way in which the crime burden is shared is matter of policy concern. To speculate, the literature is as it is because the focus has been on the administrative unit recording crime rather than the crime victim. Police commanders can get into trouble for large numbers of crimes. How they are distributed is not of central relevance. Crimes will be regarded as equal only when their sole existence are as units to be totted up by the police for onward transmission to the Home Office for inclusion in Criminal Statistics. It is not as though crimes are treated that way by front-line police officers, where, for example, particular effort may be given to preventing burglaries against the elderly, or against those who may make the most vociferous complaints to the Chief Constable.[7] Although the literature on displacement is naive about crime distributions, front-line police officers are not.

There are some social changes which may impact upon emerging patterns of crime concentration. One dimension along which people may vary is that of information-richness to information-poverty. Informed decisions taken by the information-rich in relation to where to live, how to protect themselves and their families, and so on, may well tend to concentrate crime victimisation yet further.

So what?

By what means may concerns for the fair distribution of crime opportunities be brought recognisably to bear upon crime control practice? What follows is a speculative, certainly flawed, but hopefully useful attempt to make some of the connections.

Fairness feeds on facts

The first policy implications have already been alluded to. For distributive fairness to be achieved, one must know the distribution of crime events across the social variables of interest. This is true whatever criterion of fairness one favours. If fairness involves limits on variation in the number of crimes suffered per place or household, one needs to know the number of crimes per victim. This is still difficult to determine from police crime recording systems (see Pease 1998).

Knowing the distribution of crime opportunities (whether reflected in crimes committed or crimes suffered by area residents) will not be enough to act fairly. Difficult decisions will be required as to the extent to which chosen lifestyle characteristics drive crime rates. This will require the development of an approach to crime based upon the Dworkin (1981a and b) distinction between transferable and non-transferable goods. Perhaps the development of such an approach should come before the choice of variables in terms of which crime experience must be known as a necessary condition of fairness.

Crime and Rawls' difference principle

Rawls' difference principle asserts a moral mandate to adopt those institutions which will maximise the amount of primary social goods enjoyed by those who enjoy the least of them. Restricting our attention to the supply of criminal opportunities, what would this mean for policy? Policing (as other public services) currently suffers from a surfeit of performance indicators. The difference principle might be applied by substituting one performance indicator for many of the others. This would be the ratio of crime in, say, the worst 25 per cent of households within a force area to crime in the least crime-prone 25 per cent. That ratio can (self-evidently) be reduced by increasing crime in the least crime-prone areas, or by reducing it in the most crime-prone areas. While there would be some limited scope for criming more of the events coming to police attention in the least crime-prone areas, the more plausible tactic would be the reduction of crime in the most crime-ravaged areas. Underpinning this approach is the awareness that the least crime-prone areas largely limit their own crime, by residents installing protections to their homes, ferrying their children to places rather than entrusting them to public transport, mobilising policing effort by persuasive articulation of their concerns, backed by political influence. If leverage on policing services is indeed greatest in less crime-prone homes, manipulating the ratios would perhaps be an elegant way of giving effect to the Rawls' difference principle.

This proposal, while radical in its implications, could be readily implemented, albeit in a crude form. A more refined form would be only slightly more difficult, and would rely on using individual households/premises as the unit of analysis for most property crime, and individual people for crimes of violence. Its starting point is the calculation of some form of coefficient of variability across OCUs, police forces, offence types or whatever. Offence types are chosen here. While of least direct relevance to the comparison of policing areas, there was not available data on police areas disaggregated enough to be meaningful. What is presented here is little more than an indication of what should be done. The standard form of coefficient of variability is SD/mean. This is presented for offence types in Table 9.2. The unit of analysis is the OCU. It will be noted that robbery and violence rates are most variable across OCUs, with burglary rates least variable. It is thus in terms of

Table 9.2 OCU rate variability by offence types

Offence type	Coefficient of variability
violence	2.53
sexual offences	1.65
robbery	3.51
burglary	0.62
theft of motor vehicle	1.84
theft from motor vehicle	1.70

violence that citizen experience is most varied according to where they live. By the Rawls' difference principle, areas with the highest rates of violence should be given some priority, since they define the most extreme variation by area.

It is perhaps worth noting that standard scores (mean/SD) are commonplace in the criminological literature, whereas the coefficient of variability (SD/mean) is extremely rare. In microcosm, this eloquently states that criminology has neglected the measures in terms of which distributive justice is always conceived.

Combining or uncoupling forms of disadvantage

There are two approaches to considering crime opportunities alongside the supply of other forms of good or service. One is to incorporate them all into externally occasioned hazard, as the common currency of distributive justice. This will be examined next, and followed by some consideration of crime opportunities within a 'spheres of justice' framework.

Hazard integration

This approach has been most fully developed within criminology, as the length of its exposition here suggests (see also Wiles and Pease 2000). Ironically, it will find much less favour amongst philosophers of equity. Its central element is to integrate the consideration and response to diverse externally-caused hazards. The separation of crime and disorder as kinds of harm should be avoided. This would require the repeal of the Crime and Disorder Act (1998) and its replacement by an Act which did not distinguish between harms resulting from human malice and other harms. Current arrangements will lead to, for example, intensive action to reduce pub assaults while more people are being killed on the roads. Harms should not be divided into criminal and other for the purposes of prevention. The elevation of crime to a privileged position among harms risks the 'criminalisation of social policy', and the cynical justification of programmes which may be progressive in other ways by reference to their supposed crime prevention potential.

Spheres of justice

Reducing harms to a common currency goes against the recent arguments of communitarians. Different goods being incommensurable, fairness will be achieved when status on one dimension is not associated with status on others. Communities that now suffer high rates of crime are often also characterised by poor housing, deprivation, exclusion, poor educational achievement, pollution and the like. This is not coincidence. A wide range of social and physical variables contribute to and are contributed to by crime risk, both singly and in interaction (see, for example, Tseloni *et al.* forthcoming). These variables include affluence, region, area type, parity, household composition, land use and physical attributes of a home, car or person. The establishment of causal routes through which these allied ills manifest themselves is technically difficult and probably pointless. Social variables may both drive and be driven by crime and perceptions of crime, or be manifestations of other variables, overt or subtle. For example, concentration of single parent households may be associated with crime for many reasons, including the following:

- because crime changes population composition with the more desperate moving to less desirable areas;
- because the lifestyle of single parents changes natural surveillance and other area attributes which increase crime; or
- because both single parent households and crime are attributes of an area's economic decline, which drives both; or
- because the spending power of lone parents distorts local economies, leading to the decline or change of the business profile.

The intriguing (even mind-blowing) question is: what would crime policy look like if its single aim were to uncouple risks from the risks of other types of disadvantage? How could it be monitored? It would mean that effort at crime reduction would be concentrated on those who were most crime-prone. This could most easily be achieved by a major emphasis on the prevention of repeat victimisation, since repeat victims are disproportionately to be found in areas and groups suffering most crime (see Trickett *et al.* 1995; Johnson *et al.* 1997; Pease 1998). The emphasis solely on prior victims will lead the reader to question, 'And what else?' The answer is nothing else. Why not prior victimisation occasioning high trauma? Because repeats can escalate in trauma, from robbery to murder, and because the sheer grind of chronic victimisation, even events which may dispassionately be regarded as individually trivial, is itself traumatic (see Shaw 2001). Preventing repeat crimes is the most elegant means of applying Rawls' difference principle. Not classifying victims further buys simplicity of implementation.

Prior victims are disproportionately future victims. Any other means of dispensing crime prevention help will be less efficient in identifying and helping those at risk. Let us assume that help is dispensed by geographic area. As noted above, crime is less concentrated the more aggregated an area or group. Thus an areal definition of areas needing crime reduction help will exclude individuals at high risk and include those at low risk. Dispensing crime reduction according to prior victimisation is the closest we have to a means of reducing differences in crime suffering. Recent research (Everson 2000) also suggests that it denies opportunities to those prolific offenders to whom we most wish to deny opportunities.

Parallel attention to those who are disadvantaged in other respects will reduce associations between harms. As stated earlier, this must not be restricted to the intersecting set of those suffering both harms. When the key associations approach zero, we have a distributively fair society within a set of independent spheres of justice (see Walzer 1983), and hopefully the reconciliation of justices of redistribution and recognition (Fraser 1997). Functionally, this approach and the required reduction in range of experiences of crime within an area (see 'Crime and Rawls' Difference Principle' above) will tend to the same result, if the attempt to reduce best-worst ratios as indices of performance are applied across forms of disadvantage.

Conclusion

Of the ideas presented above, the idea of best-worst ratios in crime as the basis of performance measurement seems to have immediate promise. The recognition that statistics centring on variation are rare in criminology, whereas statistics centring on central tendency are common, felt like an insight. The crude calculations of OCU and force variability contained in this chapter show that the technique is easy, the only difficult issue being the collection of the most appropriate data. Application to more disaggregated data will make the technique more useful and truer to the Rawls' difference principle.

Notions of uncoupling measures of disadvantage, taken from Walzer (1983) and consonant with the ideas of Fraser (1997; 2000), are intriguing in their implications, and could with profit be elaborated. The details of how the distribution of opportunities from the victim perspective translates into effects on criminal careers will not be simple. Single offenders commit offences against many victims, alone or with others. The impact of different tactics of reducing crime opportunities will likely be different in limiting victim harm and offender vulnerability to sanction. Past neglect of these issues makes the task a daunting one, albeit worthwhile.

Notes

The opinions expressed in this chapter are not necessarily those of the Home Office.

1   This is to assume that the ascription of offending to prior distributive injustice is more than an unfounded assumption.
2   Rape alarms and target hardening of locations prone to victimisation are usually categorised as situational prevention. The argument of this chapter may require a reconsideration of crime prevention typologies.

3 In conventional longitudinal research, one has to wait a lifetime to get a lifetime's longitudinal data, having started with a birth cohort. Sadly, criminologists get old as fast as do those whom they study. In the accelerated longitudinal design, one begins with a series of cohorts, with starting age of, say, 0, 5, 10, 15, etc. After five years, one has data on 0–5 year olds from the cohort which started at 0, data on 5–10 year olds from the cohort which started at 5, and so on. Thus, placing the cohort data together, a lifetime of data (with some qualifications) is available.

4 The smaller the unit of analysis, the greater is the inequality. This is because looking at large areas effectively averages diverse levels of risk within the area. The ultimate level of analysis relates to individual households or people. Because individual victimisation risks have not been analysed over time, this approach will overstate the concentration of victimisation somewhat, since it will include real risk differences with chance fluctuations.

5 This strengthens the case for considering the distribution of crime opportunities focusing on victims and perpetrators at the same time. Often, they are the same person.

6 In the recent rash of publications from the Home Office and the Inspectorate of Constabulary about crime statistics, place as the primary classifying variable remains unquestioned.

7 None of this should be taken to imply that displacement is typically a major problem for crime reduction programmes (see Hesseling 1994). It is rather to suggest that displacement research would (and should) have developed differently if informed by notions of distributive fairness.

References

Arneson, R. (1989) 'Equality of Opportunity for Welfare', *Philosophical Studies*, 56: 77–93.

Barnes, G. C. (1995) 'Defining and Optimising Displacement', in J. E. Eck and D. Weisburd (eds) *Crime and Place*, Monsey, NY: Criminal Justice Press.

Barr, R. and Pease, K. (1990) 'Crime Placement, Displacement and Deflection', in M. Tonry and N. Morris (eds) *Crime and Justice*, volume 12, Chicago: University of Chicago Press.

Budd, T. (1999) *Burglary of Domestic Dwellings: Findings from the British Crime Survey*, Home Office Statistical Bulletin, 4/99, London: Home Office.

Cohen, G. A. (1989) 'On the Currency of Egalitarian Justice', *Ethics* 99: 906–44.

Dworkin, R. (1981a) 'What is Equality? Part 1: Equality of Welfare', *Philosophy and Public Affairs*, 10: 185–246.

—— (1981b) 'What is Equality? Part 2: Equality of Resources', *Philosophy and Public Affairs*, 10: 283–345.

Elster, J. (1989) *Solomonic Judgements: Studies in the Limitations of Rationality*, Cambridge: Cambridge University Press.

—— (1992) *Local Justice: How Institutions Allocate Scarce Goods and Necessary Burdens*, New York: Sage.

Everson, S. (2001) *Repeat Victims and Prolific Offenders*, Ph.D. thesis, University of Huddersfield.

Farrell, G., Ellingworth, D. and Pease, K. (1996) 'High Crime Rates, Repeat Victimisation and Routine Activities', in T. Bennett (ed.) *Preventing Crime and Disorder*, Cambridge: Institute of Criminology.

Farrell, G., Tseloni, A., Wiersema, B. and Pease, K. (2001) 'Victim Careers and "Career Victims"? Towards a Research Agenda', in G. Farrell and K. Pease (eds) *Repeat Victimisation*, Monsey, NY: Willow Tree Press.

Field, S. (1991) *Trends in Crime and their Interpretation: A Study of Recorded Crime in Post-war England and Wales*, Home Office Research Study 119, London: HMSO.

Fraser, N. (1997) *Justice Interruptus*, London: Routledge.

—— (2000) 'Rethinking Recognition', *New Left Review*, 224: 107–19.

Hales, J. and Stratford, N. (1997) *1996 British Crime Survey* (England and Wales), Technical Report, London: SCPR.

Hesseling, R. B. P. (1995) 'Displacement: A Review of the Empirical Literature', in R. V. Clarke (ed.) *Crime Prevention Studies 3*, Monsey, NY: Criminal Justice Press.

Hood, R. (1992) *Race and Sentencing*, Oxford: Oxford University Press.

Hope, T. J. (1996) 'Communities, Crime and Inequality in England and Wales', in T. Bennett (ed.) *Preventing Crime and Disorder*, Cambridge: Institute of Criminology.

Johnson, S. D., Bowers, K. and Hirschfield, A. (1997) 'New Insights into the Spatial and Temporal Distribution of Repeat Victimisation', *British Journal of Criminology*, 37: 224–41.

Nussbaum, M. and Sen, A.(1993) *The Quality of Life*, Oxford: Clarendon Press.

Pascal, B. (1658/1961) *Pensées*, Harmondsworth: Penguin.

Pease, K. (1998) *Repeat Victimisation: Taking Stock*, London: Home Office Policing and Reducing Crime Unit.

Rawls, J. (1971) *A Theory of Justice*, Cambridge: Cambridge University Press.

Roemer, J. E. (1996) *Theories of Distributive Justice*, Cambridge, Mass.: Harvard University Press.

Sen, A. (1980) 'Equality of What?', in S. McMurrin (ed.) *Tanner Lectures on Human Values*,volume 1, Salt Lake City: University of Utah Press.

Shaw, M. (2001) 'Time Heals All Wounds?', in G. Farrell and K. Pease (eds) *Repeat Victimisation*, Monsey, NY: Willow Tree Press.

Sherman, L. W., Gottfredson, D., MacKenzie, D., Eck, J., Reuter, P. and Bushway, S. (1997) *Preventing Crime: What Works, What Doesn't and What's Promising*, Washington, DC: Office of Justice Programmes.

Skogan, W. (1991) 'Redesigning the National Crime Victimisation Survey', *Public Opinion Quarterly*, 23: 1–24.

Trickett, A., Osborn, D. R. and Ellingworth, D. (1995) 'Property Crime Victimisation: The Roles of Individual and Area Influences', *International Review of Victimology*, 3: 273–95.

Tseloni, A., Osborn, D. R., Trickett, A. and Pease, K. (forthcoming) 'The Lifestyle and Socio-economic Environment of Households Experiencing High Property Crime Rates in England and Wales', *British Journal of Criminology*, in press.

Von Hirsch, A. and Roberts, J. V. (1997) 'Racial Disparity in Sentencing: Reflections on the Hood Study', *Howard Journal*, 36: 227–36.

Walzer, M. (1983) *Spheres of Justice: A Defence of Pluralism and Equality*, New York: Basic Books.

Wiles, P. and Pease, K. (2000) 'Crime Prevention and Community Safety: Tweedledum and Tweedledee?', in V. McLaren, S. Ballantyne and K. Pease (eds) *Key Issues in Community Safety and Crime Prevention*, London: IPPR.

Wilkins, L. T. (1999) *Did I Really Become a Criminologist?*, unpublished manuscript.

Young, H. P. (1994) *Equity*, Princeton: Princeton University Press.

Young I. M. (1990) *Justice and the Politics of Difference*, Princeton: Princeton University Press.

—— (1999) 'Unruly Categories: A Critique of Nancy Fraser's Dual Systems Theory', *New Left Review*, 223: 147–60.

Index